Margins of Belonging

American Academy of Religion
Studies in Religion

Editor
Lawrence S. Cunningham

Number 58
MARGINS OF BELONGING

by
William A. Beardslee

MARGINS OF BELONGING
Essays on the New Testament and Theology

by
William A. Beardslee

Scholars Press
Atlanta, Georgia

MARGINS OF BELONGING

by
William A. Beardslee

Library of Congress Cataloging in Publication Data

Beardslee, William A.
Margins of belonging : essays on the New Testament and theology /
by William A. Beardslee.
p. cm. — (Studies in religion ; no. 58)
Includes bibliographical references and indexes.
ISBN 1-55540-468-5 (alk. paper). — ISBN 1-55540-469-3 (pbk.)
1. Bible. N.T.—Criticism, interpretation, etc. 2. Process
theology. 3. Process philosophy. I. Title. II. Series: AAR
studies in religion ; no. 58.
BS2631.2.B43 1991
225.6—dc20 91-18880
CIP

Printed in the United States of America
on acid-free paper

In Memory of

Jack Boozer

Table of Contents

Acknowledgements	viii
Abbreviations	ix
Introduction, by Hendrikus W. Boers	1
1. Uses of the Proverb in the Synoptic Gospels	13
2. Saving One's Life by Losing It	25
3. Listening to the Parables of Jesus	43
4. Parable, Proverb, and Koan	61
5. Robert Alter's View of Hebrew Narrative from the Perspective of New Testament Studies	81
6. Narrative and History in the Post-Modern World: The Case of the Gospel of Mark	89
7. The Infinite	101
8. Whitehead and Hermeneutic	117
9. Openness to the New in Apocalyptic and in Process Theology	125
10. Christology in Scripture and Experience: The Case of Process Theology	137
11. Recent Hermeneutics and Process Thought	149
12. Scripture and Philosophy	163
13. Men in the Post-Patriarchal World	173
14. Ethics and Hermeneutics	181
15. Christ in the Post-Modern Age	197
16. Vital Ruins: Biblical Narrative and the Story Frameworks of Our Lives	219
Afterword	237
Indexes	
Ancient Texts	243
Modern Texts	244

Acknowledgements

I wish to express my gratitude to Robert Detweiler and Lawrence S. Cunningham for taking this collection of essays into the "Studies in Religion" series of the American Academy of Religion, and to Robert Detweiler for proposing the volume. I am also deeply grateful to my friend and honored colleague Hendrikus W. Boers for his generous Introduction.

The following publishers and journals generously permitted the use of these articles (the bibliographical references for which are found at the first page of each article): *Interpretation*, "Uses of the Proverb in the Synoptic Gospels"; *Journal of the American Academy of Religion*, "Saving One's Life by Losing It" and "Whitehead and Hermeneutic"; Trinity University Press, "Listening to the Parables of Jesus"; *Semeia*, "Parable, Proverb, and Koan"; *Studia Humanitatis* and Robert Detweiler, "Narrative and History in the Post-Modern World"; Westminster-John Knox Press, "The Infinite," from *A House for Hope* by William A. Beardslee (c) The Westminster Press, 1972. Used by permission of Westminster/John Knox Press; *Process Studies*, "Openness to the New in Apocalyptic and in Process Thought" and "Recent Hermeneutics and Process Thought"; Pickwick Press, "Christology in Scripture and Experience"; *Listening: Journal of Religion and Culture*, "Scripture and Philosophy"; Scholars Press, "Ethics and Hermeneutics"; State University of New York Press, "Christ in the Post-Modern World"; *Southern Humanities Review*, "Vital Ruins."

Scripture quotations are from the *New Revised Standard Version Bible*, copyright 1989 by the Division of Christian Education of the National Council of the Churches of Christ in the USA and used by permission.

I am indebted to Anand Veeraraj, Hendrikus W. Boers, Wayne A. Merritt, John Quiring, and Kathi Breazeale, and to the staff of Scholars Press, especially Dennis Ford and Darwin Melnyk, for help in preparing the manuscript.

I have dedicated this book to my long-time colleague and dear friend, Jack Boozer, whose presence was a constant stimulus and a reminder that scholarship is required to engage our human reality.

Abbreviations

JAAR	-	Journal of the American Academy of Religion
JBL	-	Journal of Biblical Literature
JR	-	Journal of Religion
JThC	-	Journal for Theology and the Church

Square brackets indicate additions to the text made for the present edition.

Introduction

World War I destroyed the cultural security of Europe, especially of Germany, giving rise in religious thought to dialectical theology, inaugurated a year after the end of the war by Karl Barth's *Der Römerbrief*.[1] The pseudo-order which Hitler Germany tried to institute, the so-called "new order" which, in the form of the third *Reich*, was supposed to supersede all previous orders, was shattered by World War II, opening the way for a previously unknown claim to freedom and equality by all peoples of the world. That in part is the setting for these essays: the lost order and security of a past to which there is no return, but which, in Beardslee's understanding, nevertheless remains a factor in the perception of the present.

With greater conviction than many who are younger than he, William A. Beardslee accepts that there is no return to the past conception of the world as an orderly whole, but he remains equally convinced that one cannot strike out that past sense of an orderly whole without a diminished perception of reality in the present. So, for example, over against the alternatives of either "breaking the established patterns in the directionless movement of life" in Mark C. Taylor's *Erring: A Postmodern A/theology*[2] or the "strong restatement of a theology that places both Christ and the believer in a story" in Hans Frei's *The Identity of Jesus Christ*,[3] Beardslee offers a third possibility, which he considers

> not so much as in between these other two as on the third angle of a triangle—a response in which we see ourselves as deeply shaped by the post-modern world, and try to enter imaginatively into the interpretation of it offered by such writers as [Jean François] Lyotard, and yet affirm ourselves as finding our identity conferred by the history of our

---

1. Bern: G. A. Bäschlin/München: Verlag Christian Kaiser, 1919.
2. Chicago: University of Chicago Press, 1984.
3. *The Hermeneutical Bases of Dogmatic Theology* (Philadelphia: Fortress Press, 1975).

faith. A conversation arising from this kind of tension, I believe, offers the most creative possibilities for faith.[4]

Beardslee's essays do not present a final answer to the problem of the relationship of an irrecoverable past to the present and the future. A final answer would be contrary to his understanding of reality as a process. The essays represent his engagement over a period of more than three decades with the problem of an interpretation of the New Testament that moves beyond the past and present perceptions of the world as rigid alternatives.

I

Beardslee's concern comes to its most succinct expression in the title of the final essay, "Vital Ruins." He recognizes the order of the past as irreparably in *ruins*, but is convinced that it remains vital for an adequate perception of the world in the present, born as it is of the collapse of the order of the past. Thus he reaches back repeatedly as a starting point in these essays to the great nineteenth century interpreter of the parables, Adolf Jülicher, who represents that century's confidence in order and reason. The past order which finds expression in Jülicher's interpretation of the parables functions as the framework within which Beardslee tries to understand contemporary interpretations which bring to expression a breakup of order in the world.

Alfred North Whitehead's process thought provides Beardslee with the methodological tools to grapple with the problem of the opposed perceptions of the world in the past and in the present. Beardslee should not be understood as a Whiteheadian thinker who makes use of the categories of process thought to interpret the New Testament, but as a New Testament scholar who finds in the thought of Whitehead the means of coming to grips with the problems facing the New Testament interpreter. His aim is to interpret contemporary reality through the eyes of the New Testament. The unwarranted complaint against Rudolf Bultmann that his existentialist interpretation was influenced—determined even!—by Martin Heidegger's existentialist philosophy, can with as little reason be lodged against Beardslee. Beardslee's concern to incorporate contradictory perceptions in a new understanding of reality is not a product of his appreciation of Whitehead's thought. Rather, what Whitehead's

4. "Christ in the Post-modern Age," 203. Page references to Beardslee's essays, unless otherwise specified, are to the present edition.

thought does for Beardslee is that it confirms that he was correct in arguing for a view which incorporates contradictory conceptions of reality.

This openness to the validity of contradictory perceptions has been at the heart of Beardslee's thought over the years and comes to expression throughout this collection of essays. Characteristic of this openness was a statement he made many years ago in CP-400, the venerable Interdepartmental Seminar of the Graduate Division of Religion of Emory University. Faculty from a number of departments in the university participated for about three decades in vigorous discussion of topics related to the study of religion from the perspectives of a variety of disciplines—religion, theology, philosophy, history, etc. It was in that time, too, that the great controversies concerning the death of God were raging at Emory and elsewhere in the country. On one such occasion, in reaction to two diametrically opposed views, Beardslee made the following memorable remark: "I think you are both right; you see, I prefer to compromise." It would be difficult to imagine anybody else making such a remark without being considered intellectually a capitulator.

These essays reveal what Beardslee's "compromise" means, and why his remark was not taken as capitulation, but as a serious contribution to the discussion. Beardslee's "compromise" means a move forward to an imaginative new understanding in which contradicting views are incorporated as contributing elements, ironically, *without compromising* either. The roots of his concern with fundamentally opposed ideas in the interpretation of the New Testament go back to his doctoral studies. In the "Preface" to *Human Achievement and Divine Vocation in the Message of Paul*[5] he wrote, "To Paul it appeared that the achievements of the apostle or the believer were not set over against justification by faith, but were rather the fruit of the same divine purpose which is met in God's forgiveness."[6] In this statement he does not reconcile the opposed doctrines that have plagued Christian theology in general and New Testament scholarship in particular for such a long time, justification by faith and justification for the doing of good works. Instead he interprets both of them as "the fruit of the same divine purpose," recognizing both as valid.

This opposition between human achievement and divine vocation is recalled in a different formulation in the first essay of this collection: "For a long time theologians, and especially biblical theologians, . . . held

---

5. "Studies in Biblical Theology" 31; London: SCM Press, 1961.
6. *Human Achievement and Divine Vocation*, 7.

. . . that the concrete historical standpoint of faith could simply speak for itself, without taking any account of other positions. Now we see the one-sidedness of a simply confessional approach," because of its incapacity to deal "with the fact that with the passage of time standpoints change" and "its frequent failure to take its dialogue partners seriously."[7] In this formulation the opposition to a fixed confessional approach manifests itself in two ways: changing positions within the tradition of interpretation itself, and the encounter with positions from outside that tradition. In the first essay, and those that follow immediately, Beardslee concerns himself mainly with the changing positions within the interpretive tradition itself. A representative example is the third essay, "Listening to the Parables of Jesus," in which he discusses the changing understanding of the parables in the history of interpretation: Augustine's allegorical understanding, Adolf Jülicher's anti-allegorical, liberal conception, Rudolf Bultmann's existentialist interpretation, and finally the interpretations of Robert Funk and John Dominic Crossan which shatter an understanding of the world as orderly. By means of a Whiteheadian interpretation Beardslee tries to incorporate both the world-creating interpretations of Augustine and Jülicher and the world-shattering interpretations of Bultmann, Funk and Crossan.

The relationship of faith towards positions from outside comes to a forceful expression in "Vital Ruins," the final essay of this collection. Remarkably, Beardslee appeals to Whitehead's process understanding of reality relatively little in this essay, revealing that a Whiteheadian approach is not methodologically indispensable for him. The essay nevertheless has some of the clearest statements of what it is about Whitehead's thought that is important for Beardslee. For example, the following formulation which might also have pleased Heraclitus:

> There is another way to think of reality, which opens the way to connecting the imaginative, dramatic world of story to the public world. That is to think of reality as events rather than as substances. What is real is the event of experience. There is no continuing "thing" that experiences—the experience is the event, the reality. It is, of course, a momentary reality, which gives way to a succeeding moment of experience.[8]

This statement is followed by one of the most transparent formulations of Beardslee's Whiteheadian approach:

---

7. "Uses of the Proverb in the Synoptic Gospels," 13.
8. "Vital Ruins," 231.

> If what is real, however, is a series of events, each of which receives the data of its past as constitutive but not as wholly determinative, and if the event organizes these data from the past into a new experience, which in its turn becomes a datum for further experiences, we have a model which makes room for the basic ingredients of story.[9]

This last formulation reminds me of the reason for the redemption of Faust's soul in Goethe's *Faust*. It may be worth considering here as an aid to our understanding of what motivates Beardslee in his interpretation of the New Testament. Unlike most versions of the Faust legend, the hero in Goethe's drama does not in the end lose his soul to the devil. His redemption is assured by the wording of his pact with Mephistopheles. Faust pledges that if he were to encounter a moment to which he could say, "Verweile doch! du bist so schön!"[10] he will surrender his soul to the devil, or whoever else.[11] From that point on Mephistopheles' objective throughout *Faust I* and *II* is to produce such a moment. The key to the redemption of Faust's soul is the nature of the moment to which he makes his appeal to stay in his final speech in the drama: in his mind's eye he sees a people unceasingly wresting a livelihood from the wilderness.[12] It is not a static moment, but one that is in its very make-up dynamic. Faust dies, and when Mephistopheles comes to claim his soul the devil is forced into a corner by a host of angels who have come to take Faust's soul to heaven. As they ascend into heaven they announce why it had been possible to redeem Faust: "Wer immer strebend sich bemüht, den können wir erlösen."[13] Goethe's solution is a paradox, a moment which incorporates the essential features of an ever unfolding story. A hint at this solution is given very early in the drama, immediately before Mephistopheles makes his appearance for the first time, when Faust translates John 1:1, not as "In the beginning was the Word," but "Im Anfang war die Tat ('in the beginning was the deed, the act')."[14] Beardslee might propose, in the sense of Whitehead: "In the beginning was process," not "a process," but just "process."

In what might be considered an alternative description of Goethe's constantly renewing society, Beardslee sketches a community living from

9. loc. cit.

10. Will you please stay! you are so beautiful!

11. *Faust*, lines 1698-1711.

12. *Faust*, lines 11575-86.

13. "Whoever is engaged in continual striving, that is the one we are able to save," *Faust*, lines 11934-37.

14. *Faust*, line 1237.

"the Spirit of God at work in the story that comes from Jesus." This community has the potentiality of functioning as "a strong factor in the seeking and finding of those patterns that will resist the technological cybernetization of life, encourage cooperative ventures and smaller networks within the overall society, and help to reconstitute the story of our common life in such a way that it gives up its imperialistic claims, whether of tribe or nation or religious group, as well as its imperialistic claims upon the fabric of the earth, and opens the way to seek common values or at least coordinated values within the human community"[15]

Throughout these essays one finds Beardslee ready to say to a "moment" the equivalent of Faust's "Verweile doch! du bist so schön!" Time and again it becomes clear, however, that such a moment cannot be static. Beardslee wants more; he wants a moment which incorporates every moment, or, at least, a multiplicity of moments. The issue in "Vital Ruins" is the way in which orientation in life is achieved by integrating one's personal story into an overarching story of salvation. Beardslee points out how this was classically done by Augustine and in a modern version by C.H. Dodd: "The Augustinian version [of the biblical story] with its strong emphasis on a single true story line, to belong to which one had to make an unequivocal decision against a competing story line, has been typical of most Christian telling of our story since that time."[16] What he appreciates about Dodd's version is that "it expresses so clearly what has been the prevailing story pattern which we read in the Bible, a pattern which has shaped how we think and feel about finding our place in reality through story."[17] These statements brings to mind again Beardslee's comments in the first paragraph of the first essay in the present collection: "Today Christian theology is grappling again with the question of how to relate its perspective of faith, which is concrete and historical, to other perspectives from which men and women find meaning and express their deepest convictions. For a long time theologians, and especially biblical theologians, believed that they did not have to confront this problem."[18]

The statement about Dodd might suggest that Beardslee is willing to give his soul for such a moment. The further discussion reveals that this is not even a temptation. A major emphasis of "Vital Ruins" is to argue that Augustine's and Dodd's conceptions of the Christian story are inadequate

15. "Christ in the Post-modern Age," 215.
16. "Vital Ruins," 222.
17. loc. cit.
18. "Uses of the Proverb in the Synoptic Gospels," 13.

for a number of reasons. For one thing, the biblical story never corresponded very well to life, which was often more disorderly than in the story: ". . . [T]he orienting story was a better story than daily experience."[19] Beardslee points out that biblical writers themselves were at odds on the orderliness of life, quoting the optimistic statement in Psalm 37:25, "I have been young, and now am old; yet I have not seen the righteous forsaken or their children begging bread," and pointing out the bitter protest against this optimism in other Psalms and in Job. But Beardslee also notes an inverse side to this optimism in the Bible itself which reinforces the inadequacy of the biblical story: "If the stories by which the biblical people oriented themselves were, so to speak, better, more moral, than life as experienced, on the other hand, from a moral point of view, biblical writers constantly remind us that the stories on which people relied were worse than they ought to be. The prophets especially repeatedly reminded their hearers that their story was too small, that the story to which they had joined themselves had to be revised to expand their vision beyond where they were."[20] Not only do the prophets insist that the story should be able to accommodate other stories as well, but they themselves incorporate such other stories into the biblical story. So Amos, for example, shocks his readers with the statement, "Did I not bring Israel up from the land of Egypt, and the Philistines from Caphtor, and the Arameans from Kir?" (Amos 9:7), and in the vision of II Isaiah the story is expanded to the point where salvation is brought not only to the chosen people, but to the ends of the earth.[21]

For many a biblical interpreter that would settle it: the biblical story is inadequate. Not so for Beardslee. For him that is just the beginning. He focuses on Crossan's interpretation of the Parable of the Good Samaritan: ". . . [I]nstead of functioning as an overarching story which enables us to be integrated into a larger reality, the parable deals with us by breaking up the larger world to which we think we belong, for the sake of giving us a glimpse of a more profound reality than the overarching story has been able to embody."[22] He then recalls the even more radical

---

19. "Vital Ruins," 223.

20. Ibid.

21. Ibid., 223-224.

22. Ibid., 224. For a comprehensive discussion of the interpretation of this parable, beginning with Augustine, including Adolf Jülicher, Rudolf Bultmann, Robert Funk and John Dominic Crossan, see "Listening to the Parables of Jesus," (chapter 3 of this book).

interpretation of Rudolf Bultmann who eliminates narrative or story from the very heart of the New Testament message. For Bultmann the past, "including the past of the religious tradition, is imprisoning rather than liberating." And so, "There is no more story to faith, only the moment, for that is where we are free. For Bultmann the classic moment was the moment of encountering the proclamation of the Christian faith, but the same encounter could take place in meeting a fellow human being."[23]

Having in this way formulated the issue with maximum acuity, Beardslee is once more ready to come to grips with it by proposing a fresh look at the biblical story. It is at this point that the Pauline opposition of his dissertation is recalled in a slightly different formulation: "If our common life has an element of true freedom in it, then even God cannot determine the outcome. The tension between human freedom and divine determination that this comment reflects is well known within the Bible itself . . . ."[24] Beardslee clarifies this statement by an appeal to J. Coert Rylaarsdam's distinction between two concepts of the covenant, to which he referred earlier in "Christology in Scripture and Experience: The Case of Process Theology," in *Scripture in History and Theology*, the collection of essays in honor of Rylaarsdam. In Hebrew thinking about the covenant, two parallel streams developed and continued in an uneasy alliance. On the one hand, there was the covenant with Israel in which "God's promises [were joined] with the claim for obedience in a way that left the future open; it was clear that if they failed to respond, there was no assurance about how the future would turn out . . . . But around the figure of David another covenant image developed, which included the unequivocal promise that God would provide a successor on David's throne perpetually—regardless of how the ruler or the people behaved."[25]

This second conception of the covenant is what rules out other stories; it provides the basis for the understanding of the biblical story as interpreted by Augustine and Dodd. Beardslee observes that "the covenant with David was [no doubt] very reassuring in chaotic times in Hebrew history, especially after the collapse of the monarchy."[26] He brings home its illusionary effect by pointing out that it can be heard echoing in the assurance that "God would not let us destroy ourselves with

23. Ibid., 226.
24. Ibid., 227.
25. Ibid., 227-228.
26. Ibid., 228.

atomic bombs."[27] Earlier in the paper he draws attention to an even greater deceptiveness of the influence of this kind of a story: "How easily we imagine that the story of our country[28] ought to go smoothly because we are such a good country; how baffled we are when we find that we may be coming to the end of the period when things go well for us as a nation! And we are even more deeply baffled to sense that this country is not uniquely gifted by divine purpose, but is only one of many countries, all of which have equal claims to 'life, liberty, and the pursuit of happiness.'"[29]

And so Beardslee concludes, ". . . [T]he experience of our time has been unfriendly to the larger story patterns. It is not too much to say that the patterns given to us by the biblical narratives are in ruins."[30] Under the circumstances biblical scholars like Funk and Crossan have reacted by focusing on the disorienting story, not to mention Bultmann's complete negation of story in favor of the moment. For Beardslee himself, however, that story which is in ruins is nevertheless vital. Thus he proposes as a sounder pattern, "the alternation between orienting and disorienting story, which helps to keep the orienting story from becoming sterile, and this pattern has ample biblical basis."[31] By affirming both story patterns, he reveals that he is unwilling to say to a single moment, "Verweile doch! du bist so schön!"

II

The first four essays in the collection focus on proverbs and parables in the synoptic gospels. "Uses of the Proverb in the Synoptic Gospels" and "Saving One's Life by Losing It" concern the way in which proverbs function in the synoptic gospels to shatter complacent views of the world in contrast with their function in antiquity to integrate hearers and readers into an overall picture of the world. "Listening to the Parables of Jesus" focuses on the contrast between the earlier world-creating interpretations of the parables and the recent world-shattering. The same opposition between the integrating and world-shattering functions of proverbs and

---

27. loc. cit.

28. Beardslee refers specifically to the United States here, but what he says could apply equally well to a number other countries as well, even though it is in most instances kept firmly just below the surface.

29. "Vital Ruins," 224.

30. Ibid., 234.

31. loc. cit.

parables comes to expression in "Parable, Proverb, and Koan," in this case including a discussion of the Zen Koan which has a similarly world-shattering function. In all of these essays Beardslee tries to show how a Whiteheadian perspective makes it possible to accommodate both sides of these oppositions. The next two essays extend the view to include larger units of the New Testament literature. In "Robert Alter's View of Hebrew Narrative from the Perspective of New Testament Studies" Beardslee points out that the developed literary techniques found in the Hebrew Scriptures are not characteristic of the New Testament writings. "Narrative and History in the Post-Modern World" is a critical history of the interpretation of the Gospel of Mark. All of these essays are concerned with literary forms, but they are motivated fundamentally by theological issues. The rest of the essays are more specifically theological. The opposition between "human achievement and divine vocation," dominant already in Beardslee's dissertation, comes to the fore repeatedly throughout this collection.

The next two essays both have a focus on the concept of God's infinity. In "The Infinite" Beardslee points out that "Christianity (or Judaism and Christianity, more accurately) introduced into the West an understanding of infinity" which at first made it possible to understand concrete human existence as having real meaning before God, but in the course of the centuries this idea, "combined with the absoluteness and transcendence of God," developed into a conception which "did not leave any room for human beings to function with dignity."[32] The implications for eschatology of these opposed conceptions of God's infinity are clarified in "Openness to the New in Apocalyptic and in Process Theology." The same fundamental opposition is discussed again in "Christology in Scripture and Experience." In "Whitehead and Hermeneutic," Beardslee discusses those features of Whitehead's thought that are relevant for his interpretation of the New Testament.

In "Recent Hermeneutics and Process Thought" Beardslee proposes over against the alternatives of encountering the transcendent either beyond the ethical (Hans Frei)[33] or the aesthetic (Frank Kermode)[34] a third possibility "that we find a framework comprehensive enough to

---

32. "The Infinite," 114.

33. *The Identity of Jesus Christ: The Hermeneutical Bases of Dogmatic Theology* (Philadelphia: Fortress Press, 1975).

34. *The Genesis of Secrecy: On the Interpretation of Narrative* (Cambridge, MA: Harvard University Press, 1979).

include both possibilities and to set them in relation to each other."[35] The focus of "Scripture and Philosophy" is the "uneasiness of the balance between [philosophy and scripture as] sources of human knowledge [which] sprang from tension over the question of how much of our knowledge is open to all, and how much is derived from specifically Christian roots."[36] The high point of "Men in the Post-patriarchal World," a response to Catherine Keller's *From a Broken Web: Separation, Sexism, and Self*,[37] is a statement which brings out the deeply feminine in the climactic scene of the *Iliad*: When "Priam comes to plead with Achilles for the return of Hector's body, the deepest message, the 'real' message, is 'we are all related.'"[38] "Ethics and Hermeneutics" envisages an understanding of ethics that is not limited to "a single uniform community of interpreters [representing, for example, deontic or goal-oriented ethics as alternatives], but conversation among communities . . . [in which] the rigidities of each position can be questioned, yet each can speak, and frankly."[39]

In the final two essays, "Christ in the Post-Modern Age" and "Vital Ruins," Beardslee once more sets the understanding of the world as a well-ordered whole in the past history the Christian faith in opposition to contemporary perceptions of a radical break-up of that view of the world, and again shows how a Whiteheadian approach to reality makes it possible to incorporate both views into a comprehensive understanding of reality.

—Hendrikus W. Boers

35. "Recent Hermeneutics and Process Thought," 153.
36. "Scripture and Philosophy," 163.
37. Boston: Beacon Press, 1986.
38. "Men in the Postpatriarchal World," 176.
39. "Ethics and Hermeneutics," 196.

- 1 -

Uses of the Proverb in the Synoptic Gospels

Today Christian theology is grappling again with the question of how to relate its perspective of faith, which is concrete and historical, to other perspectives from which men and women find meaning and express their deepest convictions. For a long time theologians, and especially biblical theologians, believed that they did not have to confront this problem. They held that a directly kerygmatic or confessional approach was sufficient, and that the concrete historical standpoint of faith could simply speak for itself, without taking any account of other positions. Now we see the one-sidedness of a simply confessional approach, partly because such an approach has great difficulty in dealing seriously with the problem of hermeneutic: if the standpoint is simply given, it is hard to deal with the fact that with the passage of time standpoints change. Today we really cannot stand in the same "biblical" perspective as Jeremiah or Paul. Equally important in showing the one-sidedness of the confessional approach was its frequent failure to take its dialogue partners seriously. To the outsider, such a theological stance has often seemed to be one which could talk but could not listen.

In biblical theology the new interest in communication between the particular stance of the faith which is believed and other perspectives is shown in several important ways. One of the most important of these is the renewed interest in the wisdom tradition. Confessional theology and the theology of sacred history often found the Wisdom Literature to be almost an embarrassment. But wisdom has left extensive marks on the Law, the Prophets, and even the cult; and in the New Testament its influence is particularly prominent in the Synoptic Gospels. Such a tradition has to be taken seriously. Its presence and influence can in large part be understood through the fact that in the Hebraic and Jewish world wis-

From *Interpretation* 24 (1970), 61-71.

dom served precisely the function referred to above, that of building a bridge between the perspective of faith and experience outside the circle of faith.

The interpretation of existence, through which a connection could be seen between a particular faith and the meanings found by others, took place in two rather different ways in the Wisdom books, through practical wisdom and through speculative wisdom. Speculative wisdom, the Near Eastern precursor and background of philosophical speculation, attempted to grasp the meaning of increasingly wider circles of existence, and ultimately to grasp a vision of the whole. This side of the wisdom tradition was immensely important for Christian theology, particularly in providing christological categories. The early Christian faith in the universal significance of Christ was often expressed in terms taken from wisdom speculation: Logos, the wisdom of God. Speculative wisdom is not absent from the Synoptic Gospels. The interpretation of Christ in wisdom categories began very early, as early as the thinking presented in Q, where Christ is already seen as Wisdom or at least in wisdom terms.[1]

Despite the growing interest in speculative wisdom's contribution to early Christian theology and to gnosticism, the present essay will be entirely directed to the proverb, an element from the other style of wisdom, practical wisdom. This is the style which is by far the more important in influencing the Synoptic Gospels. Matthew, Mark, and Luke, quite unlike later Christian theology, draw far more heavily on practical wisdom than on the speculative tradition. Practical wisdom, the older and less technical side of the tradition, simply looked at the events of a person's life for recurring patterns. This interest in the daily human existence is characteristically shown in the Synoptics by the presence of the two wisdom forms, the proverb and the parable.

Recent study of the Synoptic Gospels has fixed a great deal of attention on the parables, and in particular on an analysis of how they "work," how they make their point. Fuchs, Wilder, Jüngel, Linnemann, Robinson, Funk, and Via are among the names which suggest the concentration of attention on the parables in the attempt to move beyond positions established principally by Jülicher, Dodd, and Jeremias in clarifying the function of the parable.

---

1. Thomas Arvedson, *Das Mysterium Christi* (Uppsala: Lundquist, 1937), 209ff.; Ulrich Wilckens, *Weisheit und Torheit* (Tübingen: J.C.B. Mohr, 1959), 197ff.

In the meantime, the proverbs in the Synoptic Gospels have received comparatively little attention, though Bultmann studied them in detail, and the discovery of many Synoptic proverbs in the Gospel of Thomas has recently turned attention to them.[2] It is easy to understand why this form has not attracted much attention. Parables are not unique in the Synoptics, but they are distinctive. It is not easy, on the other hand, to point to any distinctive marks of the Synoptic proverbs or to move backward through the layers of Synoptic tradition and make a judgment about what was characteristic of the use of the proverb by Jesus himself. Furthermore, we are still in reaction against the "moralization" of the Synoptic kerygma, and any interpretation of the Gospels which tends to reduce their meaning to mere general moral truths, as Jülicher's interpretation tended to do, for instance, is anathema to contemporary interpreters.

The present paper takes the limited task of reflecting primarily on the form and function of proverbs in the Synoptic tradition. It will also glance at the historical problem of the relation of this proverbial tradition to Jesus, without undertaking the detailed form-critical analysis which this latter problem necessarily involves when carried through thoroughly.

It is clear that the proverb is a less definite form than the parable—less specific in its function and therefore more easily capable of being transferred from one setting to another, so that the proverb, for instance, appears frequently in apocalyptic and gnostic settings as well as in wisdom settings. Nonetheless it is a striking fact that proverbs are abundant in the Synoptics, not only in the sayings tradition common to Matthew and Luke, but also in Mark. Furthermore, despite the facts that (1) these proverbs have often been combined with prophetic-apocalyptic sayings and with legal sayings, and that (2) proverbial forms like the makarism or beatitude have been shifted from a wisdom framework to an eschatological one, it is worth noting how much of the old practical wisdom setting of the proverb remains in the Synoptic Gospels. There were strong factors leading toward a utilization of speculative wisdom traditions in early Christianity, in contrast to practical wisdom traditions. In spite of this trend, the Synoptic Gospels, and especially Q as the main deposit of wisdom traditions in the Gospels, are characterized by the strong predominance of practical wisdom traditions. Although it is also

---

2. Rudolf Bultmann, *The History of the Synoptic Tradition*, tr. John Marsh (New York: Harper & Row, 1969), 69-108; Helmut Koester, "One Jesus and Four Primitive Gospels," in James M. Robinson and Helmut Koester, *Trajectories through Early Christianity* (Philadelphia: Fortress Press, 1971), 158-204.

true that the wisdom sayings have to some extent been given a specifically "religious" interpretation, even this tendency is sharply limited. Only a few of the sayings classified by Bultmann as wisdom sayings make any explicit reference to God or to the Kingdom.[3] By contrast, such a common-sense document as *The Sentences of Sextus* is far more explicitly "religious."[4] This is not to suggest that the Synoptic proverbs are secular either in the sense of the secular strand of ancient Near Eastern wisdom or in the modern sense. Practical wisdom of the proverbial type was deeply fused with faith in the Jewish tradition, and this fusion continues in the Synoptics. But the dimension of faith does not cause God and religion to appear as a separate realm. The power of the orientation of practical wisdom in the Synoptic tradition is shown by the way in which a wisdom form such as the makarism or beatitude, though transferred to a prophetic or eschatological function, still retains its practical reference to the concrete behavior of a person among others.[5]

We may enter into our discussion of how the proverb works with Bultmann's discussion of the subject.[6] He says that proverbs express general truths which can become the possession of the hearer, but that this is not the whole story; for in a particular concrete situation such a statement can lose its character of general truth and become an address to a particular person or group, qualifying the "now" of the person addressed. He points both to the coming of the Kingdom and to the encounter with opponents as elements in the situation of Jesus which could give concreteness and address-character to proverbial statements. We may take this as our starting point and work toward a further clarification.

In the first place, it is somewhat misleading to speak of the proverb as a statement of a general truth. It is a statement about a particular kind of occurrence or situation, an orderly tract of experience which can be repeated. In this sense, though it is not a narrative, the proverb implies a story, something that happens, that moves through a sequence in a way which can be known. The relation of the proverb to narrative can be

---

3. Bultmann, op. cit., 73-81.

4. See Henry Chadwick, *The Sentences of Sextus* (Cambridge: Cambridge University Press, 1959).

5. For a discussion relating the beatitude or makarism to the present theme, see William A. Beardslee, *Literary Criticism of the New Testament* (Philadelphia: Fortress Press, 1970), chap. 4.

6. "General Truths and Christian Proclamation," in *History and Hermeneutic*; JThC, IV (New York: Harper & Row, 1967), 153-62.

illustrated by noting how motifs from Old Testament proverbs are paralleled in some of the parables of Jesus:

> *Parable of the chief seats* (Luke 14:7-11, itself provided with a typical proverbial summing up at the close):
>
> Do not put yourself forward in the king's presence...;
> for it is better to be told, "Come up here,"
> than to be put lower in the presence of a noble.
> —Prov 25:6-7
>
> *Parable of the friend at midnight* (Luke 11:5-8):
>
> Do not say to your neighbor, "Go, and come again,
> tomorrow I will give it"—when you have it with you.
> —Prov 3:28
>
> *Parable of the two foundations* (Matt 7:24-27 | | Luke 6:47-49):
>
> When the tempest passes, the wicked are no more,
> but the righteous are established forever.
> —Prov 10:25; cf. 12:7

These thematic parallels, which could easily be extended to many other Synoptic parables, show the close connection between the proverb and the story—not, of course, the story of the group, but stories of a person's existence. But the main point to note is that while the proverb is a kind of generalization, it really is a prediscursive form of thought, and not a truly general statement. That is, what a collection of proverbs confronts one with is not a systematic general analysis of existence, but a cluster of insights. Part of the skill of the wise is to know when it is time to use which insight. Cautious and middle-of-the-road as much proverbial wisdom is, it does all have what may be called this existential element, the necessity of confrontation in choosing which little story or little history applies in this particular case. Hans Heinrich Schmid has emphasized this aspect of wisdom in his recent book, which provides a useful corrective to an interpretation of wisdom as "nonhistorical."[7]

The result of the above section has been to relativize the contrast between generalization and confrontation. Even the most "cracker-barrel" type of wisdom has in it an element of confrontation, and correspondingly, the confrontation cannot meaningfully take place without some kind of field or background against which it sharpens a particular demand. The fact that the imperative and the question are basic prover-

7. *Wesen und Geschichte der Weisheit* (Berlin: A. Töpelmann, 1966).

bial forms, along with the most widely used form, the statement, indicates this confrontational challenge to insight and action in the proverb.

Though there are in Mark and Q (and in material peculiar to Luke and Matthew) examples of proverbs which express a rather general folk wisdom, with its rather relaxed and sometimes even resigned attitude toward the making of choices, it is evident that in the most characteristic Synoptic sayings this wisdom is immensely concentrated and intensified. The primary means of intensification are paradox and hyperbole.

Paradox is related to the antithetical formulations which are so widespread in proverbial literature. We can bypass the antithesis between two different types of person or existence, as in Proverbs 10:1: "A wise child makes a glad father, but a foolish child is a mother's grief." The kind of antithesis which provides the background for the Synoptic paradox is the antithesis which expresses a reversal of situation. The story which lies behind the proverb is a story of reversal of fortune. This is also a very ancient proverbial form. Probably its original form, and certainly a very ancient widespread usage, was the function of expressing the disastrous consequences of exceeding one's role. "All who exalt themselves will be humbled," (Matt 23:12) in common sense wisdom is a warning against what the Greeks called *hybris*. Don't step out of place. Similar formulations appear, for instance, in a Babylonian source from about 1440 B.C.E. [The *Sittenkanon in Omenform* or Moral Rules in Omen Form](in form these sayings are derived from the "omen"): "If (he thinks,) 'I am heroic,' he will be shamed; if (he thinks,) 'I am weak,' he will become mighty."[8] These proverbs presuppose an order, and warn against transgressing it. Of this type we may cite such Synoptic proverbs as:

> For all who exalt themselves will be humbled, and those who humble themselves will be exalted (Luke 14:11; cf. Luke 18:14; Matt 23:12).
>
> Many who are first will be last, and the last will be first (Mark 10:31; cf. Matt 20:16; Luke 13:30).
>
> For what will it profit them to gain the whole world and forfeit their life? (Mark 8:36 pars.).
>
> ...[W]hoever wishes to become great among you must be your servant, and whoever wishes to be first must be slave of all (Mark 10:43-44 pars.).

Now we come to a saying which I classify as a paradox rather than an antithesis:

---

8. Ibid., 127.

> Those who try to make their life secure will lose it, but those who lose their life will keep it (Luke 17:33; cf. Mark 8:35 pars.; John 12:25).

Here the antithesis is so sharp that it can rightly be called paradox. But note that these sayings have been arranged in a kind of ascending scale of sharpness of contrast, so that one can say that gaining the whole world and losing one's life, or becoming servant of all, is paradox as well. But, at any rate, with the final saying we have reached the distinctive intensification of proverbial wisdom in the Synoptic tradition. Here the reversal of situation is so sharp that the imagination is jolted out of its vision of a continuous connection between one situation and the other.

The paradox of intensified antithesis is putting pressure on the very presupposition on which the clusters of wisdom-insights had been gathered together. This presupposition is the project of making a continuous whole out of one's existence. All the antithetical sayings about reversal of status involve some shaking up of this project, but the final one in the series involves such a paradox that the visible, or, better, the conscious continuity of the project is done away. You may humble yourself with an eye to being exalted later on, but so far as the conscious field of decision is concerned, it is difficult to hold in view the possibility of later gaining one's life while casting it away. Yet the saying is a paradox and not just a negation of the project of making a whole out of one's existence, since it affirms that in spite of all, life is conferred through this paradoxical route.

For the purpose of classifying proverbial sayings, we have defined paradox in a very specific way, as the intensification of the "reversal of status" type of antithesis which is widely known in proverbial literature. We could define paradox more broadly, but instead choose for our broader term, "hyperbole." Here we can include a wide range of intensified or exaggerated language. Once again, the phenomenon is a widespread one in proverbial literature, as one can easily discover by looking at the many parallels to the Synoptic proverbial sayings. Though these sayings fall into a variety of types, it is easy to rank them again in some kind of rough scale of intensity or exaggeration:

> Foxes have holes, and birds of the air have nests; but the Son of Man has nowhere to lay his head (Matt 8:20 | | Luke 9:58).

> ...[L]et the dead bury their own dead (Matt 8:22 | | Luke 9:60).

> ...[I]f you have faith the size of a mustard seed, you will say to this mountain, "Move from here to there," and it will move (Matt 17:20; cf. Luke 17:6; Mark 11:23; Matt 21:21).

> It is easier for a camel to go through the eye of a needle than for someone who is rich to enter the kingdom of God (Mark 10:25 pars.).

These hyperbolic passages reach their distinctive intensification in some of the longer wisdom poems of the Sermon on the Mount from which we can cite only one sample:

> Love your enemies, do good to those who hate you (Luke 6:27; cf. Matt 5:44).

In terms of its role in wisdom generally, it is often the case that hyperbole is associated with a kind of sardonic humor at the fate of the other fellow. Though I think that the question of humor in the Gospels has not been well treated, I am not going to try to enter into that subject here. In the Synoptic Gospels there is little of this sardonic humor which distances itself from the other whose fate is depicted in the proverb—though it can be seen in such a saying (not strictly proverbial) as: "You blind guides! You strain out a gnat but swallow a camel!" (Matt 23:24). On the whole, however, it is clear that the role of humor to provide distance, so characteristic of much wisdom, is not characteristic of the Synoptic proverbs; and this is not surprising, since distance is usually associated with moderation and with retaining a self-image rather than with the coming of a new self-image. In the Synoptics, hyperbole is used, like paradox, to jolt the hearer out of the project of making a continuity of life. "Love your enemies" illustrates this, and the form in which this saying appears in the Didache (1:3) illustrates the tendency of wisdom to draw even such an hyperbolic saying back into the continuity of the project of life: "Love your enemies and you will have no enemy."

From the above sketch we conclude that while many of the proverbial sayings in the Synoptics are general enough that they do not offer any distinctive clues to the specific style of life being advocated in them, the proverb does have a distinctive usage in the Synoptics in which paradox and hyperbole challenge the typical proverbial stance of making a continuous project out of one's life, but a usage which paradoxically views this challenge as itself the way of life. For the reflective interpreter, this use of paradox raises the question: To what extent can the disjunctive "jolt" or reorientation demanded by the paradox be retrospectively seen in a larger coherent framework, and to what extent must it remain as an abrupt break in perception?

As is not unexpected, the kind of confrontation sketched here for the proverb is strikingly similar to what some of the writers named at the beginning of this essay have worked out for the parable. Both are forms of faith-speech which direct the hearer to one's present existence. Wilder speaks of the secularity of the parables. Funk notes that the new logic of the parables turns out not to be an isolated entity over against the world in its everydayness, but the mundane world transmuted.[9] The proverb is not so indirect as the parable; it is too compressed for that, but it does share the parable's use of the familiar experience of everyday to jolt the reader into a new insight.

If this is a correct judgment about the intensification of the proverb by paradox and hyperbole, can anything be said about the fact that there are many proverbs which do not, so far as we can tell, share in this intensification, that simply represent the widespread tradition of practical wisdom? Briefly, yes. For one thing, the Synoptic message does not always proceed by way of reversal. ". . . [S]earch, and you will find" (Matt 7:7) is a typical proverb of continuity; and continuity also has its place in this proclamation, even though continuity does not so clearly disclose the characteristic features of the message. The presence of these more general proverbs in the Synoptic tradition is immensely significant precisely as indicating what one may call the field of intensification. For these proverbs arise from human life in its everyday existence, in its relation to the actual world, the neighbor and enemy, the family and work, and not least from one's relation to oneself. There was a tendency in the tradition for the nonparadoxical common sense to prevail over its paradoxical intensification; and for that reason students of the Gospels, searching for something distinctive, have been unfriendly toward the proverbial elements. But this situation can be viewed the other way around. The intensified proverb and even the parable find their field or setting in the context of everyday life, and the fact that this is their setting is emphasized by the presence of these more general proverbial sayings. The strongly practical orientation of the bulk of the proverbs in the Synoptics is the context from which the paradox and hyperbole arise and from which their meaning is oriented. We may contrast the situation in the Gospel of Thomas where many Synoptic proverbs occur, but for whatever reason, virtually all of those which have been cited here as most distinctive of the Synoptic orientation are absent. Reversal of situation is

9. Amos N. Wilder, *The Language of the Gospel* (New York: Harper & Row, 1964), 81; Robert W. Funk, *Language, Hermeneutic, and Word of God* (New York: Harper & Row, 1966), 195.

not the way faith is understood in Thomas, but rather clarification of situation; and at the same time situation is not understood in the practical and everyday manner of wisdom, but is interiorized.[10]

A language event is not just a verbal structure, and no doubt our interpretation has been influenced by our picture of the Synoptic message as a whole, including the presentation of Jesus' actions as well as his words—as, indeed, the interpretations of the parables are as well. But even though this essay has grouped together proverbial materials from various Synoptic strata,[11] the coherence of the picture drawn arises in good measure from its point of historical origin. If we could undertake a more detailed form-critical analysis we could show, despite all the judgments of probability involved, that the proverb, like the parable, comes into the tradition from its use by Jesus himself, and that the same is true of its intensification by paradox and hyperbole, which is the distinctive mark of the use of the proverb in the Synoptics.

For the modern interpreter, the prominent place of the proverb in the Synoptic Gospels, and presumably in the speech of Jesus himself, is important from several points of view. As noted above, even the somewhat everyday and conventional proverbs are important, as reminding the reader of the everyday field of concern to which faith and action must relate. The characteristic thrust of the Synoptic proverbs, however, is not the cautious and balanced judgment so typical of much proverbial literature. Such middle-of-the-road style has as its presupposition the project of making a continuous whole out of one's existence. The intensification of the proverb in paradox and hyperbole functions precisely to call this project into question, to jolt the hearer out of this effort, and into a new judgment about one's own existence.

---

10. A study of the function of the proverb in the Gospel of Thomas would be a separate project, but it is nonetheless indicative of a different stance from that of the proverbs chosen above to illustrate paradox and hyperbole, that so few of the sayings chosen above appear. Only Logion 4 (many first shall be last) and Logion 86 (foxes have holes) appear in Thomas. Reversal sayings do occur, such as Logia 5, 6 (what is hidden will be manifest) and hyperbolic ones as well, e.g., Logion 26 (mote and beam) and Logion 45 (grapes from thorns). [See also William A. Beardslee, "Proverbs in the Gospel of Thomas," pp. 92-103 in David E. Aune, ed., *Studies in New Testament and Early Christian Literature: Essays in Honor of Allen P. Wikgren* (Leiden: E. J. Brill, 1972).]

11. A sketch of wisdom elements in several Synoptic strata is offered by this author in "The Wisdom Tradition and the Synoptic Gospels," *JAAR* 35 (1967), 231-240.

It is evident that the gnomic, proverbial form cannot express the whole framework or perspective from which the challenge to insight and action issues. The perennial efforts to bring the perspective to expression lead, so far as the present subject is concerned, rather in the direction of speculative wisdom. This effort is an inevitable task, but the direct speech of the proverb, like that of the parable, simply bypasses it. Both proverb and parable presuppose that the hearer's own perspective already gives her or him a basis from which to respond to the challenge being given.

Since the proverb assumes that there is a common human body of experience on which to comment, the use of this form tends to point in the direction of a hermeneutic based on a common human nature. This direction has often been followed in Christian theology, and despite the view of some modern thinkers that there is no constant human nature (within limits this is certainly correct), this line of interpretation is still an important one. Such a hermeneutic would not necessarily have to flatten the distinctively Christian perceptions. But it would recognize that the same reality which is described in explicitly Christian or christological terms can also be spoken of in other ways, and that a significant response to the substance of the message of faith can be made without the expression of or response to any explicitly christological affirmations.

If we can recognize the authentic speech of the gospel in a paradoxical or hyperbolic proverb, we should be prepared to recognize that there is no one standard form of Christian speech, but that the point of the message may be made in a great variety of ways in various circumstances.

The "intensification" of the proverb, as has been pointed out, has to do with the shifting of its function from that of identifying some repeatable tract of experience, useful to know about when engaged in the project of striving to make a coherent whole out of one's existence, to that of jolting the hearer out of this hoped-for continuity into a new judgment about one's existence. The term intensification suggests that impossible standard which is set so often in the Synoptics. Here we cannot examine the question of the "practicality" of the Synoptic message, but can only comment on one facet of this question. The intensification of the proverb is, of course, related to the use of proverbs in an eschatological framework. Eschatology often has a large speculative component, partly derived, in fact, from speculative wisdom. That the Synoptics have little of this speculative expression of eschatology, and instead set it forth through the intensified proverb (as well as in other ways) is an important clue to the kind of eschatological faith that they present. In particular it is worth noting that speculative eschatological dualism often leads to detachment from present existence, a detachment that is heightened in gnosticism. The Synoptic proverbs, for all their intensity, do not fall into this pattern of detachment, but instead keep the hearer very much in this world. It is sometimes said that a radical eschatology is radically world-denying, or that it anticipates a total reversal of existence. The presence of these intensified wisdom sayings, however, shows that such an analysis is far too oversimplified. Though eschatological urgency may easily take the direction of abandonment of the present, this kind of eschatological hope produces a faith sharply focused on the present, and ready to make demands on the present which are (as we can say without carrying the subject further) beyond common sense possibility.

Finally, the proverbial form itself cannot answer the question raised above, whether the jolt or challenge to make an abrupt break in one's relation to oneself and one's neighbor can retrospectively be brought into some unified vision, or whether it has to remain an outright "leap." It has been suggested above that in the Wisdom Literature there is no absolute break between the generalized statement and the existential challenge. The sayings themselves fix attention on another point, and the shift of vision which they demand is one which leaves the self open to the claim of the other. Since the other's existence is not just momentary, but itself needs continuing coherence, the quest for coherent vision is not excluded by the paradox and hyperbole of these central Synoptic sayings. They do insist that one's vision of a coherent world of faith not close one off from the demand of the world outside.

- 2 -

Saving One's Life By Losing It

> For those who want to save their life will lose it, and those who lose their life for my sake, and for the sake of the gospel, will save it (Mark 8:35; cf. Matt 16:25; Luke 9:24).
>
> Those who find their life will lose it, and those who lose their life for my sake will find it (Matt 10:39).
>
> Those who try to make their life secure will lose it, but those who lose their life will keep it (Luke 17:33).
>
> Those who love their life lose it, and those who hate their life in this world will keep it for eternal life (John 12:25).

One of the traditional forms of speech which Jesus used was the proverb or saying (aphorism). We do not need to distinguish here between the "proverb," widely used in popular speech and taken from it by a speaker, and the "saying" or "maxim," coined in pithy form by a speaker or writer and then perhaps adopted by popular speech. Both forms appear in the Synoptic Gospels; often we do not know enough of their histories to distinguish them. We may assume that Jesus used both.[1] The present study will reexamine some aspects of the use of the proverbial form in the Synoptic Gospels and in the speech of Jesus, concentrating on the saying about finding life by losing it which is cited at the head of this essay.

From *Journal of the American Academy of Religion* 47 (1979), 57-72.

1. This distinction contrasts with the structural definition of Nigel Barley, "A Structural Approach to the Proverb and Maxim with Special Reference to the Anglo-Saxon Corpus," *Proverbium* 20 (1972), 737-750, which separates the proverb as expressed in concrete imagery from the maxim which is a generalization. In Barley's frame, our saying is a maxim. Barley's useful distinction, however, does not affect the argument which follows.

In an earlier study [now chapter 1 of this volume] I tried to show that the saying or proverb has its usual function as a comment on or a glimpse into the way to make a whole out of one's life; it discloses a repeatable pattern that can be imitated or shared on the proper occasion. But in the Synoptic Gospels and in the speech of Jesus himself, insofar as we can get back to it, although this function of pointing toward ways of shaping life does appear, the characteristic use of proverbial sayings is to challenge and break open the project of making a whole out of one's life. Paradox and hyperbole are the rhetorical means by which the shattering of the vision of one's life as a whole takes place. The saying chosen for study is a central example of a paradoxical saying.

A broader view would correctly note that proverbs often function simply as observations about life, and are not necessarily so closely involved in the effort to direct life as my formulation supposed. Nevertheless, the selection of proverbs for use in the Near Eastern and to a lesser degree in the Hellenistic teaching traditions was indeed shaped toward the aim of making a whole out of one's life which is shattered by the paradox and hyperbole of the gospels.

In that earlier essay I raised but did not try to answer the question whether this challenging or shattering function of the paradoxical or exaggerated proverb had to remain opposed to the recomposition of vision that can follow such a transformation, or whether the total thrust of the new insight is to be seen as disorienting, breaking the vision of the whole. This question of the connection between challenging of vision and recomposition of vision will be central to the present study.

In recent scholarship the function of the Synoptic proverbial sayings has received further attention from several scholars. Norman Perrin treated the proverbial sayings of Jesus at some length, and he summed up his discussion in part by saying, "When seen in connection with the Kingdom sayings, these proverbial sayings seem to serve the function of preparing the hearer for an experience of God in terms of radical questioning, of reversal, of a conflict both personal and eschatological. To use a phrase I owe to Dominic Crossan [Perrin continues], it is as if Jesus was proclaiming the Kingdom, not in terms of the end of the world, but in terms of the end of world itself. . . . [A] pattern begins to emerge. It is a pattern which has as its center the claim to mediate an experience of God as King, an experience of such order that it brings world to an end. On the one side there is the symbolic language of the Kingdom with its enormous evocative power, and on the other, the various metaphors of response."[2]

We should note that Perrin reconstructs the earliest form of the saying about losing and finding life as something like: "for whoever would save his life will lose it, and whoever loses his life for the sake of the Kingdom of God will find it."[3] Though he regards the phrase "for my sake and the gospel's" as a modification made by the church, shifting attention from the Kingdom to Jesus, he does not find it unlikely that Jesus' saying should have included a reason for the challenge.

One of Perrin's main aims is to bring out the symbolic character of such sayings as the one on which we are concentrating. They offer "metaphors of response," and are set in the context of the "enormous evocative power" of the "symbolic language of the Kingdom." These phrases all point to some larger context for the choice demanded by the Kingdom. At the same time, Perrin's understanding of the symbolic language of the Kingdom, with its emphasis on God as King, minimizes any further referential value such language may have. Hence he is cautious, indeed skirts the question, about what new vision may come from the "end of world" spoken of in these sayings. His main emphasis is on "radical questioning."

Paul Ricoeur approaches the same territory in a recent study. His summary makes the following points: "The transmutation of worldly existence, which Robert Funk[4] speaks of with respect to the parables, is accomplished in the proverb by the strange strategy which I will call *reorientation by disorientation*. The parable takes the round-about way of fiction; the proverb takes that of an impossible possibility. But both presuppose a field of common experience, 'a basis from which to respond to the challenge,'[5] hence, a 'field of intensification'[6] which has already been oriented by traditional wisdom."[7]

Ricoeur adds, "Perhaps it is necessary to say of the parable what we have said here of the proverb, that it of itself furnishes neither the practi-

---

2. Norman Perrin, *Jesus and the Language of the Kingdom* (Philadelphia: Fortress Press, 1976), 53-54.

3. Ibid., 52.

4. Robert W. Funk, *Language, Hermeneutic, and Word of God* (New York: Harper & Row, 1966), 195.

5. Ricoeur is citing what is now chapter 1 above, p. 23.

6. Ibid., 21.

7. Paul Ricoeur, "Biblical Hermeneutics," *Semeia* 4 (1975), 114.

cal way in which it would be possible to reinsert the impossible model within the course of existence, nor a way of incorporating this abrupt rupture within some unifying vision."[8] Ricoeur here follows a course similar to that which I took in my essay on the proverb, though insisting even more strongly that the primary speech forms of Jesus, proverb and parable, do not offer an opening toward a reunified vision. At the same time he notes that if the paradoxical saying about gaining one's life by losing it were not a true paradox, "we would have a simple negation—either skeptical or ironical, for example—of the project of existence."[9]

John Dominic Crossan, to whom we have already heard Perrin refer, deals with this same saying about gaining and losing one's life, correctly noting that the tradition was not very happy with this "dark aphorism."[10] He sees the earliest version of the saying in its shortest form in Luke 17:33, in which we find the simple antithesis, "try to make secure...lose/lose...keep," with no directing "reason," for the act. Perrin, we recall, had allowed a "reason," a phrase like "for the sake of the Kingdom of God," to stand in his reconstruction of the earliest form of the saying.

Crossan sums up his view: "Jesus is using the paradoxical aphorism or antiproverb to point beyond the proverb and beyond wisdom by reminding us that making it all cohere is simply one of our more intriguing human endeavors and that God is often invoked to buttress coherence. There is nothing wrong with making a whole out of one's existence as long as one does it in conscious knowledge that world is our supreme play and that we encounter the Holy in its eschatology."[11] By eschatology Crossan of course means "end of world," of the whole project of there being a coherent world to live in.

There is a remarkable coherence in these four treatments of the paradox and hyperbole by which the sayings of Jesus challenge at least our accepted visions of coherence. So far as the direct impact of these sayings is concerned, all agree that these proverbs aim to interrupt the flow of the moments of life in continuous connection, to break the vision which orients this flow. That God or the Holy is particularly known in

---

8. Ibid.

9. Ibid., 113.

10. John Dominic Crossan, *Raid on the Articulate: Comic Eschatology in Jesus and Borges* (New York: Harper & Row, 1976), 71.

11. Ibid., 73.

such moments of discontinuity is also a point in common. The response which the sayings evoke does not focus upon the longer-range question of "what then?" Yet from the point of view of theological interpretation of the gospels, this question is of central importance, as is evident, for instance, in the interpretation of Crossan, which effectively excludes God from the field of the knowable. This radical conclusion from the emphasis on the break in continuity which the gospel sayings attempt to achieve is coherent with a modern context of interpretation which emphasizes the gap between subjective and objective knowledge, and which concentrates attention in interpretation on the phenomenological structures of self and world, and is reluctant to venture ontological statements. We must try to test this sort of conclusion and the interpretive stance which accompanies it, in terms of its appropriateness to the gospels themselves as well as in terms of its adequacy to the whole task of interpretation.

There is no doubt that the tradition remembered the saying about losing and finding life in the definite context of the challenge to become a disciple. Mark (8:34-35) and most probably Q as well (Matt 10:38-39; Luke has a different order) associate this saying with the one about taking up one's cross. Erich Dinkler has shown that this latter saying is to be regarded as a genuine saying of Jesus, although the distinctive religious meaning of the cross did not emerge until a later period. As a saying of Jesus, the word about taking up the cross referred to receiving the mark (the "x") of Jesus, a mark of identification and initiation. Though the association of these sayings is an early one, we cannot assume that they were joined by Jesus himself; further, the cross saying has been reinterpreted by the cross of Christ.[12] What is significant is that the saying about taking up one's cross, even when interpreted as accepting an initiatory "x," does strongly imply a context; the break with the old life implies a setting and a direction that entail loss and are full of risk, but which also express purpose and a vision of the future.

It will help us to assess the "dark aphorism," as Crossan calls it, if we look at the motif of finding life by losing it as it appears elsewhere. For this saying did not come into the language of Jesus from nowhere. The evidence is not as full as in the case of the Golden Rule, which Albrecht Dihle has shown came into Jewish and Christian speech from an original

12. Erich Dinkler, "Jesu Wort vom Kreuztragen," pp. 77-89 of *Signum Crucis: Aufsätze zum Neuen Testament und zur christlichen Archäologie* (Tübingen: J. C. B. Mohr, 1967).

formulation in sophistic ethics.[13] Nevertheless, the widespread use of sayings about gaining one's life by losing it, and vice versa, in ancient culture does provide an important context. In what follows we shall be dealing with a "motif" rather than with a "form," since the forms of the sayings vary widely. But the motif does bear strongly on the sayings of the gospels.

The prevailing early context within which one finds such sayings is that of the participation of the individual in the struggle of a community for survival. The functional setting of the motif of gaining one's life by losing it is the setting of exhortations in the course of wars between communities. A typical example would be Xenophon, writing a bit pompously after the event about some good advice which he gave when his army's fortunes were at a low ebb:

> [T]hose who are anxious in war to save their lives in any way they can, are the very men who usually meet with a base and shameful death; while those who have recognized that death is the common and inevitable portion of mankind and therefore strive to meet death nobly, are precisely those who are somehow more likely to reach old age and who enjoy a happier existence while they do live. (*Anabasis* 3.1.43; cf. also *Cyropaedia* 3.3.45.)[14]

Xenophon does speak explicitly of the recognition that death is the common lot of all, and of the heroic effort to die well, as a wider framework. Unspoken is the assumption that the individual's life finds meaning in the group. On this assumption he grounds his common-sense exhortation about courage leading to survival.[15]

That such exhortations passed into wisdom teaching we can see from a Jewish collection of maxims from the Roman period, the Syriac Sayings of the Wise Menander:

> Lose not courage!
> Despair not in war!

---

13. Albrecht Dihle, *Die goldene Regel* (Göttingen: Vandenhoek und Ruprecht, 1962.

14. Xenophon is cited from Carleton L. Brownson, *Xenophon: Hellenica, Books VI & VII; Anabasis, Books I-III*; "The Loeb Classical Library" (London: Heinemann, 1932).

15. Xenophon's reference to the common fate of death suggests the affiliation of this saying with the many Greek sayings about the preferability of death to life, e.g., "[T]he god showed through them that it is better for a man to die than to live," the conclusion of the story of the sacrificial death of Cleobis and Biton in Herodotus (1.31); cf. the references in the notes *ad loc.* in W. W. How and J. Wells, *A Commentary on Herodotus*, vol. I (Oxford: Oxford University Press, 1912).

Whoever despairs not in war
and offers himself to death
Directly wins life, fame therewith,
and is celebrated.[16]

Here the relation to the group is expressed, in terms of fame which was so prominent in that culture. The gaining of life is also explicitly mentioned, but may have been transposed from the common-sense probability of survival that Xenophon mentions, to a hope for eternal life.

A much later example, and a more paradoxical one, shows the endurance of the motif. Frederick the Great is exhorting his faltering troops: *Kerls, wollt ihr denn ewig leben?* (Rascals, do you want to live forever?).[17] Gregor Sebba, in discussing this saying, notes how widespread the use of such exhortations is, and comments following Sorel, that the claim requires a setting in myth, or we may say, a vision of life. The modern reader is far more painfully aware than the ancient, of the variety of myths that may induce men and women to give up their lives, and of the ambiguity of such a claim. Yet C. S. Lewis could still adduce this situation of literal battle, with its claim upon one's life, as evidence of a universal moral claim upon humanity.[18]

In making this use of the claim, Lewis was following an ancient tradition. The shift from an unreflective myth or vision of life to the giving of one's life for "principle" was an easy step. Socrates provided the classic example, and his career as a soldier was not forgotten as his death was reflected upon.[19]

Noteworthy, too, is the fact that the case of Socrates brought into focus an aspect of the individualizing of responsibility which was involved in the process here described, which has not been thoroughly discussed in Christian theology: the close relationship between dying for something and suicide. In the *Phaedo* (61C-63B), Socrates is at pains to disavow suicide, understood as one's own individual act; one waits until a god sends some necessity (62C), as in his own present case.

---

16. *Menander* 56; Paul Riessler, *Altjüdisches Schrifttum ausserhalb der Bibel* (Augsburg: Benno Filser, 1928), 1054.

17. Gregor Sebba, "Symbol and Myth in Modern Rationalistic Societies," pp. 141-168 in Thomas J. J. Altizer *et al.*, eds. *Truth, Myth, and Symbol* (Englewood Cliffs, NJ: Prentice-Hall, 1962), 145.

18. C. S. Lewis, *The Abolition of Man* (New York: Macmillan: 1947), 19.

19. See the reference to running away in battle in Plato, *Apol.* 39AB, and to Socrates' military career in Epict. *Diss.* 4.1.10.

This theme was extensively discussed in later popular philosophy which tended (like the corresponding social practice) to be more permissive toward the taking of one's own life than Socrates is represented to have been in the *Phaedo*. The emphasis in much of this later discussion on individual freedom (among the Cynics) and on pride (as in Seneca) moved this discussion away from the question of paradoxical finding by losing. But when, as in Epictetus (*Diss.* 1.29.29) the emphasis is on responding to the divine command, the justification for taking one's own life remains in the realm of "sacrifice" as in Plato.[20] Christian thinking has been reluctant to bring together the images of suicide and sacrifice, though this juxtaposition is familiar in other cultures.[21]

More significant for our purpose is the way in which the move from the concrete, "practical," military exhortation to the ground of "principle" was used in later popular philosophies as a generalized example of courage and the exercise of freedom. Thus Epictetus cites the case of Menoeceus, who gave his life to save his native city, Thebes:

> Do you think that Menoeceus derived but little good when he died? . . . did he not maintain the patriot that he was, . . . the man of fidelity, the man of honor? And had he lived on, would he not have lost all these? (*Diss.* 3.20.5-6).[22]

Epictetus comes to the same point again in a lengthy discussion of the case of Socrates; the general context is human "freedom" (*Diss.* 4.1.165); he says of Socrates, "he is saved by death (*apothnêskôn sôzetai*) and not by flight."

The specific risk of losing life was not lost sight of in these passages, but the image of living by dying, taken from this context, becomes in the popular diatribe a generalized but still vivid and paradoxical image of the ethical way. Thus Philo offers a typical use of the metaphor (here a scoffer is speaking): "The so-called lovers of virtue are almost without exception obscure people, looked down upon, . . . in training for dying" (*The Worse Attacks the Better* 34).[23] The powerful antithetical passage, II Cor 6:7-10,

---

20. J. M. Rist, *Stoic Philosophy* (Cambridge: Cambridge University Press, 1969), 233-55; see also Adolf Bonhoeffer *Epiktet und die Stoa* (Stuttgart: Ferdinand Enke, 1890), 29-39, 188-192.

21. See James M. Plumer, "Suicide and Sacrifice," *The Art Quarterly* 10 (1947), 254-261. Plumer takes Matt 10:39 as the epigraph for his article.

22. Epictetus is cited from W. A. Oldfather, *Epictetus: His Discourses*; "The Loeb Classical Library," 2 vols. (London: Heinemann, 1928).

23. Philo is cited from F. H. Colson and G. H. Whitaker, *Philo*; vol. 2; "The Loeb Classical Library" (Cambridge, MA: Harvard University Press, 1958).

has often been seen to have been drawn from this rhetoric of the diatribe; its culminating passage, "as dying, and see—we are alive," strongly parallels the passage we are studying.[24]

In addition to the context of war and the derived context of principle with its related symbolic uses, a third context for sayings about giving up one's life should be noted: the relationship of loyalty in friendship or love between two persons.[25] This is a motif expressed very widely in folklore and in literature; we can note two examples, one from Pindar and one from Euripides. To Pindar's Polydeukes we could add such figures as Herakles and Asklepios. Pindar's Nemean 10 recounts the death of Castor and Polydeukes' willingness to share his lot: "Bid me also die, O King, with this my brother" (77).[26] Polydeukes' willingness to die results in the renewed life of his brother Castor. Pindar's rendering of the story carries us far beyond the scope of death as an expression of human, brotherly solidarity and of life as within the other. Curtis Bennett has recently taken it to be a paradigm of incarnation and resurrection in the Greek context.[27] But this theological use springs from a universal motif of death for love which appears in most if not all cultures.

The closely related motif of death for love between woman and man we can cite from Euripides' *Alcestis*. Again, the widely-used motif has been shaped by the poet for his particular purposes. The movement back to popular culture is shown by the fact that a line from the play (301) found its way into the popular collection of Greek maxims, *The Sentences of Menander*: "There is nothing more valuable than [one's] life."[28] Note the parallel to Mark 8:37, "Indeed, what can they give in return for their life?", which is placed in the context of the saying which we are studying, and which was recognized as proverbial already by Wettstein.[29] The

---

24. Cf. Hans Windisch, *Der zweite Korintherbrief*, ed. Georg Strecker (Göttingen: Vandenhoek und Ruprecht, 1970), 208; Hans Leisegang, *Pneuma Hagion* (Leipzig: J. C. Hinrichs, 1922), 137; Gustav Stählin, "'Um mitzusterben und mitzuleben': Bemerkungen zu 2 Kor. 7,3," pp. 503-522 in *Neues Testament und christliche Existenz: Festschrift für Herbert Braun*, ed. Hans Deiter Betz and Luise Schottroff (Tübingen: J. C. B. Mohr, 1973).

25. See Stählin, op. cit.

26. Pindar is cited from John Sandys, *The Odes of Pindar*; "The Loeb Classical Library" (Cambridge, MA: Harvard University Press, 1968).

27. Curtis Bennett, *God as Form* (Albany: State University of New York Press, 1976), 218-259.

28. *Menandri Sententiae*, ed. Siegfried Jaekel (Leipzig: Teubner, 1964), 843.

29. J. J. Wettstein, *Novum Testamentum Graecum* (2 vols.; Amsterdam: Dommerian, 1751-52), 1:434, on Matt 16:26.

motif of self-giving for love, of course, also found clear expression in the New Testament: No one has greater love than this, to lay down one's life for one's friends (John 15:13).

The Hebrew Scriptures at many points assume the same conviction that participation in the life of a community opens a context within which life may be claimed and thus fulfilled when given up. For example, the rulings in Deut 20:5-9 about who shall and who shall not go out to battle, and the reference to the "volunteers" in the War-Scroll (1QM 7.5) presuppose this perspective. The lack of specific exhortations on this theme in most Jewish wisdom literature is probably related to the predominantly nonmilitary situation in which it was compiled. The narratives about the Maccabean heroes, as in 2 Maccabees and 4 Maccabees, are different from the motif we are following only in that they make the purpose explicit, e.g., "because of his laws," (2 Macc 7:11); "rather than transgress our ancestral commandments" (4 Macc 9:1).

The moralized transfer of the language which we have noted also occurs in Jewish literature, as in the Talmud.

> He [Alexander the Great] said to them: What shall a man do to live? They replied to him: Let him mortify [kill] himself. What should a man do to kill himself? Let him keep himself alive.
> (*b. Tamid* 32a).[30]

In this case, the "killing" or "mortifying" refers to wearing oneself out by the study of Torah, while "keeping oneself alive" means "living it up."[31]

In our first part we surveyed a number of efforts to understand the effect of the saying about finding one's life by losing it, which approached the saying, so to speak, from within, by a careful examination of the conscious and preconscious response which the saying calls for; in a word, we first studied it by using a phenomenological-literary approach. The consistent result of the New Testament scholars, including myself, who have followed this route is to see the saying in terms of breakup of world, of orientation by disorientation, of challenge to the project of making a whole out of one's life.

---

30. I. Epstein, ed., *The Soncino Talmud: Seder Kodashim* (London: Soncino, 1948).

31. My colleague, David R. Blumenthal, indicates that this motif was not widely explored in the rabbinic literature, though Rabbenu Gershom, Rashi, and Rabbi Asher ben Yehiel comment on the above passage.

When we turned from phenomenological-literary analysis to a historical literary approach, however, the saying appeared in a wholly different light. I am not thinking of the fact that from this point of view one could construct a history of the saying, making clear the movement from one context to another, although that surely can be done, and we have made some suggestions about it as we went along. More important for our purposes however, is the fact that when we view the saying with the historical-literary presuppositions which prevailed in the second part of this essay, at any point in the process the act of finding by losing does appear in a definite context, and that means that from this point of view one can think about what one is losing one's life *for*, precisely the item that tends to fall out of the picture from the phenomenological approach undertaken first.

It is not surprising that the two lines of interpretation come out so differently. The gap between phenomenological and historical approaches runs deep in biblical studies, and there has been a marked shift toward the phenomenological as a result of the seeming objective barrenness of the historical. To counter the self-enclosed nature of the phenomenological approach, some types of literary analysis have as their aim the rooting of conscious perceptions and the structures which can be perceived behind consciousness more firmly in language, and in an ontology of language. This is a promising and useful sort of criticism. But my own perception of it is that it is still so limited by Kantian presuppositions that it does not succeed in bringing together the phenomenological and the diachronic-historical.

Thus we shall conclude the exploration of the gospel saying with an essay in process or Whiteheadian interpretation, in the hope that such a perspective may help to overcome the chasm, or at least to build some bridges, at a point very important to biblical studies and to humanistic studies generally.

In an later essay in this collection I sketch some of the outlines and aims of such an approach.[32] In contrast to the phenomenological effort to work backwards to a stage prior to the "subject-object split," the process approach will accept both subjective and objective aspects of reality as valid clues. It will criticize the identification of objective with "clearly-perceived," with, in Whiteheadian terms, the realm of presentational

32. [The reader may wish to turn to chapter 8 below, "Whitehead and Hermeneutic."]

immediacy, as noted in that essay. Objective reality does offer itself to us directly, but in the mode of causal efficacy which is not, so to speak, directly before our vision. Such a course will open the way to doing more justice, in the present case, to both styles of perception of the meaning of the saying in question: the style that examines it at work in the moment of transformation or disorientation, and the style that looks for a cultural setting and a history, including the kind of diachronic cultural history we have outlined as well as the internal history, the past, and the projection of the future, of the person struggling with the saying.

A statement in language evokes a bundle of propositions in the hearer. By propositions I mean concrete possibilities or proposals. There can be no one-to-one correspondence between a statement in language and the propositions which stand behind it, since the propositions are not theoretical, abstract entities created in the process of analysis in order to account for the concrete linguistic effects; on the contrary, the propositions are part of the actual experiences of the hearer or reader. They are not just subjective, although the way in which they are experienced is subjective. They are precisely something experienced, and their grammatical subjects are already existent. They are concrete possibilities which the hearer deals with in the process of perceiving and dealing with the statement. In the case of a statement like "the one who loses life shall find it," the explicit grammatical subject is in the third person. It is evident, however, that the thrust of the saying derives in large measure from the interplay between propositions which have a third-person, "distanced," subject, and propositions of which the subject is the experiencing center of activity itself. Such a tension is characteristic of many statements in the form of "address," which call for enactment by the hearer.

Further, it appears that such a statement as "you/I will find life by losing it" gains in intensity by reducing the scope of associated explanatory propositions. Thus the element of risk in accepting the propositions as dealing with oneself is heightened. At the same time, what are here termed explanatory propositions, meaning propositions which deal with relationships, which set the bare statement in some framework, are evidently presupposed and suggested by the various settings in which sayings about finding and losing life were used in ancient culture: propositions about the worth of the community in which one participated and about the manner of sharing in its life, for instance, were intended to be perceived as the frame within which one group of such sayings were heard. Similarly the early Christians set this saying in a context which enabled the hearer to associate it with a field of propositions or concrete possibilities about the Kingdom or the community, and also about the remembered speaker, Jesus.

While it may appear at first sight that the maximum effect of, in Ricoeur's excellent phrase, "orientation by disorientation,"[33] will occur if attention is narrowed as sharply as possible to the proposition about one's own existence, with a renunciation of concern about the field which gives meaning to the act, closer inspection causes us to see that the matter is not so simple. If the act of perception is always an act of self-creation, and one in which the various elements perceived have to be brought into some kind of contrasting unity, then it appears that too extensive a reduction of the associated propositions will result in a flattening of the challenge, an elimination of contrasts.

Further, "losing" and "finding" are not simple notions. They are both relational; they mean losing and finding "for" something. Though what they are "for" may recede from the center of consciousness, to eliminate that element would shift the felt propositions into a dominance of self-concern which is foreign to such sayings in all their settings.

At the same time, the reduction of attention to the surrounding framework does point us toward an essential feature of such sayings. They are sayings about self-transcendence. The self-transcendence spoken of by Jesus and that understood by the early Christians who composed the gospels has much in common with that self-transcendence urged by other sayings expressing this motif; it is for this reason that such similar sayings continue to be used. The difference in the sort of self-transcendence reached for cannot be determined from the sayings themselves, but requires an evaluation of their respective settings. The inward, phenomenological analysis cannot tell the whole story. Here Perrin does well to associate these sayings with "the language of the Kingdom with its enormous evocative power."[34]

This saying is extremely revealing of the interweaving of self-concern and self-transcendence which has characterized Christian existence from the beginning. Here there is a clear parallel with the use of the motif in Hellenistic culture; both the Hellenistic and the early Christian uses represent a movement away from the loss of self unreflectively in a group, toward a self-transcendence which is preoccupied with self as it moves

33. [Ricoeur's actual phrase was "reorientation by disorientation."]
34. Perrin, op. cit., 54.

beyond self. Our saying focuses upon the self; it evokes propositions of which the self-creating occasion of experience is the subject; while at the same time it calls for a loss of self into the larger reality which is for the moment only peripherally visible. Thus the radical self-transcendence of which the saying speaks could be brought to expression only by focusing attention on the self. In the saying under discussion, this situation is created not only by the structure of the saying itself (for in a less self-conscious world the "seat of existence," as Cobb puts it,[35] would remain principally in the unconscious, and the saying would not evoke self-preoccupation), but by the saying in its setting of expectation. To counter the concentration on the self, other, related propositions which focus attention on other reality have to function along with those evoked by the questioning of the self's existence. Otherwise, the call for self-transcendence will result in self-preoccupation. This is another indication that a complete erasure of context is not a fruitful way to understand the radicality of these sayings.

We may approach the matter differently by reflecting on how an occasion of experience—a self at any moment—may hypothetically affirm itself as the subject of a proposition of which the predicate is some sort of loss of self. If this possibility is held at sufficient distance from one's immediate unreflective choices, then we find the stance of irony. James Williams has suggested (in correspondence) that the radically hyperbolic and paradoxical sayings of Jesus are to be understood from the background of the stance of irony in Hebraic wisdom. There is indeed an important issue here. Irony is characteristic not only of much Hebraic and Jewish wisdom, but preeminently of the popular Cynic-Stoic diatribe, and at least Paul incorporates irony as an aspect of his paradoxical antitheses which include "dying, and see—we are alive."[36] Sayings about transcendence of self are often found in ironic speech. And the gospel sayings can be read ironically. But it is necessary to conclude that the ironic reading is a "second" reading, a distancing of oneself from the intended thrust of the saying which does not, in its setting, permit the distancing of irony.

Thus we are led to a different view. The entertainment of an "impossible possibility" by the self at a moment of experience means an

---

35. John B. Cobb, Jr., *The Structure of Christian Existence* (Philadelphia: Westminister Press, 1967), 54.

36. See above, pp. 30-31, on 2 Cor, and E.-B. Allo, *Saint Paul: Seconde Epître aux Corinthiens* (Paris: Gabalda, 1937), 178.

interruption of (at least some) of those elements by which the successive moments of experience had connected themselves meaningfully with their predecessor occasions, and had thereby also projected a desired future. The whole range of meanings seen in death need not be explored here, even though literal death was in view in many settings of the saying including some early Christian settings. Whether taken to refer literally to death or not, the same sort of disorientation is intended. The saying is a call to give up the connection with the past and with the intended future by which one's own identity has been established. At the same time the context confers a new or larger identity.

If this line of interpretation is correct, then the risk and disorientation, the radical questioning, which such sayings aim to invoke, need not be related to the unknowability of ultimate reality, as in Crossan's interpretation. Rather, the risk is related to the genuine freedom and openness which inhere in the process of interrelated decision making which constitutes human existence. It is for the reason that human experience, at any rate, tends to solidify itself into routes of inheritance which are only marginally open to risk and renewal of vision, that such radical questioning as this saying expresses is required.

What we have sketched above is put in general terms, suitable as an interpretation of the saying in a wide variety of settings in which the human self is coming to a new stage of self-consciousness. The message of the early Church and that of Jesus as well belong in this class. The saying's presence in the tradition is a forceful reminder of the degree of disorientation and discontinuity that is called for in the style of perception and life which these messages proclaim. At the same time, our study has clearly shown that many different sorts of meaning can be associated with such disorientation. Indeed,if one concentrates on the linguistic effect of disorientation alone, the saying of Jesus could be seen as doing the same work as the disdainful, cynical maxims of La Rochefoucauld, which, as a recent writer notes, "offer us the added bliss of being surprised, thrown off balance, jolted to a new level of observation by the unexpected celebration of a countertruth."[37] Both groups of sayings do have in common an assault upon the continuity of the ego, but with very different intentions.

To sort out the particular intention of this saying thus requires attention both to the impact of the inner act required by its form, and also to

37. Francine dePlessix Gray, "A Few Well Chosen Words," *New York Times Book Review*, October 31, 1977, 3, 48-49.

the background or setting that established the particular expectation associated with the response. In the present case that would mean inquiring into the meaning of the Kingdom of God, for Jesus, and the meaning of the cross and of the figure of Christ, for the early Christians. Of course this inquiry is reflexive or circular: the meanings of the Kingdom and of the figure of Christ are in turn enriched and in part defined by the saying and its impact. The fruitfulness of this inquiry is indicated by the close proximity of this saying to the symbolism of the cross, both a physical proximity in the arrangement of the sayings in the gospels, and a symbolic proximity. Without more than briefly sketching this question we can say (1) that the context within which one loses oneself is here extremely rich in positive images of fulfillment, in comparison with many other settings in which the saying was used: Kingdom, resurrection, and Christ are charged with positive expectation, drawn from eschatological hope; and (2) in comparison with the setting in Hellenistic philosophy, with which it otherwise has much in common, in terms of the tension between self and "beyond self," the gospel saying is set in a highly dynamic framework, a processive setting in which narrative images prevail. In both cases, the claim for loss of self is set in a framework of "rightness"; in the one, the rightness is perceived as eternal principle, in the other, as participating in the interactive processes of reality.

Finally, we need to consider the listening of the modern reader or hearer. Our study has presupposed that there is value in reconstructing an earlier situation in the effort freshly to grasp the saying in its original force. This effort assumes that the original setting was at a confluence of forces where depths were touched, and where new possibilities emerged, that may renew insight repeatedly.

At the same time, we need not expect to be content simply with a renewal of insight. Each hearing, even of so abbreviated a form as a proverbial saying, contains the possibility of new insight. To attend seriously to the past may well be a powerful clue to the emergence of the new; in the case of this saying precisely because it is a paradigm of dislocation, of being shaken free from previously-chosen directions. To say this much is to remain attentive to the structural-phenomenological properties of the saying, properties which remain relatively constant from culture to culture.[38]

---

38. Barley, op. cit., 746.

Along with this relatively constant factor are changing ontological insights, changes in the quest to know reality, that provide the settings in which the saying is perceived. We may say that the disruption of the continuity of existence which this saying aims to effect opens the hearer to a glimpse of a complex experience of mystery. This complex experience of mystery was perceived in the Hellenistic and early Christian worlds predominantly in terms of a vector, a reach toward "rightness." That was the aspect of this glimpsed mystery which was explicated, whether in the Stoic doctrine of the logos or in the Christian doctrine of God. And the element of rightness is an aspect of mystery which, though sometimes with ensuing unfortunate rigidities, can be related to the ongoing continuities of life. But this experience of mystery also includes a component of an unformed creative void, and thus the move of the Stoic and early Christian users of our saying is not exhaustive of it as a presentation of the experience of mystery. Many contemporary persons who allow themselves to be grasped by the saying, but who find that traditional explications of "rightness" in mystery are rigid and inadequate, tend to explicate the mystery into which they are launched in terms of a vector toward "creativity" (in Whiteheadian terms) or "emptiness" (in Buddhist terms). For the proposal of a complex model of the ontology of mystery I rely primarily on the work of John B. Cobb, Jr.[39] and Masao Abe.[40]

The liturgy and theology of Christianity have been strongly directed toward cultivating the sense of rightness in mystery. To recur to "rightness" in a contemporary exploration of "losing oneself" (as I do) is to be convinced that the ontological basis of the experience of rightness is capable of further creative clarification and exploration. To turn from "rightness" to "creativity" or "emptiness" is to parallel a course which has been explored in Western metaphysics and mysticism, and profoundly explored in the East. The two courses have often been seen as contradictory. I believe that they have much to teach each other, but this consequence of our study cannot be pursued here.

My proposal is that careful attention to the various ways of perceiving the experience of mystery occasioned by the disruption of the continuity of our experience will compel us (1) to develop an understanding of reality which not only has room for varieties of experience, but also for

39. "Buddhist Emptiness and the Christian God," *JAAR* 45 (1977), 11-25.

40. "Non-Being and *Mu*: The Metaphysical Nature of Negativity in East and West," *Religious Studies* 11 (1975), 181-192.

a pluralistic model of transcendence, a transcendence constantly active but best glimpsed in moments of disruption and change; and (2) to recognize that the most adequate interpretation will hold in contrasting tension and interaction as much as possible of the rich complex of mystery opened to us by the creative disruption of our continuities, rather than quickly opting for a clear and simple perception. To consider the mutual possibilities of those perceptions of the ultimate which we have tended to fuse or partially eliminate is the ontological frontier to which a study of this saying has brought us.[41]

41. I am indebted to the Society of Biblical Literature for a grant to support my work at their then Claremont Center in 1976-1977, where the research for this paper was carried out.

- 3 -

Listening to the Parables of Jesus An Exploration of the Uses of Process Theology in Biblical Interpretation

The force and simplicity of the parables of Jesus always have enabled them to speak directly to ordinary people, and this special character still does. Yet the simplicity and directness of the parables have not enabled them to tell the same story to every audience. People have heard them in very different ways at different times. Scholars have provided insight into the reasons for the variation in understanding the parables, thereby suggesting what the possibilities of listening are in a given state of culture. This variety in hearing and the reasons for it are the concern of this essay.

What kind of world do the parables disclose? How far do they reinforce the vision of the world which the hearer brings to them, or how far do they undermine or overturn the vision of the world of the hearer? If they do challenge the hearer's world, do they offer an alternative vision, or does that have to come from elsewhere than the parables themselves? These are the sorts of questions which will be addressed. A particular aspect of the vision of the world found in the parables which will be considered is the relation between gift and demand that vision.

To explore and reflect on the different ways the church has listened to the parables, the interpretation of one well-known parable will serve as illustration. Four different modes of interpretation characteristic of, though not limited to, different historical periods in the church's history demonstrate not only the variety in listening to the "sample" parable chosen for this study, but also the progressive reduction of the world within which the hearer's response to the parable is expected to take

From W. Eugene March, ed., *Texts and Testaments: Critical Essays on the Bible and the Early Church Fathers: A Volume in Honor of Stuart Dickson Currie* (San Antonio: Trinity University Press, 1980), 201-218. This volume is now distributed by Mercer University Press.

place. Reduction or loss of world means the erosion of a sense of a coherent environment within which a human response to the word of God in the parable can take place. In the light of the reduction of world so characteristic of the more recent interpretations of the parables, this essay will inquire whether a perspective governed by process theology has the possibility both of overcoming the oppositions so often affirmed between contrasting interpretations of the parables and of opening a path toward a legitimate affirmation of "world," of an environment which is responsive to the hearer's response. What is at stake is the doctrine of creation, which has been badly eroded in much recent New Testament scholarship. To sharpen the differences and clarify the manner of listening employed in each mode in order to reach this goal is the aim of this essay, and a consideration of some of the history of the interpretation of the parable of the Good Samaritan will be the means.

Allegorical interpretation has a tradition many centuries old in the church. It still persists and, in fact, is more highly regarded today than it was a half century ago. The great function of the classic allegorical interpretation of the parables was to integrate them into the life of a religious community, the church.

Consider the parable of the Good Samaritan, Luke 10:30-35:

> A man was going down from Jerusalem to Jericho, and fell into the hands of robbers, who stripped him, beat him, and went away, leaving him half dead. Now by chance a priest was going down that road; and when he saw him, he passed by on the other side. So likewise a Levite, when he came to the place and saw him, passed by on the other side. But a Samaritan while traveling came near him; and when he saw him, he was moved with pity. He went to him and bandaged his wounds, having poured oil and wine on them. Then he put him on his own animal, brought him to an inn, and took care of him. The next day he took out two denarii, gave them to the innkeeper, and said, "Take care of him; and when I come back, I will repay you whatever more you spend."

Luke places the parable in a framework in which it answers the questions, Who is my neighbor?, and in which the concluding point is, Go and do the same thing yourself.

For the moment the setting will be bypassed, to hear how the parable sounds when it is taken allegorically. This is Augustine's interpretation:

> *A certain man went down from Jerusalem to Jericho*: Adam himself is meant; *Jerusalem* is the heavenly city of peace, from whose blessedness Adam fell; *Jericho* means the moon, and signifies our mortality, because it is

> born, waxes, wanes, and dies. *Thieves* are the devil and his angels. *Who stripped him*, namely of his immortality; *and beat him*, by persuading him to sin; *and left him half-dead*, because in so far as man can understand and know God, he lives, but in so far as he is wasted and oppressed by sin, he is dead; he is therefore called *half-dead*. The *priest* and *Levite* who saw him and passed by, signify the priesthood and ministry of the Old Testament, which could profit nothing for salvation. *Samaritan* means Guardian, and therefore the Lord Himself is signified by this name. The *binding of the wounds* is the restraint of sin. *Oil* is the comfort of good hope; *wine* the exhortation to work with fervent spirit. The *beast* is the flesh in which He [Christ] deigned to come to us. The *being set upon the beast* is belief in the incarnation of Christ. The *inn* is the Church, where travelers are refreshed on their return from pilgrimage to their heavenly country. The *morrow* is after the resurrection of the Lord. The *two pence* are either the two precepts of love, or the promise of this life and of that which is to come. The *innkeeper* is the Apostle (Paul). The supererogatory payment is either his counsel of celibacy, or the fact that he worked with his own hands lest he should be a burden to any of the weaker brethren when the Gospel was new, though it was lawful for him "to live by the Gospel."[1]

Of this lengthy interpretation, it is initially important to note one thing: Adam is you and I. The listener comes into the parable as the man lying in the ditch, in Augustine's interpretation of the parable. There he or she finds the point of contact in life for the elaborate theological interpretation that Augustine offers. Secondarily, of course, one must follow the example of Christ and act like a Samaritan; but this is a second hearing of the parable as Augustine listens to it.

To criticize this kind of interpretation is easy, and people have been doing so for seventy-five years or more. Clearly the story has nothing to do with Paul's views on celibacy or working for a living. But emerging today once more is a period in which one can appreciate the purpose of the older allegorical interpretation, oriented to the life and faith of the church. The elaborate set of correspondences between the parable story and the larger story of the Christian faith seemed natural to the allegorical interpreter, who lived in a coherent world, a *cosmos*. The parable gave the listener access to this cosmos as did other versions of the Christian story. A concentration on the often very arbitrary details misses the point. The basic stance of allegorical interpretation is the confidence that the dif-

1. Augustine, *Quaestiones Evangeliorum*, 2, 19, as cited and abridged by C. H. Dodd, *The Parables of the Kingdom* (3rd ed.; New York: Scribner's, 1936), 11-12.

ferent versions of the story of faith cast light on one another, so that one can interpret back and forth within this network of meanings.

In this setting, the work of the parable upon the listeners is to help them find their place. The story shows where the individual belongs. In this case, the initial reading of the story focuses on Adam and Christ, but the hearer who knows this way of listening to the parables knows that the story comes home when heard from Adam's point of view. That does not exclude the possibility of other readings; identification with the priest and the Levite suggests a peril to be avoided or a sense of sin to be confessed; and since Christ is example as well as redeemer, the hortatory, imperative interpretation so familiar in other ways of listening to the parable is not excluded. But the indicative reading, a description of how things are, a declaration of God's grace, is more fundamental than the imperative in this allegorical interpretation of the parable.

Putting it differently, one notes that all story-telling balances the experience of belonging in an orderly sequence with the experience of risk and movement as choices are made within the sequence of action. Allegorical interpretation, when set as it was within the context of an established faith, tended to put the emphasis on the first of these two dimensions of story-telling—that of experiencing the sense of belonging in a sequence of events. Yet this reading of the parables did not give up the dimension of risk and openness. In contrast to some modern interpretations of the Christian faith, however, the allegorical interpretation of a parable, as in this example, did set the hearer in an ongoing story where decision and action were believed to have dependable results. Choices had appropriate consequences. The eschatological element in the allegorical interpretation of the parables served to insure this dependability amid the risk and confusion of life, and thereby better identify the place of the hearer.

In shifting from the allegorical interpretation of the parables to the ethical interpretation, the name of Adolf Jülicher, whose interpretation of the parable of the Good Samaritan will be examined, is important. It should be noted that the turn away from allegory was not purely the result of studies of literary form such as those of Jülicher; this turn was already underway in other writers of the time, even as the faith in a coherent world interpreted by the Christian story was receding. Jülicher made clear on literary grounds what was already coming to be sensed by readers with less exact knowledge of literary style. Thus while the decline of allegorical interpretation was associated with the rise of literary analysis, crucial also was the collapse of the traditional Christian vision of which allegory was the vehicle. For Jülicher, as for many in that period, the replacement for the older Christian story was a strong confidence in the absoluteness of moral claims.

As for the Good Samaritan, our chosen example, Jülicher brushed aside all the elaborate churchly and doctrinal elements which figurative and other allegorical interpreters had seen in it. For him, the parable was an example story or illustration—an illustration precisely of how to act. Indeed, it was Jülicher who brought this parable, along with three others in Luke, into this category and made the classification current in New Testament interpretation. The distinction, still drawn, is that a parable is a metaphor which offers an analogy of how one should respond—the Kingdom is like a treasure hidden in a field, which someone found, for instance. The example story or illustration is not metaphorical but directly supplies an example of how to act, which one is to follow literally.

Jülicher described allegory as improper (*uneigentlich*) speech that did not say what it meant and contrasted it with the proper (*eigentlich*) speech of the actual parables, which meant what they said and not something else.[2] He summed up his view of the Good Samaritan in this way: the parable or, more properly, example story was genuinely from Jesus, but setting it in the framework of the question about "who is my neighbor" was Luke's work. Removed from Luke's setting, the meaning is: "the self-sacrificing exercise of love creates the highest value in the eyes of both God and humans, and no position of advantage of office or birth can substitute for it. The merciful person, even if a Samaritan, deserves salvation rather than the Jewish temple official who is the slave of egotism (cf. Rom. 2:14ff.)."[3] If this sounds a bit bare and general, Jülicher was well aware of how much more directly the story said it. But general principles impressed Jülicher. Of example stories as a class he concluded: "they illustrate a religious idea in its inescapable universal validity, in the form of an especially favorable chosen example."[4]

In his opposition to allegory, Jülicher developed the well-known "one-point" interpretation of the parable. He insisted that there is in a parable only one legitimate comparison to be drawn between the story and the intended religious application. Later interpreters have been

---

2. Adolf Jülicher, *Die Gleichnisreden Jesu* (Leipzig: Mohr, 1899), 1, 49.
3. Ibid., 2, 596.
4. Ibid., 2, 585.

favorable to this emphasis until recent times when scholars have once more begun to examine the many-sidedness of the symbolic language of the parables.[5] But long before wide criticism of the one-point theory, many writers on the parables criticized Jülicher for his plan of looking—as he did regularly, and as the illustration has shown—for a general moral or religious truth as the one point of a parable.[6] Many readers of the parables felt that something more than general truth was intended. Probably part of the criticism of Jülicher on this point arose from the correct perception that his interpretation of the parables involved a marked shift from the "indicative" setting of the hearer in a coherent world to the "imperative" of a general truth that tells people what they should do.

If it is correct to qualify Jülicher's position so as to find more than general truths in the parables, and to deny that a dramatic narrative can ever be successfully reduced to a static proposition, why was so keen and able a critic as Jülicher so well satisfied with this way of listening to the parables? Two aspects of his approach help us understand the appeal of his position.

In the first place, Jülicher was engaged in establishing a less christological interpretation of the parables. The example here showed how, in allegorical interpretation, the parable easily became the vehicle for a message about the Christ. Jülicher discerned that the christological affirmations of most of the parables were minimal if not altogether lacking. The parables, he saw, spoke to the human without making christological claims as such. Jülicher attempted to release the parables from a dogmatic rigidity by substituting a moral claim for a christological claim.

Jülicher was right in his effort to release the parables from christological exclusiveness, both historically and, we may venture to judge, in terms of the theological situation to which he spoke. Despite various attempts made since his time to reaffirm an explicit christological claim in the parables, those who interpret them today say, like Jülicher, that the language of the parables is not the only bearer of the reality to

---

5. John Dominic Crossan, *In Parables: The Challenge of the Historical Jesus* (New York: Harper & Row, 1973); Norman Perrin, *Jesus and the Language of the Kingdom* (London: SCM Press, 1976); Dan O. Via, Jr., *The Parables: Their Literary and Existential Dimension* (Philadelphia: Fortress Press, 1967); cf. the articles in John Dominic Crossan., ed., *Semeia* 9: *Polyvalent Narration* (1977).

6. Dodd, *Parables*, 24-25; Joachim Jeremias, *The Parables of Jesus*, tr. S. H. Hooke; rev. ed. (New York: Scribner's, 1964; tr. from German 6th ed., 1962), 18-19.

which it testifies. At the same time, the relation between the "message of Jesus" with its possible indirect christology and the "message about Jesus" is only indicated and not resolved by this insight.

A second aspect of Jülicher's view must be noted: general principles may not be very impressive to us, but they were to him and to many in his time. Cited above was Jülicher's phrase, "a religious idea in its inescapable universal validity." For the listeners of his time, the Kantian assertion of the absoluteness of the ethical demand, and its presence as an avenue of access to the ultimate, to God, still held power. If the move from the cosmos of the allegorical interpretation to the general moral truths of Jülicher reflected a shrinking world, a further shrinking is signaled in moving to the contemporary scene in which it is difficult to apprehend the seriousness of the universal moral or religious claim as Jülicher and many of his time perceived it. In his time there was still a sense in which a "moral truth" or "religious truth" embodied an indicative element. It was a statement about how things are as well as an imperative. This aspect of Jülicher's hearing of the parables, which may easily be missed by readers today, made them exciting to the hearers of his time.

In coming to the existential interpretation, a type of reading of the parables which is still current and vital is encountered. In this view, the listener is not in a structured world of moral claims, but in a world which is simply given, without any inherent meaningful structure. There are, indeed, structures of existence that recur, but these structures of existence only offer the field within which meaning is found in the act of decision.

Such a view strongly emphasizes the "imperative" over against the "indicative." Responding to the parable means risk and decision. Decision is taken with neither the sense of a surrounding dependable world assumed by the allegorical interpretation nor even the support of the "inescapable universal validity" of a religious (or moral) idea.

Rudolf Bultmann is the scholar many remember as at the center of existential interpretation. The "imperative" of the call to response was absolutely central to Bultmann, particularly in his interpretation of the parables. He looked elsewhere in the New Testament, especially to Paul and John, for a clear statement of that which is prior to the imperative, the indicative of grace. Following an old Lutheran theme, Bultmann considered the Gospels in general and the parables in particular too close to the imperative of law to be a firm base for the gospel.

Bultmann's interpretation has the great strength of moving away from Jülicher's notion of general truths toward a powerful focus on the confrontation of the individual and the actual concrete moment of existence. The moment which real listening to the parable evokes is a unique moment on which rests the weight of the hearer's destiny.

This powerful insight is gained at the cost of virtually eliminating the sense of drama in life, the fateful movement of life through a series of events which successively shape the possibilities that follow. To Bultmann such a dramatic vision of existence threatened the wholeness of the confrontation of the moment. To picture life as a process tending in a certain direction deprives the moment of its unique weight, and gives the person making the decision some leverage and control against the moment that, rightly, requires a total commitment. The root of this tension between dramatic sequence and existential moment lay in Bultmann's interpretation of sequences as what he thought of as natural events, cause-and-effect sequences. He did not think that one could participate in ongoing life "dramatically," but only in the moment, "existentially." The consequence of this judgment is particularly clear in his treatment of eschatology. He rejected any image of hope for future fulfillment because he believed that any vision of fulfillment would give the believer a leverage with which to manipulate the moment instead of giving oneself wholeheartedly to it.

Bultmann commented only briefly on the parable of the Good Samaritan. He followed Jülicher in taking it as an example story or illustration. He went so far as to say that these example stories "have no figurative element at all."[7] Like Jülicher he thought that the parable had been put in its present setting by Luke and that the point of the parable was the contrast (addressed to Jews) between the unloving Jews and the loving Samaritan. He saw the parable as a polemic against any notion of ethnic superiority. About this general point he said: "the Jew as such has no claim before God. Consistently with this Jesus proclaims a call to decision and repentance. Consistently, too, Jesus can elsewhere picture a Samaritan as putting the true Jew to shame (Luke 10: 29-37)."[8] More specifically Bultmann interpreted the parable of the Good Samaritan as follows:

> Such a man, who in contrast to those learned in the Law really understands what is demanded of him in the given situation, is depicted in the story of the good Samaritan. Luke reports it, pertin-

---

7. Rudolf Bultmann, *The History of the Synoptic Tradition*, tr. John Marsh (New York: Harper & Row, 1963; German 3d ed. 1958), 178.

8. Rudolf Bultmann, *Jesus and the Word*, tr. Louise Pettibone Smith and Erminie Huntress Lantero (New York: Scribner's, 1934; German ed., 1926), 45.

> ently for content if somewhat awkwardly from the point of view of style, as told by Jesus in answer to the evasive question "Who is my neighbor?"[9]

Bultmann wrote these words more than fifty years ago. In the meantime, a host of very good books on the parables have been published. To my mind, the key works were those of C. H. Dodd and Joachim Jeremias.[10] Focusing on the question of the relation of the parables to Jesus' action and message as a whole, both perceived that the parables offered the best avenue in the quest for the historical Jesus. Time has confirmed their judgment in this respect: nearly all the serious subsequent efforts to speak of the intention of Jesus concentrate on the parables. It is tempting to explore all the numerous solid interpretations of the parables that have been offered, but this is not possible.

Instead, a survey of the current development in interpretation, in which there is a strong concentration on language and its effects, will be undertaken. The linguistic interpretation will be discussed as a mode that succeeds the existential approach, even though many components of the existential interpretation are being carried forward into the various types of linguistic interpretation. To avoid the narrowness of the term "linguistic," perhaps one should speak of a period of "literary and linguistic" interpretation. Varied as the studies are, they include an effort to pay close attention to how language works, to how it achieves its effects, and to how the parables can be set more fully in the context of recent studies of language. These include a variety of emphases such as the concern for literary analysis by some American critics, continuing linguistic analysis, and the contributions of French structuralism.

As samples, contributions by John Dominic Crossan and Robert W. Funk will be considered. This choice means passing over other equally important work such as that of Dan O. Via, Jr. and Daniel Patte,[11] but the choice of Funk and Crossan serves well to relate the recent mode of parable interpretation to the earlier styles sketched above.

As noted, both Jülicher and Bultmann were keen students of the form of the parables. Neither of them, however, saw any problem in the notion that along with metaphorical parables like the Sower or the Hidden Treasure, there should be among the parables of Jesus also illustra-

---

9. Ibid., 96.

10. Dodd, *Parables*; Jeremias, *Parables*.

11. Via, *The Parables*; Daniel Patte, ed., *Semiology and Parables: An Exploration of the Possibilities Offered by Structuralism for Exegesis* (Pittsburgh: Pickwick Press, 1976).

tions or example stories like the Good Samaritan in which the point is made not metaphorically but directly. Some of the linguistic interpreters have questioned this assumption and have argued that the parable is by its nature metaphorical; therefore there are no example stories among the parables of Jesus. Thus, to hear the story of the Good Samaritan as it was meant to be heard, it must be heard as a metaphor, a true parable, and not as an example of proper behavior.

Both Crossan and Funk agree in this judgment. Crossan studied this parable and all the "example stories" or illustrations, and concluded that the Good Samaritan was not, as originally told by Jesus, an example of behavior to be followed at all (even though, of course, Luke understood it in that way). Rather, he concluded, it was a parable and must have a metaphorical point. Crossan followed most interpreters in saying that the point of the story was bound up with the unexpected goodness of the Samaritan. He summarized: "The original parabolic point was the reversal caused by the advent of the Kingdom in and through the challenge to utter the unutterable and to admit thereby that other world which was at that very moment placing their own under radical judgment."[12]

Crossan's analysis of the force of the language of the parable was based on the critical judgment that the church and the Gospel writers did not understand the original radical force of the parables. Instead, they tamed them, making them less extreme and more bearable—in this case converting an authentic parable about a surprising manifestation of goodness into a mere example of good behavior. Jülicher and Bultmann had already held that Luke modified the parable. Crossan was thus not following a new course. But he rigorously separated the Gospel of Luke's version of the parable from the original version of Jesus with the assumption that the uniform tendency of the Gospel writers was to take the effect off Jesus' parables, to domesticate them, so to speak, in the church. Such a view enabled Crossan to maintain that the parables, as Jesus used them, were not only metaphorical, but that they had the specific metaphorical function of leading to the point where the hearer's vision of the world is shattered.

The world in which the hearer lives must be broken for the hearer to have the possibility, the momentary opportunity, to glimpse the ultimate, the mystery of God. Crossan described this basic process of coming to insight in the following way: the seeming naturalness of a parable compels

---

12. Crossan, *In Parables*, 66.

a hearer's assent and leads into involvement in the story, only then to shock the hearer with the discovery that to give assent to the story necessitates abandoning the vision of the world the hearer originally brought to the event. Radical judgment and the possibility of redemption can suddenly but momentarily be glimpsed.

The historical analysis behind this way of listening to the Good Samaritan is basically the same as Jülicher's. Crossan separated the parable from the framework in which Luke had set it and made some acute observations about how the points of emphasis were to be located in the parable. At bottom, however, he simply listened to it differently from Jülicher, being convinced that a parable must be a surprising metaphor and not merely an example of something good.

Robert W. Funk's analysis of the Good Samaritan arrived at much the same result as Crossan's although he worked out the details differently.[13] Funk, like Crossan, considered the parable of the Good Samaritan metaphorical and not an example story. His approach to understanding the metaphor has a very simple—and important—basis: with whom, asked Funk, is the listener to identify? His answer: not with the Samaritan, but with the man who is lying in the ditch. The question is not "Can I be a Samaritan?" but "Am I willing to let myself be served by a Samaritan?" Thus the parable tells a story of a person at the end of the rope; all who are truly victims, truly disinherited, have no choice but to give themselves up to mercy. If the hearer, concluded Funk, as Jew, understands what it means to be the victim in the ditch in this story, the hearer also understands what the Kingdom is. The meaning of the parable cannot be made more explicit, because it is nonliteral; it lacks specific application. In this, Funk has rejected Jülicher's interpretation of the parables as expressing general truths. About parables generally, Funk wrote,

> The parable does not, therefore, involve a transfer of information or ideas about an established world from one head to another. In this parable reality is aborning; the parable opens onto an unfinished world because that world is in course of conception. This means that both narrator and auditor *risk* the parable; they both participate [in] the narrative and venture its outcome. He or they do not tell the story; it *tells* them.[14]

---

13. Robert W. Funk, "The Good Samaritan as Metaphor," *Semeia* 2 (1974), 74-81.

14. Ibid., 76.

Funk's simple but important point that one great clue to the meaning of a narrative lies in asking how an individual identifies with the characters is extremely helpful in clarifying how people hear the parables. The point of the story is missed if one does not or cannot identify with the man in the ditch. It is equally clear to me, however, that one is also to identify with the Samaritan. Why limit identification to only one character in the story? Funk believes that in any hearing of the story one makes a primary identification with one character who is taken to give the central perspective. Part of the richness of the narrative form itself, however, is that it invites multiple perspectives: What is it like to be the man in the ditch, the Samaritan, the priest or Levite? From any of these identifications proceeds a primary hearing of the story. The same is true of the central Christian story, the story of the crucifixion; a study of various liturgies and theologies would show the force of hearing the story in terms of various primary identifications with the different characters in the narrative.

Funk's emphasis on hearing the parable of the Good Samaritan through an identification with the man lying in the ditch ironically brings us full circle back to Augustine's allegorical interpretation which had the same thrust; this despite Funk's vigorous rejection of allegory.[15] Both interpretations have in common the primary emphasis on "indicative," on the surprise of grace that comes into the situation before one expects it and in a way not anticipated. The other obvious identification, with the Samaritan, naturally puts the emphasis on "imperative," explicit in Luke's interpretation: go and do the same thing yourself.

There is, of course, a difference between Augustine and Funk. From the allegorical interpretation through the ethical and existential to the linguistic, can be seen a progressive "loss of world," a progressive loss of the sense of a coherent environment within which the receptiveness of faith and the act of decision were understood to take place. The allegorists knew that the world was created by God and redeemed by Christ, and within this context they heard the parable. Those who employed the ethical interpretation had lost much of this sense of stability, but they still had a world of dependable moral principles. The existentialists saw the world

15. Robert W. Funk, *Language, Hermeneutic, and Word of God* (New York: Harper & Row, 1966), 214 n. 67: "It is for this reason that the parables should not be allegorized (allegory: reduction to a congeries of ideas or concepts, for which the narrative elements are ciphers), but it is also the reason why the parables cannot be reduced to a leading idea . . . or understood to teach 'spiritual truths.' Rationalization in any form maims the parabolic image."

as constituted only by the act of repeated, individual decision. The linguistic interpreters whose works have been sketched here are still largely existentialists in their theological approach to the parables; if there is a shift, it is toward an even stronger negativity toward structure, toward the notion of a world on which one can depend, as a vehicle for the ultimate.

What is surely inherent in this history of interpretation, this history of reduction of world, is the sharp challenge to cultural security confronting the church. The parables are shocking, disconcerting, to those who are at home in their world in the sense of the given cultural structures. But there is a difference between the shattering of cultural security and what I call a "reduction of world." For the shrinking world which the more recent interpreters offer as the context within which one listens to the parable is a world in which neither the "other" in the sense of the neighbor nor the "Other" as God is visible. All the more necessary and challenging is the need to listen yet more attentively to the parables, to rediscover an authentic wider context, a framework of interaction between humans and God, a world hidden within or behind the way the parables are heard.

Simple as they are, the parables nonetheless are rich and complex enough to speak powerfully through a whole series of sharply different interpretations. To think that we can discard these earlier views to find at last the one true interpretation would be foolish. Instead, I raise some questions and make some suggestions toward a more comprehensive interpretation.

In the first place, as a more language-oriented interpretation of the parables is developed, it is important to reexamine the presuppositions that we bring to the analysis of language. In my view, linguistic analysis is much more neutral, and not necessarily freighted with the existentialist, Heideggerian views that Crossan and Funk have joined to it. To put it more positively: the Heideggerian vision of the poetic creation of the world through language is a powerful general framework for approaching the detailed linguistic analysis of religious speech, in this case the parable. But the very concentration on language as world-creating event may close the interpreter to other dimensions of the actual events which take place in hearing the parable, notably the interchange between language and the constraints imposed by non-linguistic reality.

If the act of listening is thought of as a part of the repeated act of self-creation, and especially as a response to the text which arouses in us a bundle of concrete possibilities or proposals, possibilities which are suggested by the text as related to the tradition in which the text is heard, a model emerges which allows us to take seriously a variety of readings of the text and to develop a framework for evaluating and relating the various possibilities. Putting the emphasis on the reader's or hearer's act of self-creation allows us to leave a place for the full work of figurative analysis, but reminds us that the linguistic effect is in interaction with a host of nonlinguistic factors. Above all, by positing an element of freedom in each act of self-creation, however routine and repetitive most such moments may be, the harsh break between scientific analysis, conceived as casually determined, and humanistic analysis, which strives to avoid determinism, can be avoided. Further, since the concrete possibilities suggested by a text are combinations of subjects abstracted from previous experience with hypothetical predicates, this model provides a fruitful way of relating the empirical and the imaginative.

Such a model sees that historical reconstruction, important as it is, is a special, abstract kind of listening. The emphasis is on the present quest for meaning. The reason for listening to a text is that it may open possibilities for the listener, possibilities which have not yet been experienced or which need to be recalled and reexperienced.

The sensitive insights of the schools of interpretation sketched here are invaluable. Each successive type of interpretation has brought forth a valid and authentic way of hearing the parables. Yet one cannot fail to see that each type was able to make available from the parables an interpretation that was already congenial within the acknowledged possibilities of that culture. Serious listening to a scriptural or other important text must take place within contemporary culture, but one hopes that the culture will not decide in advance what can be heard in the text. The reason for listening to such texts is that they may renew a vision of what is possible, re-structure the vision of the culture. The Whiteheadian or process model here suggested as a mode of interpretation does not, I believe, impose a process reading on the parables, but, on the contrary, has the capacity to be more open to the unexpected, the culturally rejected, possibilities that may be heard in the text.

For instance, the gains in understanding in the positions sketched above have been won at the price of a progressive loss of an element which did not seem valid to the cultures which shaped the readings, namely, the sense of a coherent world as a field for human solidarity. This becomes even more striking as one moves from the earlier to the later readings.[16] The more open model for listening suggested here could bring this element back for serious consideration.

We move from a proposal about how to think of the process of interpretation to a proposal about the theological content. Funk's emphatic rejection of allegory, noted above, has its center in a point well illustrated by the particular parable we have been studying: he has argued that allegory must be rejected because it tends to transform the parables into stories about God. This position reflects a modern view that the realm of speech is the human realm and that God is beyond speech. To me this does not sound like Jesus and the Gospels. At the same time I see the very good reasons for the move Funk made. The God of whom he was afraid is the God allegorically represented by the authoritative figures in the parables, particularly the father who appears in a number of them (though not, of course, here). Such a God is a threat to human freedom. To learn both from the New Testament and from process theology to grasp a different view of God—God as the persuader rather than as the absolute ruler—opens the way for a more comprehensive theory of metaphor in which metaphors can really point to God and tell us something about God's reality.

Some of the most imaginative New Testament interpreters, and Funk and Crossan are among them, have been so strongly taken with the poetic, metaphorical character of language that they have given up the possibility of speaking non-metaphorically about the substance of the parable. Funk has argued that a specific meaning cannot be given to the parable of the Good Samaritan. Such an insistence on the total irreducibility of metaphor, however, must be rejected. True, symbolic language has a richness that can never be reduced to propositional statements (using the term propositional in its usual sense). Yet the interchange between dense, symbolic speech and carefully constructed abstract speech has long been a principal way of enlarging our world and of testing the vision of faith for its coherence with the whole of our experience. The task of enlarging our vision of the world by keeping these two forms of speech in dialogue with each other is still crucial.

The parable of the Good Samaritan is a fine illustration of the problem. Bultmann said it had "no figurative element at all," since it was an

---

16. The sense of social responsibility in the parables is emphasized by Charles E. Carlston, *The Parables of the Triple Tradition* (Philadelphia: Fortress Press, 1975).

example story.[17] Crossan and Funk tried to identify it as something other than an example story, so that it might have a figurative element. Would it not be wiser to say that, even as an example story, the Good Samaritan does indeed have a powerful figurative, symbolic element, calling up the world of risk and of love, throwing open the unfinished and unlimited nature of the claim which living together in a social world lays upon us? Even though God is not figured at all in this story, God's love is in the background, the ambience of the world depicted by the story. While true parables have a much stronger metaphorical element, we have been misled, from Jülicher onward, in thinking that example stories are non-metaphorical. Funk rightly saw that "Christian" benevolent righteousness easily becomes self-righteousness. He did well to point out that only the person who is able to accept is really able to give. This is no new point, of course; recall Deut 5:15: "Remember that you were a slave in the land of Egypt." But is this the exclusive point of the story? Dan O. Via, Jr., who argued that there really are example stories among the parables of Jesus, has much the better of it.[18] What becomes clear is that the hearer who listens attentively and struggles with the parables can hear it both ways.

This leads to a further point. Is it really true, as Funk says, that the truly disinherited have no choice but to give themselves up to mercy? I do not hear the marginalized from society speaking this way in North American Black theology or in Latin American theology of liberation. The disinherited find in listening to the parables a dignity and hope which enable them to act![19] It is true that the message of Jesus as set forth in the parable of the Good Samaritan calls for a very difficult kind of action, that of putting oneself in the place of the other, which is often very difficult to hear in times of conflict. But one of the reasons for the deep power of this story is its effectiveness both at the level of receptivity and at the level of the call to action. As such it fully represents the complexity of the interplay between the divine and the human as represented throughout the Gospels.

So far we have not explicitly touched on the question, whether the parables can be taken "just as they are in themselves," or how far they

---

17. See above, p. 50, n.7.

18. Dan O. Via, Jr., "Parable and Example Story: A Literary-Structuralist Approach," *Semeia* 1 (1974), 105-133.

19. See James H. Cone, *A Black Theology of Liberation* (Philadelphia: Lippincott, 1970), 222; José Porfirio Miranda, *Marx and the Bible: A Critique of the Philosophy of Oppression*, tr. John Eagleson (Maryknoll, NY: Orbis, 1974), 70.

require a setting in the message of the Gospels as a whole for full understanding. Such a question, if really pursued, would lead again to the question of christology: how or to what extent do the parables require the figure of Christ? Here we can only indicate some directions for the exploration of this question. Surely it is the case that there is no escape from the interpretive circle between the concrete text and the larger context. The larger context does not have to be that of the Gospels; the parables of Jesus can, for instance, be set in the context of a modern collection of parables such as that edited by Howard Schwartz.[20] If so, the impact on interpretation is to highlight the reading of the parables of Jesus in terms of multiple perspectives and ambiguous meanings. Most New Testament interpreters would probably defend the "Jesus" context as the proper one for listening to the parables for historical reasons. Jesus' message of the Kingdom of God and his action on behalf of the Kingdom were the context that, so to speak, provoked the parables. The approach suggested here also favors testing a spontaneous reading of the parables against the best understanding of their original function, not simply to give priority to the first meaning, but because the New Testament setting has repeatedly shown its paradigmatic power and its ability to renew the vision of a later age. Thus, though the parables say little directly, or even indirectly, about their speaker, our understanding of them and response to them is clarified and deepened as the world they evoke is related to the world evoked by Jesus' other words and actions. If this context is problematic, so much so that some interpreters allow little beyond the parables to guide us about Jesus, nevertheless a reader of the New Testament will hear the parables in this context and try to establish it as adequately as possible.

Recent writers, many of whom have followed the same line as Crossan and Funk, have heard the parables primarily as "indicative" rather than "imperative." They have done so precisely for the reason that the finding of a place, the vision of a world in which we can place ourselves, has become so problematical in our time. Approaching the matter through the hermeneutic of a vision of language creating a fragile, temporary place for the human, they have in fact been questing in the depths of the "primal" insights that lie buried behind the rigid and concealing structures built through the centuries by Western culture including Christian theology. Their quest for liberation from the rigidity of

---

20. Howard Schwartz, *Imperial Messages: One Hundred Modern Parables* (New York: Avon, 1976).

traditional forms has taken place through a discarding of baggage, a simplifying, precisely a reduction of world, in the faith that the minimal and transitory world revealed by the shock of recognition of the parable will be truer than the much more visible forms offered by tradition. Not all, but many of the sharply defined linguistic studies operate from a faith similar to this.

That such a stance is liberating can be seen from the widespread resonance that it evokes. I do not follow a different path in order to adhere more fixedly to tradition, but because I find that recourse to the "primal," the pre-rational and pre-cultural resources of the spirit, does not fully release the movement toward hope and the new. The aim is to work toward an interpretive stance which is more consciously open toward the emerging new word and not only to that which is in the depths of the spirit and prior to cultural formulation. Such a quest is more fully in touch with the future-oriented renewing power that shows itself in the New Testament. I do not, in addition, share the negative view of a structured world that is presupposed by so many recent interpreters. Seeing that for all the weight of the past, the present does always embody momentary elements of freedom to reshape and reuse the past, one may believe that the most creative stance is not that of searching back for the primal reality, but the stance of hope, of sensitizing oneself to the world that may come to be. Such a stance will find it natural to value positively both the receptiveness that discovers or allows the world to be broken and remade in the vision of faith, and the human activity without which hope cannot be realized. Such a stance should be a productive one for listening to the parables, and one that may allow them to be foundational in the vision of the world that is coming to be. In this sense Funk is correct that "reality is aborning" in listening to the parables. The goal is to discover a listening which can effect a connection between the moments of experience such that action and hope may result from listening. In the specific case of the parable of the Good Samaritan, as noted above, such a stance listens attentively to what it says about human solidarity.[21]

---

21. My exploration has been stimulated by a group which met in Claremont in 1977: John B. Cobb. Jr., David J. Lull, Russell Pregeant, Theodore J. Weeden, Sr., and Barry A. Woodbridge. For bibliography on process thought and New Testament studies, see John B. Cobb, Jr. with David J. Lull and Barry A. Woodbridge, "Process Thought and New Testament Exegesis," *JAAR* 47 (1979), 21-30.

- 4 -

Parable, Proverb, and Koan

The parables of Jesus have claimed constant attention from interpreters of the New Testament; the proverbs in the gospels on the other hand have been attended to only intermittently. Also the parables have been interpreted a in great variety of ways, while there are fewer options open in interpreting proverbs. Since the parables stand between narrative and gnomic saying, they may be interpreted toward their narrative function or toward the similarity of their function to that of sayings or aphorisms. Proverbs, too, commonly imply a background story, but the narrative element is clearly less prominent.

Presuppositions of Interpretation

In this essay we shall concentrate on some of the presuppositions which lie behind an older and a more recent style of interpretation of parables and proverbs. If we can perceive these presuppositions more clearly, we may be able to criticize our own in ways that will alter our own perspectives and thus our interpretations. The discussion will center on the question of the relation of parable and proverb to the perception of order, and on the question of the relation of the transcendent to order.

The modern period of parable study began with allegorical interpretation, which strongly aligned the parables with their narrative aspect, indeed seeing them not only in the framework of the overarching dramatic story of salvation, but often also as brief resumés of it or of some aspect of it. Augustine's interpretation of the parable of the Good Samaritan, as cited by Dodd,[1] will serve as an example of this incorporation of the parable into the dramatic story of salvation. In this view, the parable clearly expresses the purpose of a God who creates and renews the order of the world, though standing far above it.

From *Semeia* 12: *Festschrift for Amos Niven Wilder* (1978), 151-177.

1. C. H. Dodd, *Parables of the Kingdom* (New York: Scribner's, 1936), 11-12.

It was not only a better perception of the form of the parables, but also—perhaps at a fundamental level even more—a loss of participation in the story of salvation which led, around the beginning of this century, to the abandonment of this earlier, somewhat naive interpretation of the parables. Adolf Jülicher is the name rightly associated with this shift. Indeed, he established the classification of the parables which, though it has been much discussed and modified, still governs our appreciation of their form. His book included a sharp attack upon allegorical interpretation, and he is usually thought of as the one who overturned it, though others were working along similar lines.

It was Jülicher's work which turned attention to the parables as didactic, as teaching general truths, therefore as similar in function to proverbs. The modern reader who is not much thrilled by general truths should remember that at that time the perception of duty, of the universal moral demand as a basic and universal element of humanness, was still felt as a powerful and as a transcendent claim. It seemed that by interpreting the parables as vehicles of such a universal moral and religious claim, they were being made available to a world which was less and less impressed by christological exclusiveness. Jülicher observed, in the course of a discussion of the origin of Mark's theory of the purpose of the parables, that Jesus used parables (in contradiction to the Marcan theory) in speaking to all sorts of audiences, because he found that this "form was peculiarly suited to intensify the clarity and convincing power of his ideas (*Gedanken*)." Jesus was not put off by the fact that the same form was used in profane speech, just as in his own, to "clarify the unknown by the generally known, to lead from the easy to the difficult."[2] Thus the parables functioned, in his view, as aids in the process of perceiving the deeper ordering processes of life.

A few years later, in 1905, Dean William Wallace Fenn was giving his lectures on "The Theological Method of Jesus" at Harvard. Essentially he pictured Jesus as a wisdom teacher. Fenn used both parables and proverbial sayings to present the message of Jesus, the gist of which he summarized in part as follows: "As God deals with men in nature, so he deals with the soul of man."[3]

---

2. Adolf Jülicher, *Die Gleichnisreden Jesu* (Leipzig: J. B. C. Mohr, 1899), 1, 146.

3. William Wallace Fenn, *The Theological Method of Jesus: A Course of Lectures in the Summer School, Harvard University, 1905* (Boston: Beacon Press, 1938), 65.

The various studies of Q which were made about this time and even much later thought of it as a didactic writing, and in these studies the proverbial sayings of Jesus (and of the early church) were explored as condensing and thereby making available the continuities of experience, albeit a higher or highest form of experience. Streeter, for instance, referred to Q as a "collection of 'wise sayings' of Christ, comparable to a book like Proverbs or Pirke Aboth."[4]

The studies of proverbs and parables of this period were aware of the element of surprise and paradox in at least some of these sayings, though they were sometimes uncomfortable with it.[5] But they characteristically saw this element of surprise in a context of overarching meaning which could be re-established in fuller form after the moment of shock. An interpreter in this tradition was Henry J. Cadbury, whose lifelong study of Jesus was the basis of *Jesus: What Manner of Man*. Cadbury was a keen student of rhetoric (in this book he also draws on Amos Wilder's *Eschatology and Ethics in the Teaching of Jesus*).[6] He quotes Fenn with approval, yet he mediates between the earlier and the later types of interpretation in that, like the newer interpretation, he throws into the foreground the intensity and extremeness of Jesus' words, which he sums up at one point as the "demand for a surplus."[7] But this insight does not separate him from the claim that these parables and proverbs stand in an important continuity with a whole experience of life. "The facts of religion and of ethics may be directly observed in nature and in man since all of life is homogeneous and mutually analogous."[8]

Bultmann, who studied the parables and proverbs of the gospels with great care, adopting Jülicher's classification of the parables and giving a formal analysis of the proverbial sayings which is still current, fully recognized their "wisdom" affinities. Yet he understood the more traditional sayings which expressed the continuity noted by Cadbury, to be for the most part background material later incorporated into the gospels, in accordance with his principle of dissimilarity. He turned his interpreta-

---

4. B. H. Streeter, *The Four Gospels: A Study of Origins* (New York: Macmillan, 1924), 286.

5. As Jülicher was uncomfortable with the parable of the Workers in the Vineyard; cf. Jülicher, op. cit., 2, 466.

6. Rev. ed. (New York: Harper, 1950; lst ed., 1939).

7. Henry J. Cadbury, *Jesus: What Manner of Man* (New York: Macmillan, 1947), 30.

8. Ibid., 54; cf. also Dodd, 21-22.

tions of the parables and proverbs strongly toward those elements which lifted the demand of a saying out of the continuous context of life into an existential confrontation.[9] This double aspect of his work so provoked an American interpreter, still strongly in the tradition of continuity, that he said, "Bultmann does not seem to apprehend the significance of his own statements."[10] This was hardly the case, but the difficulty of mutual understanding does point to an issue with which we must still try to deal.

Amos Wilder's *Eschatology and Ethics in the Teaching of Jesus* has an important role to play in the movement from the earlier to the more recent range of concerns in the interpretation of parable and proverb, even though that work was not specifically addressed to these speech forms. In common with the earlier view, Wilder presented Jesus as making an "appeal to reason and conscience [which] necessarily evokes a moral order in which the consequences are patent and inescapable."[11] But his perception of the eschatological aspect of Jesus' message opens the way for him to give a place to real breaks in the expected continuities of life. His appreciation of eschatological symbolism also enables him to move beyond the tendency to reduce faith to the ethical dimension, a tendency which was strong in the earlier period.[12] Consequently his work offers a fuller appreciation of the radical, extreme sayings which break the continuities of life; but he emphasizes both that extreme sayings usually spoke to particular situations, and that as symbolic language they had to be taken seriously but were misunderstood if taken literally.[13] Many of these themes were more fully developed in *Early Christian Rhetoric*.[14]

Throughout this period, it was assumed that the context within which parables and sayings were spoken was the context of a partly-knowable divine purpose. As we move through the period, we find that this presupposition becomes more problematic.

---

9. Rudolf Bultmann, *Jesus and the Word*, tr. Louise Pettibone Smith and Erminie Huntress Lantero (New York: Scribner's, 1934), 57-120; *The History of the Synoptic Tradition*, tr. John Marsh (New York: Harper & Row, 1963), 69-108, 166-205.

10. Elmer W. K. Mould, *The World View of Jesus* (New York: Harper & Row, 1941), 22.

11. Wilder, op. cit., 136.

12. Ibid., 198-202.

13. Ibid., 133-35.

14. Amos N. Wilder, *Early Christian Rhetoric: The Language of the Gospel*, reissue with new Introduction (Cambridge, MA: Harvard University Press, 1971).

More Recent Interpretation

More recent interpretation has arrived at its concerns through a history which we cannot sketch here, though the references to Rudolf Bultmann and Amos Wilder have indicated some of its features. The earlier scholars often had a strong perception of the disorienting, surprising claim of the sayings of Jesus. In general, they grasped the movement of disorientation in a context of a larger process of growth in orientation; they tended to see the transcendent element as "beyond" the continuities which are supportive of the human. But recent study looks both to parables and to proverbs for their function of disruption, of creating discontinuities, rather than for clarifying or establishing continuities. This very substantial shift in direction reflects a change in cultural sensibility, a quest for an interpretation of the gospels and of Jesus which will be viable in a world which does not find the testable or commonly-experienced continuities of life to be transparent to the Spirit or the divine. Many of the essays in the present collection[15] are themselves eloquent testimony to this shift; for instance, Roger Hazelton's on the problem of analogy (analogy is mentioned above, in the quotation from Cadbury, and presupposed in many of the earlier interpretations), and Sallie McFague's on narrative (we have noted the orienting importance of narrative in connection with allegorical interpretation).[16] In an earlier article Sallie McFague wrote: "It may be that the parable, while itself a story of a certain kind, is a more appropriate genre for our time [than the extended narrative], for unlike the more developed narrative it does not call for the same degree of faith in cosmic or even societal ordering."[17] Disconnectedness and surprise are also characteristics of the aphoristic saying which have made it attractive to many recent writers.

Recent studies of the parable by Funk, Perrin, Ricoeur, Crossan, and others have provided powerful exegetical clarification of how parables disconcert, and Perrin, Ricoeur, and Crossan as well as the present author have shown how the hyperbolic and paradoxical proverbial sayings

---

15. [The reference is to *Semeia* 12 and 13 (1978), which were a *Festschrift* in honor of Amos Niven Wilder.]

16. [Roger Hazleton, "Theological Analogy and Metaphor," *Semeia* 13 (1978), 155-176; Sallie McFague (TeSelle) "Imaginary Gardens with Real Toads: Realism in Fiction and Theology," *ibid.*, 241-260.]

17. Sallie McFague TeSelle, "Parable, Metaphor, and Theology," *JAAR* 42 (1974), 641.

in the gospels aim to break up the project of making a whole out of one's life.[18]

Alas, our study has to bypass the extremely rich formal analyses of both parable and proverb, and in taking this course we risk meriting the displeasure of the authors cited above, who may find that we have not paid attention to their central contributions. They will rightly hold that their emphases on disjunction, on shattering of vision, are grounded in formal studies which they have carried out with great care. Nevertheless, we must accept this risk, in order to move at once to reflect about the presuppositions which these studies of form embody, the more so because the contrast with the earlier interpreters is so apparent.

The Issue of Underlying Presuppositions

The earlier treatments of parable and proverb set the element of surprise in the context of an ongoing process of the ordering of life. They saw the sayings as presenting a vision of the world in which the transcendent God was the ultimate source of the ordering process, a vision in which God was continually at work in the world, even though the work of God was or could be particularly evident in moments of crisis or alteration of direction. It is precisely this presupposition which is rejected or at least bracketed by the newer interpreters, in differing degrees or ways. A first formulation of the issue, a formulation which has governed our discussion this far, casts the problem in terms of "continuity or discontinuity." This way of viewing the question derives from the crisis theology. That we are all so indebted to Bultmann in our thinking about parables and proverbs helps to account for the fact that a formulation in terms of continuity or discontinuity is still the prevalent framework of discussion. Ricoeur's relating of the concept of "limit" to the transcendental imagination of hope[19] is also related to this antithesis of continuity and discontinuity, and makes clear how deeply related the crisis theology was to Kant.

---

18. Robert W. Funk, *Language, Hermeneutic, and Word of God* (New York: Harper & Row, 1966); Norman Perrin, *Jesus and the Language of the Kingdom* (Philadelphia: Fortress Press, 1976); Paul Ricoeur, "Biblical Hermeneutics," *Semeia* 4 (1975); John Dominic Crossan, *In Parables: The Challenge of the Historical Jesus* (New York: Harper & Row, 1973); *The Dark Interval: Towards a Theology of Story* (Niles, IL: Argus Communications, 1975); *Raid on the Articulate: Comic Eschatology in Borges and Jesus* (New York: Harper & Row, 1978); for William A. Beardslee, see chapter 1 of this volume.

19. Paul Ricoeur, "Biblical Hermeneutics," 138-45.

The language of discontinuity, and that of limit, reflect an effort to speak of a response to the transcendent without talking about the transcendent directly. To move beyond this language is to raise the question whether it is possible to avoid trying to speak about the transcendent. The assumption that one could speak about the response to the transcendent without speaking about the transcendent presupposed that there was one authentic way to respond to the transcendent because there was one definitive revelation of the transcendent. The matter may not be so simple as this.

The significance of Crossan's work lies particularly at this point. While retaining the starting-point in discontinuity and in the disruptive effect of parable and proverb, he enriches his interpretation by a much fuller reflection on how he understands the context of expectation which suggests the impact of the saying. The context of expectation for the sayings of Jesus, for instance, is presented by associating the parables of Jesus with those of Jorge Luis Borges, which are fuller narratives that, with great imaginative power, bring the reader into a thoroughly ambiguous world, a world ambiguous because language has no secure referent, a world based on play or game.[20] In Crossan's view, Jesus and Borges have in common a "comic eschatology," a playful rejection of the false securities of structure and order. "End," the central apocalyptic symbol, is here interpreted in purely negative terms, since all stable structures of human culture are linguistic creations, and it is only in their deconstruction that we can glimpse the transcendent nothingness which is their creative ground. As Crossan says in an earlier work:

> The parables of Jesus are not historical allegories telling us how God acts with mankind; neither are they moral example stories telling us how to act before God and towards one another. They are stories which shatter the deep structure of our accepted world and thereby render clear and evident to us the relativity of story itself. They make us vulnerable to God. It is *only* [italics mine] in such experiences that God can touch us, and only in such moments does the Kingdom of God arrive. My own term for this relationship is transcendence.[21]

We are at an opposite pole from the earlier interpreters, not merely with an emphasis on discontinuity, but with a new ontology of transcendence, a transcendence which does not sustain the structures of humanness, though it may, by shattering, renew them, and a trans-

20. Crossan, *Raid on the Articulate.*
21. Crossan, *The Dark Interval*, 121-22.

cendence which can be glimpsed only in moments of disorientation. Amos Wilder comments, as part of a larger, appreciative response to Crossan's work: "Jesus' mythos of the Kingdom of God has more content to it than this kind of ontological reversal."[22] Such a statement presupposes that "mythos," or organizing story which wrests order out of chaos, and its "content" are not necessarily completely opaque to the transcendent.

The sayings of the desert fathers

Before we try to assess the contrast between older and newer interpretations of the sayings of Jesus, it is worth asking whether ancient Christianity offers any texts in which the interpretation of the transcendent as creative nothingness would be more clearly affirmed by the context as well as by the text. While we do not quite find "creative nothingness," we do find something close to it—aphoristic sayings used with the intention of shattering the continuities of experience of the hearer and of opening the hearer to an experience of pure negativity and formlessness as far as both ego and world are concerned. I am speaking of the *Apophthegmata patrum,* the sayings of the desert fathers, coming from the oral tradition arising in late fourth-century Egypt. (We leave aside the parable since this form was not widely used in ancient Christianity.)[23] The apophthegms of the desert fathers are, like the gospel apophthegms, usually more extended narratives than the very brief question and answer which provides the setting for a pungent saying in the usual apophthegm of popular Greek philosophy. Often the point is carried by the story rather than by a particular saying. But the aphoristic saying is central to the collection all the same.

These sayings include many elements of paradox and surprise, but not often in the form of a rhetorical paradox which makes its immediate effect by the overthrow of expectation at the moment of hearing. The immediate effect is rather, for most of the sayings, that of a lapidary simplicity which reinforces or renews insight into what is already known to be affirmed.

---

22. Amos Niven Wilder, *Theopoetic: Theology and the Religious Imagination* (Philadelphia: Fortress Press, 1976), 77 n. 1.

23. But cf. Robert M. Johnson, "Greek Patristic Parables," *SBL Seminar Papers 1977* (Missoula, MT, Scholars Press, 1977), 215-229.

> A brother asked an old man, "How cometh the fear of God in a man?" And the old man said, "If a man have humility and poverty and judgeth not another, so comes in him the fear of God."[24]

The element of surprise is often present in the way in which that which is rejected is spoken of, as for instance in the motif of admiration for the dedication of "loose women" in this extremely anti-sexual literature:

> Athanasius of holy memory besought the abbot Pambo to come down from the desert to Alexandria; and when he had come down, he saw there a woman who was an actress, and he wept. And when those who stood by asked him wherefore he had wept he spoke. "Two things," said he, "moved me. One, her perdition; the other, that I have not so much concern to please God as she hath to please vile men."[25]

But on the whole the elements of surprise are infused into the whole collection by its resolute opposition to the "world's" value system. The rhetoric of hyperbole and paradox does not need to be used because this opposition is so well known to all hearers. The sayings deal with a difficult choice between two seemingly well-known alternatives.

Nevertheless, it is not surprising that the sharp retort is also used to open the hearer to the new world which the sayings deal with.

> A certain brother came to the abbot Moses in Scete seeking a word from him. And the old man said to him, "Go and sit in thy cell, and thy cell shall teach thee all things."[26]

> A brother asked an old man saying, "Father, give me some word." The old man said to him, "When God struck Egypt, there was no house that had not mourning."[27]

> There came three brethren to a certain old man in Scete, and one of them asked him, saying, "Father, I have committed the Old and New Testaments to memory." And the old man answered and said, "Thou hast filled the air with words." And the second asked him, saying, "I have written the Old and New Testaments with my own hand." But he said to him, "And thou hast filled the windows with manuscripts." And the third said, "The grass grows on my hearthstone." And the old man answered and said, And thou hast driven hospitality from thee."[28]

---

24. Helen Waddell, *The Desert Fathers* (London: Constable, 1936), 90.
25. Ibid., 96-97.
26. Ibid., 94.
27. Ibid., 97.
28. Ibid., 149.

> The abbot Pastor said that when brother Zachary was dying, the abbot Moses asked him, saying, "What seest thou?" And he answered, "Naught better, Father, than to hold one's peace." And he said, "It is true, my son, hold thy peace."[29]

> In the beginning of his conversion Abbot Evagrius [Ponticus] came to a certain elder and said, "Father, tell me some word by which I may be saved." The elder said, "If you want to be saved, . . . do not speak until [some one] asks you something."[30]

The apophthegm concludes with Evagrius' confession: "Believe me, I have read many books and have never found anywhere such learning."

Appropriate as a put-down of a cultivated and theologically literate scholar, who had been a disciple and friend of the great Cappadocian fathers before he retired to Egypt, this apophthegm is also significant for its reference to silence, so central to the actual discipline of the fathers and in negative theology.

We have introduced Evagrius Ponticus (ca. 345-399) because it was he who provided the most thorough theological and practical interpretation of the asceticism which lies behind the sayings of the desert fathers. He is little known, since his work was condemned along with that of Origen, whose theological disciple he was. Nevertheless, his works on prayer and ascetic discipline have been truly foundational in the development of both Eastern and Western Christian spirituality.[31]

For our topic of the paradoxical aphorism, Evagrius shows much the same pattern as we noted in connection with the popular sayings of the desert fathers. He wrote in a gnomic style, but most of his sayings are simple maxims, generalizations which point the reader away from the concrete to the more general. Such generalizing was felt to be an appropriate way of approaching that which cannot really be spoken in gnostic and neo-platonic spirituality as well as in ancient Christian spirituality. For beyond the general stands the unspecifiable.

> The spirit that possesses health is one that has no images of the things of this world at the time of prayer. (*Praktikos* 65)[32]

---

29. Ibid., 167.

30. Thomas Merton, *The Wisdom of the Desert* (New York: New Directions, 1960), 69-70.

31. Louis Bouyer, *The Spirituality of the New Testament and the Fathers* (New York: Desclée, 1960), 380-94.

32. John E. Bamberger, *Evagrius Ponticus: The Praktikos, Chapters on Prayer* (Spencer, MA: Cistercian Publications, 1970), 15.

> Do not represent the divinity to yourself when you pray, nor let your mind undergo the impression of any form; but as immaterial go to the immaterial, and you will understand. (*On prayer* 66)[33]

This last may have been directed toward the simple piety of some of the "anthropomorphite" monks who thought of God in human form. But regardless of this specific application, the interpretation given the piety of the desert by Evagrius stands at a critical turning-point in the development of Christian thought, namely, the effort to relate the biblical, confrontational-dynamic images of God to the quest for or toward Being. A recent writer speaks of Origen's effort to "formulate a theology of the new conception of a wholly transcendent God."[34] Origen's follower, Evagrius Ponticus, clarified the piety of the desert by seeing its pungent aphorisms as leading the hearer toward radical transcendence. Evagrius himself so sharply moves beyond concrete, incarnational imagery in his theological maxims that Hans Urs von Balthasar remarks of him in exasperation, "There is no doubt that the mysticism of Evagrius, carried to the strict conclusion of its premises, comes closer, by its essence, to Buddhism than to Christianity."[35]

Interestingly enough, it seems that in Evagrius' rhetoric, paradox is most appropriate at the final state of spiritual development. So he says:

> Blessed is he who has arrived at infinite ignorance. (*Third Century* 88)[36]

This is a genuinely paradoxical aphorism, the more so since it is found in the exposition of a theological system. At the same time the saying is also explainable in terms of Evagrius' theology of ascetic discipline, in which a long period of discipline is followed by the reaching of a higher, undifferentiated state.[37] We must also note that the text of this saying is also read quite differently in another, and on the whole better, version:

---

33. Bouyer, op. cit., 380; cf. Bamberger, op. cit., 66.

34. Ivor Leclerc, *The Nature of Physical Existence* (London: Allen & Unwin, 1972), 65.

35. Cited in Bouyer, op. cit., 381.

36. Bouyer, op. cit., 390; W. Frankenberg, *Evagrius Ponticus*; "Abhandlungen der königlichen Gesellschaft zu Göttingen," Phil.-hist. Klasse, N.F. 13.2 (Berlin: Weidmann, 1912), 257.

37. Richard Reitzenstein, *Historia Monachorum und Historia Lausiaca*; "Forschungen zur Religion und Literatur des Alten und Neuen Testaments," N. F. 7 (Göttingen: Vandenhoek und Ruprecht, 1916), 124-33.

> Blessed is he who has arrived at infinite knowledge.[38]

But the two statements are not as different as they sound, as can be seen from the comment of the Syrian Babai (commenting on the text we cited first):

> Blessed is he who, in the purification of his soul by ascesis, has come so far that he has surpassed all knowledge of things, and in him the light of cognition has transcended all cognitions. . . . [H]e stands at the foot of the mountain of the unsearchable and enters the bright cloud of the unsearchable riches of Christ.[39]

The vision of life expressed in the pungent, lapidary sayings of the desert fathers can be interpreted in more than one framework. The general framework originally intended was that of the ascent of the soul (itself a complex vision, as can be seen from the sketches of the views of Gregory of Nyssa, Gregory of Nazianzen, Origen, Plotinus, and Valentinus offered by Ekkehard Mühlenberg).[40] We may read this saying too readily in the light of negative theology, when the controversy with Eunomius about the knowability of God may have been more directly in mind.[41] Nevertheless, the radical transcendence of the ultimate forces the negation of all concrete forms including especially all forms of self and world. The rhetorical function of the dislocation effected by the apophthegms of the fathers is aimed to help the hearer (reader) along this path of letting go.

This magnificently disciplined spirituality did successfully express the reality of "distance," of separation from the self-projection which supplies the context of the common-sense wisdom from which most popular aphoristic sayings arise. Whether or not it dealt successfully with the reality of "participation" is a serious question.[42] Thomas Merton has grappled with the same issues as a modern representative of aims very

---

38. Antoine Guillaumont, *Les six centuries des "Kephalia Gnostica" d'Evagre le Pontique*; "Patrologia Orientalis" 28.1 (Paris: Firmin-Didot, 1958), 134-35; cf. Antoine Guillaumont, *Les "Kephalia Gnostica" d'Evagre le Pontique* (Paris: Editions du Seuil, 1962), 27 n. 39.

39. Frankenberg, op. cit., 257.

40. Ekkehard Mühlenberg, *Die Unendlichkeit Gottes bei Gregor von Nyssa*; "Forschungen zur Kirchen- und Dogmengeschichte," 16 (Göttingen: Vandenhoek und Ruprecht, 1966), 147-82.

41. So Guillaumont, *Kephalia Gnostica*, 118 n. 167 on the related saying, 3.63.

42. Waddell, op. cit., 17-18, 30-32.

resonant with those of the desert fathers.[43] It is possible to interpret the message of Jesus about the Kingdom of God along a similar path of letting go of self and world (to this we shall return in closing), and to see the paradox and hyperbole of the gospel parables and proverbs in this context. The strong element in them of what we have termed "participation," of continuing reentry into the human social context, may not be adequately represented by this line of interpretation, however.

The Zen Koan

Before we return to the interpretation of the gospels, it is worth looking at another context in which aphoristic sayings are used in a discipline of seeking for a realization of creative nothingness. The affinity between the sayings of the desert fathers and the Zen koan has been noted by Thomas Merton among others, and the parallel aroused the interest of D. T. Suzuki.[44] Thus we turn for our final examples to a very different setting for the paradoxical aphorism. In the koan the element of witty needling, witty needling with the aim of disorientation, is clear enough:

> There was another master who, bringing out his staff, made this enigmatic declaration: "When you have a staff, I'll give you one; when you have none I'll take it away from you."[45]

Typical koans carry paradox and contradiction to the extreme. They aim to move attention beyond the conceptuality expressed in the aphorism itself.

> A monk in all earnestness asked Joshu, "Has a dog a Buddha nature or not?" Joshu retorted, "Mu" [no, nothing, non-being].[46]

This dialogue turns attention away from the answer as answer toward meditation upon the key phrase, *Mu*, which becomes itself a koan set for the disciple by the master. Many koans arose from such short dialogues. But in the disciplined use of the koan, the direction of the dialogue is reversed; the koan becomes a problem set for the disciple by

---

43. Thomas Merton, *The Wisdom of the Desert*; *Mystics and Zen Masters* (New York: Farrar, Straus & Giroux, 1967).

44. Merton, *The Wisdom of the Desert*, 9; see also Merton, *Zen and the Birds of Appetite* (New York: New Directions, 1968), 99-138.

45. D. T. Suzuki, Erich Fromm, and Richard de Martino, *Zen Buddhism and Psychoanalysis* (New York: Harper & Row, 1960), 44.

46. William Johnston, *The Still Point: Reflections on Zen and Christian Mysticism*. (New York: Fordham University Press, 1970), 6.

the master. The form of meditative discipline thus extracts and concentrates upon the kernel of the earlier dialogue.

We should also note that the koan has moved beyond the usual function of the aphorism in another way. For it is not expected that its effects will result from the immediate rhetorical impact of the saying (as in Aristotle's and in subsequent analyses of rhetorical effect). Rather, the result is anticipated in the course of a period of spiritual discipline, and may come only after long struggle and meditation. In a much more informal way, something like this was also the expectation for the sayings of the desert fathers.

Koans are quite varied, gathered from a long history. If their content is distinctive, in comparison with other aphoristic sayings, it is in their tendency to push paradox to outright contradiction or utter inconsistency.

> A monk asked Tung-shan, "Who is the Buddha?" "Three *chin* of flax."[47]

> A monk asked Chao-chou, "What is the meaning of the First Patriarch's visit to China?" "The cypress tree in the front courtyard."[48]

> Hakuin . . . used to raise one of his hands before his followers, demanding, "Let me hear the sound of one hand clapping."[49]

> "What is the teaching beyond the Buddhas and the Patriarchs?" He said, "Pancake!"[50]

There are many such aphorisms, discursively contradictory or "meaningless," which have become traditional in Zen discipline. Johnston rightly speaks of their "mockery of reason."[51] Hyers interprets the koan in the framework of comedy's breaking of conventional categories:

> "Comedy is therefore a trespasser upon the holy ground of spheres which we expend a great deal of energy in defining and in keeping separate, only to have them thrown back precipitously into the same knapsack with odd bits of everything."[52]

---

47. D. T. Suzuki, *Essays in Zen Buddhism: Second Series* (London: Rider, 1950), 84.
48. Ibid., 84.
49. Suzuki, Fromm, and Martino, *Buddhism and Psychoanalysis*, 49.
50. Chun-Yuan Chang, *Original Teachings of Ch'an Buddhism* (New York: Vintage Books, 1971), 272.
51. William Johnston, *The Still Point*, 6.
52. M. Conrad Hyers, *Zen and the Comic Spirit*, (Philadelphia: Westminster Press, 1973), 59.

But the aim of the koan is not only epistemological, to pass beyond the subject-object separation presupposed by reason, but also ontological, to pass beyond cosmic ordering toward a creative nothingness from which all the transient forms of order arise.[53]

Zen thinkers insist on atheism, since God is an ultimate ordering factor, a factor that would interfere with the goal of complete egolessness, since order points to distinction, to the irreversible, to life as a project. As Masao Abe puts it:

> Being beyond duality, the view of one who has attained *nirvana* is not monistic but rather non-dualistic. This is why Buddhism does not proclaim only one God, but speaks of Sunyata (Emptiness). Emptiness is realized by going beyond one God and thus is not the relative emptiness of a mere vacuum. Being beyond one God, Emptiness is identical to, or, more strictly speaking, "non-dualistic" with respect to individual things, making them truly individual. Indeed, in Emptiness, all is all in the sense that all is as it is and at the same time all is equal in its as-it-isness. The following question-and-answer dialogue between the Chinese Zen master, Joshu (778-897), and a monk illustrates the point. The monk asked Joshu, "All things are reduced to the One; what is this One to be reduced to?" Joshu replied, "When I was in the province of Tsin I had a monk's robe made that weighed seven pounds." That which is ultimate or universal is not the One to which all things are reducible but a particular thing, absolutely irreplaceable, which has a particular weight and is made at a particular place at a particular time. The universal and a particular thing are paradoxically one in the realization of Emptiness, which goes beyond the understanding which sees all things as reducible to the One.[54]

Abe's quotation from Joshu and his interpretation of it admirably illustrate how the koan moves the hearer beyond conceptual communication, yet at the same time requires ontological reflection as a secondary reaction.

We have thus come far from the earlier interpreters of the parables and proverbs of Jesus who were, perhaps too unreflectively, confident that those sayings were spoken in a context of divine purpose, in which time is not reversible, and in which God is an ordering presence not wholly unknowable. The sayings of the desert fathers, set in the context of

---

53. For insight into the function of the koan I am indebted to an unpublished paper of my colleague John Y. Fenton.

54. Masao Abe, "Buddhist Nirvana: Its Significance in Contemporary Thought and Life," *The Ecumenical Review,* 25 (1973), 160-61.

the theology of Evagrius, are in a middle position, symbolized by Abe's reference to the One.[55]

The newer interpretation of Jesus is more congenial to seeing his words in a context in which they serve to open the hearer to an experience of the creative Nothing, the transcendent creativity which escapes all conceptualization and is known, as Crossan puts it, only in moments when structure is broken.

The newer context of interpretation makes it not surprising that not only the sayings of the desert fathers, but also the sayings of Jesus, have been brought into juxtaposition with the Zen koan. William Johnston has cited the following as koans of Jesus:

> Let the dead bury their dead and come, follow me! [Matt 8:22| |Luke 9:60]
>
> He that loves his life will lose it. [Mark 8:35| |s]
>
> I am the vine and you are the branches. [John 15:5]
>
> This is my body. [Matt 26:26| |s][56]

He cites a Zen master identifying the saying, "Before Abraham was, I am"[57] as the "great enlightenment of Jesus," his recognition not of his empirical selfhood but of the "'I' of the universe that came surging up from the depths of his being."[58] At the same time, Johnston sees clearly that Christian and Zen discipline are based on different foundations. In a line of thinking related to that of Teilhard de Chardin, he hopes for a convergence between Christianity and Buddhism.[59]

Transcendent Contexts for the Interpretation of Parables and Sayings

The gospel sayings have been interpreted, except in gnosticism and in some types of mysticism, in relation to the Kingdom of a God who creates, judges, and renews the order of the world. God as a principle of

---

55. Ironic aphorisms function widely in other religious traditions as well, and could fruitfully be brought into comparison with gospel materials. For Hasidism, cf. Louis I. Newman, *The Hasidic Anthology* (New York: Scribner's, 1938); for Sufism, cf. Idries Shah, *The Way of the Sufi* (New York: Dutton, 1970).

56. William Johnston, *Christian Zen* (New York: Harper & Row, 1971), 63.

57. John 8:58.

58. William Johnston, *Silent Music: The Science of Meditation* (New York; Harper & Row, 1974), 163.

59. Ibid., 169-74.

rightness, however variously conceived, has been a basic presupposition of the central strand of the interpretation of these sayings. The mysticism of Evagrius Ponticus fused this presupposition with another one, that the ultimate is beyond existence and distinction. The doctrine of the Trinity, developed in the context of the controversies which were under way in Evagrius' time and in which his work was condemned, attempted to express a pluralistic understanding of the transcendent which would do justice to the variety of perceptions of it. But the transcendent as pure creative negativity was not included within the pluralism of the Trinity, though the mystical tradition in both Eastern and Western churches has approached this perception. The tension between these presuppositions about the transcendent has persisted, as can be clearly seen in the theology of Tillich.[60] Problems with the traditional doctrine of God have opened the way for a fresh grappling with the symbolization of transcendence, a situation which is clearly reflected in the newer interpretation of the parables and proverbs of Jesus.

At the same time contemporary interpretation is carried on with the aid of greatly sophisticated tools of understanding of language and rhetoric. The thesis of this paper is that an adequate interpretation cannot be achieved by concentrating on linguistic and rhetorical effects alone, since the rhetorical effects themselves, without concentrating on the ideological content, require some assumptions about the transcendent out of which they arise and to which they point.[61]

It is easy for us to see the shortcomings of the earlier interpretations of Jesus' parables and proverbs which too easily integrated them into a vision of a stable order which derived from God. Surely it is also the case that the experience of mystery, of the transcendent, is indeed a complex one. It is wise to assume that this complexity has real ontological roots, and is not just a matter of varieties of experience. The doctrine of the Trinity was an exceptionally creative venture in its incorporation of diversity in the transcendent. Yet we clearly sense a distancing from the traditional Christian doctrine of God in much of the recent interpretation of parables and proverbs.

---

60. Paul Tillich, *Biblical Religion and the Search for Ultimate Reality* (Chicago: University of Chicago Press, 1955).

61. Another dimension of these sayings which requires attention to other than strictly linguistic factors, a dimension which unfortunately can only be mentioned here, is the situation in which all these groups of sayings originally functioned: the situation of the master-disciple relationship.

We have sketched a variety of settings within which such sayings may be interpreted. We cannot now return to the gospels and reexamine the sayings there which have inspired these reflections. But the directions which we should wish to follow can at least be indicated. These rhetorically simple materials help us to rediscover the complexity—the diversity—of transcendence itself, for they lead us to an experience so complex that it cannot be reduced to a simple notion of the transcendent.

My own path is to relate the surprise and dislocation, the letting go, evoked by the parables and the paradoxical sayings of Jesus to a transcendent reality characterized by "rightness," as did the earlier interpreters of the gospels. They were not wrong in presupposing this connection, but in thinking in too simple a manner about the rightness of God and its disclosure in our life in the world. In point of fact, some of the most profound insights of the gospels about the interrelatedness of God and the world were concealed by the developed doctrine of the "wholly transcendent God." We are now in a position to relate these insights about the suffering of God to a contemporary understanding of reality. In my view a "process" perspective is especially fruitful from this point of view.[62] One reason why I choose the path of rethinking a point of view in which God and the world interact is that it seems to me to be the most adequate in showing why, after the moment of fracture of the continuity of life, faith leads to a reentry into the continuing social relationships of men and women. Despite the need for the dislocation, the "jolt" which the speech forms in question aim at, the continuities of life are not totally separated from the transcendent. Even though many in our culture perceive the gap between the transcendent and the "daily" to be insuperable, it is one task of the contemporary interpreter of the New Testament to see and to show how the gap can be bridged.

To relate this conviction to historical study of Jesus would require a separate study. We cited Amos Wilder's view above[63] that Jesus' "mythos" of the Kingdom of God has more content than ontological reversal, and we concur in this judgment. A study of the relationship between the gospels and contemporary social hopes would strengthen this conviction.[64]

---

62. William A. Beardslee, *A House for Hope: A Study in Process and Biblical Thought*, (Philadelphia: Westminster Press, 1972).

63. See p. 68.

64. William A. Beardslee, "New Testament Perspectives on Revolution as a Theological Problem," *JR* 51 (1971), 15-33.

If one takes this position, it is all the more important to recognize the validity of the other direction of interpretation, toward the transcendent as a creative negativity or Emptiness. This perception is a real possibility as one listens to these sayings. The sayings themselves do not foreclose either line of interpretation. Such a view of the transcendent as creative negativity has its own way of conferring freedom and acceptance amid the precariousness of life.

It is not useful to identify the two paths of interpretation, since the respective strengths of each come more clearly to light if we work with a model which allows each its own integrity. But it is possible to hope and to explore toward convergence. The recent work of John B.Cobb, Jr., developing a model of the ultimate or transcendent which includes and also distinguishes between the principle of rightness (God) and that of creativity (Emptiness) is suggestive in the light of the interpretation made above about the ways in which aphoristic sayings may function in relation to the transcendent.[65]

Amos Wilder's work will play a creative role for anyone who is reflecting about the linkage between rhetorical and ontological perceptions, and about the possibility of convergence between differing ontological presuppositions. For he has long insisted that we be sensitive to what is here termed "creative disruption" in the rhetoric of the gospels, and he has seen the need for working from a given stance while at the same time responding to the demand for letting go. Further, his interest in poetics and rhetoric has assumed that religious language involves ontological commitment. Thus his work is extremely illuminating in bringing to attention what I have called the context of expectation in which parable and proverb are heard. It is not surprising that his work is pathbreaking both to those who find that the exciting task is working for a fresh view of the transcendent as an ordering factor, and to those who work for a new imaginative grasp of the transcendent as a creative nothingness.

---

65. John B.Cobb, Jr., "Buddhist Emptiness and the Christian God," *JAAR* 45 (1977), 11-25.

- 5-

Robert Alter's View of Hebrew Narrative from the Perspective of New Testament Studies

In his book,[1] Professor Alter has vigorously, not to say pungently, expressed his opinions of other scholars, and it would be appropriate to comment in kind on his book. But I shall not enter into a direct critique of most of his elegant and illuminating analyses of biblical texts. The truth is, I do not know enough about the Hebrew Scriptures to do so. I shall speak of how one who works with New Testament texts is challenged by *The Art of Biblical Narrative*, in the hope that this indirect approach will cast light on Alter's methods and presuppositions.

A first reaction is that this book opens important vistas on unfinished work in New Testament studies. Alter's chapter on composite artistry deals with a question with which scholars of the New Testament must deal as well as scholars of the Hebrew Scriptures. Since the early nineteenth century, students of the New Testament have recognized the composite nature of at least some New Testament books. But at least since William Wrede's work on the messianic secret, the main interest has been in the *theological* aims that guided the conjoining of different sources. When redaction criticism reopened the question of the meaning of the gospels as wholes, it was again with an eye to their theological purposes that the gospels were studied. More recently, fully literary study of the gospels has mostly simply treated them as wholes and bracketed out the possible meaning of the "aesthetics of montage." To study the gospels in terms of "montage" is an exciting possibility. I mention this specific area as only one illustration of the fruitfulness of Alter's work for New Testament studies. Others can be seen in his study of characterization and in his analysis of the handling of the pace of narration.

Previously unpublished. An earlier version was presented at the 1983 Annual Meeting of the Society of Biblical Literature.

1. *The Art of Biblical Narrative* (New York: Basic Books, 1980).

At the same time, the literary differences between the Hebrew Scriptures and the New Testament soon appear forcefully as one reflects on Alter's book. To put it simply, we have always known that the Hebrew Scriptures had all the good stories. Alter has helped us to see why they are such good stories. Both canons share the presentation of human life in the tension between an overarching and (as it is sometimes presented, at least) overruling divine purpose and a stubborn honesty about the reality of the human situation and the mystery of human freedom. But the particular traits of the biblical Hebrew narrative upon which Alter fixes his attention are not really characteristic of the New Testament. The subtlety of characterization in parts of the Hebrew Bible would be a prime example of the contrast. Parenthetically I note that there are, of course, as some of Alter's critics have pointed out, other kinds of narrative in the Hebrew Scriptures besides those which he discusses, but most of these would not get us any nearer to the New Testament. Apocalyptic narrative would be an exception.

One obvious entrée into this question is the observation that the New Testament writers do not allow their characters enough time for the kind of portrayal that Alter discusses in the Joseph and David stories. I want to explore this question further, but first to look at a related one: the question of the relation between the oral background and the written text. For it is a clear presupposition of Professor Alter that, though some of the techniques which he discusses may have originated in the oral stage, the subtle and nuanced handling of them which we find in Genesis or Samuel could only have been achieved by a writing author who was able to take a reflective overview of the whole. Though the works in question may have been largely intended for hearing rather than for reading in our modern way, these ancient hearers may be expected, especially upon repeated hearing, to have perceived intuitively the subtleties of presentation, the alterations of substance as a point is spoken by different characters, etc. But the analogy with the modern author is required to understand how these subtleties got into the text in the first place.

I do not wish to try to resolve the question of the degree to which the literary conventions of biblical prose (whether of the Hebrew Scriptures or of the New Testament) can be ascribed to the oral stage of literature, nor, of course, do I wish to suggest that what would be an appropriate solution for one text is correct for another. What I do want to point out is the quite different assumptions that different scholars bring to this question. For Professor Alter, the oral stage is judged negatively because it is seen as limited in its capacity to create an imagined world of sufficient complexity. The oral world would be a world of stock epithets, flat characters, and type situations, a necessary background indeed for the complex, ambiguous, yet purposeful world that is created by the biblical stories. The greater control which the author can exercise upon the written text (Alter explicitly draws the comparison between God and the author) is a prerequisite for the creation of a more real world, a world so real indeed that it still exercises its influence upon how stories are told today, and not only so, but a world which commands attention for its moral valuation of human beings as well as for its theological implications.

Professor Alter does not present the issue quite in these terms, but I hope that I have done justice to the implications of his work.

How different it looks when we follow Werner Kelber in his analysis of the oral and the written gospel.[2] Kelber, like students of the Hebrew Bible, is dealing with a written literature which had an oral stage behind it. He believes that he can analyze out the characteristics of each stage with substantial clarity. But the valuation of the two—the oral and the written—is exactly the opposite of what we find in Alter. For Kelber, the oral stage is the stage of presence, the stage which is fluid precisely because the immediacy of the divine presence is sensed (the living Word present in the community), and there is a major loss when this fluid and charismatic tradition is frozen into the Gospel of Mark.

It is evident that what Kelber is looking for is very different from what Alter sees. Alter sees an imagined series of situations in which a character can live and interact with others and deal with himself or herself so that the hearer or reader may become aware of, indeed may participate in, the complex and ambiguous task of becoming human. He notes that, although God is in the background and is occasionally an actor in the narratives, the presentation of the human person is close to "dominant modern notions" in its perception of character as often unpredictable, sometimes impenetrable, and constantly emerging from and slipping back into a penumbra of ambiguity.[3] Among the complex requirements which make possible this presentation is the written medium.

---

2. Werner Kelber, *The Oral and the Written Gospel* (Philadelphia: Fortress Press, 1983).

3. Alter, op. cit., 129.

For Kelber, on the other hand, the written medium is less lifelike than the oral. As one of the epigraphs for one of his chapters he cites Walter Ong, "The association of writing with death is not total, but it is manifold and inescapable." And just below in another epigraph he quotes Herbert N. Schneidau, who associates "literature" with "an absence at the core, not communication and presence."[4] In the early Christian world that Kelber evokes, the oral stage was the stage of presence precisely because it was fluid and did not aspire to the fixity of form which makes the Genesis narratives—as Alter views them—possible.

Of course the two authors are working on very different fronts and presupposing extremely different forms of oral literature. And it would be worth asking whether there are other parts of the Hebrew Scriptures that—regardless of the oral versus written question—would be appropriate texts in which to explore the question of immediate presence, the latter prophets, for example. But what strikes me about these two contrasting approaches is that the New Testament scholar, who himself quotes Paul Ricoeur to the effect that, "Thanks to writing, man and only man has a world and not just a situation,"[5] emphasizes that this world was created by distanciation from oral dialogue and remembering, which up until then had been the vehicle for Jesus's presence.

Kelber's work is not at issue here, but I bring it in to emphasize that Alter is at ease with the fictional world of writing, that he finds it, I think it would be fair to say, giving us more reality. He would, I suppose, freely agree about the indirectness of access to reality in the written medium; he explicitly discusses this question in connection with the presence of God in the narrative—God usually sets the frame, or the author alludes to God's purpose in setting the frame, and then gives the human person scope to struggle humanly with his or her problem. Similarly, Alter's work does not display the longing for the directness of personal human presence which supplies part of the model to which Kelber appeals. We know literary characters better because of our distance, in part because the written form enables us to become more clearly aware of the gaps in our knowledge.

A closely connected point is one which I mentioned above—the contrast in the handling of time, as we compare the biblical narratives discussed by Alter with the narrative portions of the New Testament. With

---

4. Kelber, op. cit., 184.
5. Ibid., 215.

few exceptions, the New Testament writers simply do not allow their characters time enough to become human beings in the way that Alter has shown us happening in Genesis and Samuel. There is plenty of time in these latter stories, and the authors need this time in order to present the subtle exchanges which are analyzed in *The Art of Biblical Narrative* (though of course there are also briefer narratives in these books, which cannot display this trait). It would interesting to study Luke-Acts from this point of view, for it is about the only place in the New Testament where comparable narrative time is plotted out—and in that work we would find such traits as differentiation of groups of characters by stylistic means, and brief units at least approaching the "type-scene" in nature, for instance, the "narrow escape," which occurs in the stories of Jesus, Peter, and Paul.

The category, "type-scene," taken from Homeric studies by Alter and applied with great effectiveness to the stories he studies, is fruitful also for students of the New Testament. Indeed, it has been used to good effect by Robert Tannehill in studies of Luke and Acts.[6] But it is important to be aware of differences in the respective collections of narratives. In the New Testament as in the Hebrew Scriptures variations in the development of a type-scene open up the varied possibilities of human response.[7] The Homeric type-scenes as well as those in the Hebrew Scriptures mark significant turning-points in the lives of their heroes, and the particular emphases of a specific scene, as Alter shows, illuminate the character of the person in question. This could be said as well of the New Testament, but in this latter case, the development of character, so carefully analyzed by Alter in the Joseph and David stories, is not of interest to the writers. Though the New Testament healing story, for instance, is an established type which no doubt aroused certain expectations in the hearers, it does not function as the type-scenes do as noted above. Further, the fact that the Hebrew Scriptures were canonical writings for New Testament readers means that the looser term, "literary allusion," is appropriate for many New Testament references to the stories which

---

6. Robert Tannehill, "Paul Outside the Christian Ghetto: Stories of Intercultural Conflict and Cooperation in Acts," pp. 247-264 in Theodore W. Jennings, ed., *Text and Logos: The Humanistic Interpretation of the New Testament: Festschrift for Hendrikus W. Boers* (Atlanta: Scholars Press, 1990); *The Narrative Unity of Luke-Acts*; 2 vols. (Philadelphia and Minneapolis: Fortress Press, 1986-1990), esp. 1, 170-171; 2, 201-263.

7. Tannehill, *Unity*, 1, 170.

Alter discusses. An example would be John 4, Jesus and the Samaritan woman at the well, which has connections with the betrothal scenes discussed by Alter, but which cannot be understood as the same "type."

But we would look in vain in the New Testament for the kind of characterization which we find in the great narratives of the Hebrew Scriptures. Alan Culpepper has shown, in his recent book on the literary character of the Gospel of John, that all of the characters of the fourth Gospel, with the exception of Jesus, are flat or typical characters, and that Jesus is a wholly static character.[8]

It is no accident that Bultmann could virtually reduce the significant time in the New Testament to the moment of decision. Though this was an exaggeration, it does give us a clue to the contrast I have in mind. The New Testament writers are pushing their characters—and their readers—harder than the writers whom Alter discusses.

I suspect that this contrast in the handling of time gives us a clue to one reason why Christian readers found and still find so necessary and valuable to them what they call the Old Testament. If one pushes the shortness of time to its ultimate conclusion, then there is no sense in the growth of stable character, such as we see in the great Hebrew narratives, and it becomes exceedingly difficult to hold in view the persisting complexity and mixed character of human selfhood.

I found myself asking when it was that a Christian writer probed the ambiguities of the self over a long stretch of time with a depth comparable to what we find in the narratives under discussion. The work that came to my mind is Augustine's *Confessions*. Scholars debate the question how far this is a fictional work, just as they do in the case of the biblical narratives. Augustine's focus has shifted—to first person narration. The New Testament probing of the self—the disruption of its continuities that is so much emphasized in a recent New Testament study—has much to do with this shift. But Augustine certainly needs both portions of his Bible. His work shifts back and forth between narrative and speculation, and is, indeed, very different from the Hebrew narratives in many ways. But he follows their lead in allowing his principal character—himself—the time needed to struggle humanly with himself and to disclose, in his own ways, the ambiguities of human existence and the mysteries of the depth of character.

---

8. Alan Culpepper, *Anatomy of the Fourth Gospel: A Study in Literary Design* (Philadelphia: Fortress Press, 1983).

I hope that it is apparent from these remarks that I find the broad outlines of Professor Alter's work persuasive. It may be that we should think of some of the authorial judgments as more intuitively made than Alter describes them to have been; this is a hard question to decide. It may be that we should attribute a higher degree of direct historical memory to parts of the David story than he does. It is clear that Professor Alter has tried to counter the clarity with which many theologically-oriented interpreters think that they can understand both God and human beings with an emphasis on the indeterminacy and ambiguity of the biblical narratives, and he may have overdone this. But to press such points would miss his central emphases. Fundamentally his approach is friendly to an historical perception of reality. For he does not treat narratives as existing in a wholly enclosed world of language. The knowledge which they share with the reader is indirect, both with respect to God and with respect to human beings. We may say that these narratives function as proposals—incomplete ones indeed, but proposals to be tested out against not just other language, but against moral experience as well—not that the two can ever be disentangled, yet they may be distinguished.

Probably Professor Alter would concede with Nathan Scott that contemporary writers make us aware there is "an absurd discrepancy between all plots, even the most knottily complicated, and the human actuality."[9] Put the other way about, that means that there is an element of play in the very exercise of creating a plot. But it does not follow that these stories are merely fanciful. They embody and reveal moral and, ultimately, religious values which are proposed as basic possibilities for being and becoming human, and they do so by setting people and events in a world of chancy events and yet ultimately ruled by God's moral purpose. The link between plot and character is not merely a literary device, but also an essential enabling element in there being character, for character makes sense only if one can take seriously the interplay of memory, present experience, and expectation. That is why I find Alter's treatment of the Hebrew narratives so stimulating also for the student of the New Testament. Though New Testament scholars have often fixed attention on other elements in the texts with which they deal, and are to an extent justified in doing so by the nature of the texts themselves, it will

---

9. Nathan A. Scott, Jr., "The Rediscovery of Story in Recent Theology and the Refusal of Story in Recent Literature," pp. 139-155 in Robert Detweiler, ed., *Art/Literature/Religion: Life on the Borders*; "JAAR Studies," 49, 2 (Chico, CA: Scholars Press, 1983), 143.

not be well for us to lose sight of those elements of narrative which Professor Alter has analyzed in so skillful a way.

- 6 -

Narrative and History in the Post-Modern World
The Case of the Gospel of Mark

Whether or not Biblical Studies counts as a full-fledged member of the humanities disciplines, it certainly participates significantly in their languages, perspectives, and methods. Hence it follows that Biblical Studies has been involved in—has contributed to and suffered from—the "crisis of the humanities." It is appropriate, therefore, to sketch in this essay the vicissitudes of a recent phase of this troubled relationship by examining the treatment, in the last one hundred and fifty years, of a key document from an early stage of the encounter, namely the Gospel of Mark.

In the formative years of Christianity, and for many centuries thereafter, Mark received no special attention from scholars or from the church. It had made its contribution to the orienting Christian story, but Mark's creative place in the formation of that story was not recognized, and since it was the shortest of the gospels it was largely overlooked. It was about a century and a half ago that all this changed—as a result of what was then a new form of humanistic research. The new method was the historical method, which both reached a peak of methodological precision and came to be the focus of great scholarly enthusiasm in the first half of the nineteenth century. Specifically, historical literary criticism such as that engaged in by Weisse and others showed that Mark was the first gospel to have been written.[1] Roman Catholic and conservative Protestant scholarship were slow to take up this view, but it has increasingly prevailed down to the present time.

From *The Crisis in the Humanities: Interdisciplinary Responses*, ed. Sara Putzell-Korab and Robert Detweiler; "Studia Humanitatis" (Madrid: José Porrúa Turanzas, 1983), 47-60.

1. Christian Hermann Weisse, *Die evangelische Geschichte kritisch und philosophisch bearbeitet,* 2 vols. (Leipzig: Breitkopf and Härtel, 1838); see Werner Georg Kümmel, *The New Testament: The History of the Investigation of Its Problems*, tr. S. McLean Gilmore and Howard C. Kee (Nashville: Abingdon Press, 1972).

Even though the evidence is not unequivocally clear, and the position is still challenged, the placing of Mark as the first gospel has become a foundation of most types of inquiry into the history of early Christianity.[2] The immense weight which this discovery placed upon the Gospel of Mark was increased by the fact that at about the same time, studies of the Gospel of John were convincing historically-minded scholars that John is not an historical record of Jesus but a theological interpretation of him. Traditionally the historical outline for the life of Jesus had been derived principally from John. Now the inference was drawn that Mark, being the earliest gospel, was to be the foundation for life of Jesus research. Mark was taken to be a substantially historically accurate record of Jesus' ministry. Little thought was given at first to the study of the gospel genre. Mark was valued because it was transparent, not rendered opaque by heavy Christian theological interpretation such as was seen in John. The presupposition was that the historian could see human realities as they really were. At the same time, the coherence and the significance of the story of Jesus were assured to these scholars, both by an evolutionary-developmental vision of Jesus as the highest possibility of the human, and by the confidence that Mark's story could be interpreted in terms of another developmental pattern: the growth of Jesus' self-understanding in reaction to the events of his ministry. It was presupposed that Mark displayed a strong narrative consistency, but what was of interest was the "actual" narrative of the story of Jesus as reconstructed on a more human basis by scholars. Though they were revising the traditional biblical story of existence, there was no question that human existence fitted readily into a narrative pattern, both in the case of the individual and in that of the community.

The image of Mark as transparent historically and thus transparent upon ultimate reality was forcefully stated by H. J. Holtzmann in the mid-nineteenth century.[3] Of course there were dissenting voices, not only from the conservatives but notably from D. F. Strauss, who perceived the

2. William R. Farmer, *The Synoptic Problem: A Critical Analysis,* (New York: Macmillan, 1964) is one who challenges the primacy of Mark. See also William O. Walker, "The Son of Man Question and the Synoptic Problem," *New Testament Studies* 28 (1982), 374-88.

3. Heinrich Julius Holtzmann, *Die synoptische Evangelien: Ihr Ursprung und geschichtlicher Charakter* (Leipzig: Engelmann, 1863). Holtzmann's view is expressed in English in Oskar Holtzmann's *The Life of Jesus,* tr. J. T. Bealby and Maurice A. Canney (London: A. & C. Black, 1904).

mythical element in the gospels and thus paved the way for many twentieth-century questions about Mark.[4] But the effort to combine the best humanistic scholarship with a concern about religious reality and ultimate truth was classically expressed in the interpretation of Mark as a history of Jesus' growing self-consciousness, a history transparent to the presence of the divine.

Thus Mark came on the scene abruptly, after centuries of neglect. At first the book was valued because it was supposed to be an accurate record of a life of special significance. The tools of humanistic research, critically applied, could open the way to an understanding of God's purpose, through a study of the life of the supreme human person.

Toward the end of the century, different sorts of sharp challenge were thrown at the bold "liberal" reconstruction of the Christian story. Johannes Weiss and Albert Schweitzer undermined the whole project by showing that it lacked rigor in its own terms.[5] The focus of attention upon Jesus' supposed growing self-consciousness was not sufficiently historical to bring out the great difference between the world of the scholars and the world of Jesus and the early Christians. The message of the Gospel of Mark and of most early Christian documents sprang from a very different dynamic from that seen by the Holtzmanns and their associates. Jesus, said Weiss and Schweitzer, acted and spoke out of a vision of the coming massive transformation of existence, a vision of the end of the world. These scholars saw that an eschatological vision such as that of Jesus or Mark entailed not just the question of individual destiny, but the reshaping of the structures of existence. Recognition of the eschatological character of early Christianity indirectly raised the question of the narrative coherence of life. For radical eschatology presupposes a disrupted narrative sense, an existence which would be terribly alienating but for the hope for a drastically different future.

Weiss and Schweitzer were pointing to a limiting factor in humanistic research—the difficulty of taking account of a fundamental vision radically different from that of the student. From their time to the present, the struggle to interpret early Christian (and Jewish) eschatology

4. David Friedrich Strauss, *The Life of Jesus Critically Examined,* tr. George Eliot (Philadelphia: Fortress Press, 1972).

5. Johannes Weiss, *Jesus' Proclamation of the Kingdom of God,* tr. Richard H. Hiers and David L. Holland (Philadelphia: Fortress Press, 1971); Albert Schweitzer, *The Quest of the Historical Jesus,* tr. William Montogomery (New York: Macmillan, 1968).

has been a central problem of New Testament studies. The transparency of Mark to ultimate reality was becoming problematic, and in the process the question of how to deal with a distant and different experience came into focus.

At about the same time, at the beginning of the twentieth century, William Wrede attacked, from a different point of view, the assumption that Mark is a straightforward historical account.[6] He showed that, far from being an unsophisticated chronicle of events, Mark is a complex reflection of the church's interpretation of Jesus. Like John, it is theology, rather than descriptive history. Wrede's clue was the "messianic secret," the way in which Jesus' messiahship is a secret to most of the characters in the narrative, though obvious to the author and intended to be clear to the reader. Wrede held that this puzzling feature of Mark resulted from the author's combination of two types of tradition about Jesus, one of which recognized him as Messiah during his earthly life, while the other was completely non-messianic so far as the earthly Jesus was concerned. To Wrede, this latter was the earlier type of tradition, but the main point is that, while Wrede continued the historical study of Mark, he looked in it primarily for the history of the time at which the author wrote the book. Now Mark lost its supposed transparency to the story of Jesus as history. It was seen to be in the first place a source for the history of the church. Later scholars have been dissatisfied with the details of Wrede's analysis, but more and more his view has prevailed that Mark has to be read in the first place as a theological interpretation of Jesus rather than as a descriptive historical record.

It is not surprising that again at about this time, the end of the nineteenth century, a third major criticism of the "historical transparency of Mark" was framed. Though they did not receive much attention until later, the issues raised by the work of Martin Kähler have proven to have a methodological importance similar to those raised by the discovery of eschatology and the emphasis on Mark as a creative theological reinterpretation of Jesus.[7] Kähler was critical of the ability of distanced, neutral historical analysis to seize the dynamic unity of the story of Jesus. He was not particularly concerned with Mark in distinction from the other gospels, but his position applied to it as well as to the others.

6. William Wrede, *The Messianic Secret,* tr. J. C. G. Grieg (Cambridge: Clark, 1971).

7. Martin Kähler, *The So-Called Historical Jesus and the Historical, Biblical Christ,* tr. Carl E. Braaten (Philadelphia: Fortress Press, 1964).

Kähler believed that the story of Jesus as read, shall we say, naively in the community of faith could be a life-orienting narrative, despite the dissection of the gospels by scholars. He saw that the vital, orienting elements in Mark and the other gospels were precisely those that are perceived in the believing and liturgical use of the gospels. The abstract constructions of historical scholars—the "so-called historical Jesus"—could not provide anything like the unifying power of the "historic biblical Christ." To Kähler it was humanistic scholarship that was opaque, not the gospels. Not opposed to historical scholarship as such, Kähler held nevertheless that those characteristics that made the gospel story a meaningful whole could not be extracted piecemeal from the records of early Christianity by detached scholarship. To put it in terms of the present inquiry, Kähler saw that the narrative coherence of Mark and the other gospels was threatened by the project of reconstructing an "historical Jesus" along the lines of the new historical work. We might say that for Kähler the story in question could be perceived in its wholeness and deeper meaning only from the inside, by one who actually participated in it. Kähler's work was a strong claim that the current interests of the humanities should not simply set the agenda for religious and theological inquiry.

The work of Kähler represented an attempt to affirm a coherent narrative meaning of the story of Jesus (and thereby of the story of the believer) against the assaults on narrative coherence exemplified by the course of the investigations sketched above. His claim that this meaning was understood by participating in it was not a new one, but it gained new significance in the face of the increasing attacks on the traditional narrative version of Christian faith which had been responded to by the scholars we have noted.

However, for the mainstream of critical New Testament inquiry, the principal course of research took a different tack in the first half of the twentieth century. The main line of the new probing moved in the direction of reducing still farther the narrative element in the gospels. So-called "form criticism," which studies the forms of the constituent elements of the Gospels (such as miracle stories, parables, proverbial sayings, controversy stories, the passion story) had a low regard for the overall narrative pattern of the gospels and particularly of Mark. The gospel authors were regarded as collectors who loosely organized the small units which were available to them. Thus attention was turned away from the story as a whole. While many of the component elements of the gospels were themselves narratives, this aspect of them did not attract much attention from the form critics. Their main interest was to discern the function in the community of the various literary forms.

The last statement is not wholly correct as far as Rudolf Bultmann is concerned, since he did give close attention to many aspects of the narrative form of the parables and miracle stories.[8] Nevertheless, the thrust of his work and influence was in the other direction. He was the leader in a thorough rethinking of the way to interpret the Christian faith which had the net effect of de-narratizing it. Bultmann's existentialist theology reflected the loss of continuous narrative meaning which was widely sensed in Europe at the time. His reconstruction of the Christian vision to reduce the elements of narrative in it to their barest minimum of "openness to the future," and to concentrate all the weight of ultimacy in the moment of decision, is illuminated by the neo-Kantian background of much European Protestant thought of the time, which saw the characteristically human as the will.[9] Bultmann interpreted the past and memory under the theological heading of "law" and in terms of a deterministic chain of causation as the characteristic which we see in the past. Expectation the future and hope were also rejected insofar as the future had any cognitive content, since the attempt to grasp the future would rob the moment of its significance. This perspective renounced the dramatic interplay of memory, expectation, and the present moment as they are known by the participant in a story, in favor of the moment which could be free because it was set free from past and future by the Christian proclamation.

It would be fair to view Bultmann's achievement as one of the great modernist reconstructions of our Western heritage. His was a far more drastic reshaping of tradition than the steps which preceded it. Confronted with a loss of accepted meaning, Bultmann reshaped the materials of the past to give a unified vision of human meaning in the perspective of faith. We might say, in language which would have been highly objectionable to Bultmann, that he worked to create a new myth, a myth without story but nonetheless a whole vision with a center. The close contact between this theological effort and the wider humanistic scene is

8. Rudolf Bultmann, *The Presence of Eternity: History and Eschatology* (New York: Harper & Row, 1957); *The History of the Synoptic Tradition,* tr. John Marsh (New York: Harper & Row, 1963).

9. See Amos N. Wilder, *Jesus' Parables and the War of Myths,* ed. James Breech (Philadelphia: Fortress Press, 1982).

shown by Bultmann's adaptation of Heideggerian categories to his theological task—an adaptation for which he was censured by many of his colleagues, but one which was fully justified to him by the ability of these categories to cut beneath the traditional Christian forms and release the power intrinsic to them. Bultmann, here again like other modernists, separated as sharply as possible the central vision which provided ultimate meaning from other penultimate sources of meaning, which were strongly relativized.

Mark was recognized by Bultmann as the originator of the gospel genre, but this genre's narrative quality had no interest for him. Coherently with this, Jesus' "story" was insignificant for theology. Only "that" he was, not "what" he was mattered. A major transformation of Christian vision shifted it out of its long-established diachronic, narrative idiom into a frame where disconnected moments may open themselves to meaning. Correspondingly, Mark was viewed from a literary point of view as a collection of short units which could provide the occasion for such illumination. We should note that this episodic use of gospel materials was not the invention of existentialist theology, since it has an ancient background in the liturgical use of the gospels in short units.

As we move into the second half of the twentieth century, the post-modern period as we say, we come to a much more pluralistic world, a world that has become skeptical of organized visions with centers. More modest claims tend to be made for encounters with ultimacy or even for encounters with meaning. At the same time, the inadequacy of the "moment" as the bearer of the whole weight of meaning is increasingly recognized.

In Marcan studies the post-Bultmannian period has been marked by a renewed interest in the overall contour of the book. In the jargon of the field, "form criticism" was succeeded by "redaction criticism," a field which was pioneered for Mark by Willi Marxsen.[10] Here the interest was in seeing how the special concerns of the author appeared in the modifications of tradition which were made by the author. Such an approach was not yet interested in the literary design of the work as a whole; it looked at specific sections thought to reflect the author's special interest. But the author of Mark now became again a real author, not a collector. A point of view, a selective principle, governed the resulting work.

---

10. Willi Marxsen, *Mark the Evangelist: Studies on the History of the Gospel,* tr. James Boyce (Nashville: Abingdon Press, 1969).

Redaction criticism has been succeeded by an outburst of interest in literary criticism, in the study of the organization of Mark as a whole. Mark became interesting again as a narrative. Some of the scholars who have been developing literary interpretations of Mark have tried to relate the work to its original audience, thus preserving a large degree of the earlier historical orientation as they developed a literary approach (Theodore J. Weeden, Sr.; Werner Kelber).[11] Others have worked more with the categories of new criticism or structuralism (Dan O. Via, Jr.; Robert Tannehill; Norman R. Petersen; John Dominic Crossan, and others).[12]

We cannot here survey all this important work. What is striking about it is that, despite the differences in method and results in detail, all of these authors find Mark to be a remarkably coherent narrative—whether with Petersen attention is directed to narrative point of view, with Tannehill to the function of narrative roles, with Weeden and Kelber to intended impact on the audience, with Via to the movement of the plot, or with Crossan to the eschatological implications of absence for faith. Mark emerges as a strong narrative, not a collection of "beads on a string" as the form critics had supposed.

Further, these various interpretations inspired by literary criticism also have a high degree of similarity in what they see Mark to be: a work which brings the reader into a vision which is highly critical of "resolution," of the simple "happy ending" of the conventional narrative (this remark does not apply equally to them all). It is the element of suspense in the sense of the suspension of the final resolution which these authors find to be characteristic of Mark's narrative vision. Though the nineteenth century readers who "discovered" Mark were struck by its transparency, the contemporary readers see its opaqueness, or at least its challenge to any premature transparency. In Crossan's striking term, the gospel genre was created by Mark as a "form for absence." Of course, the

11. Theodore J. Weeden, Sr., *Mark: Traditions in Conflict* (Philadelphia: Fortress Press, 1977); Werner Kelber, *Mark's Story of Jesus* (Philadelphia: Fortress Press, 1979).

12. Dan O. Via, Jr., *Kerygma and Comedy in the New Testament: A Structuralist Approach to Hermeneutic* (Philadelphia: Fortress Press, 1975); Robert Tannehill, "The Gospel of Mark as Narrative Christology," *Semeia* 16 (1979), 57-95; Norman R. Petersen, "Point of View in Mark's Narrative," *Semeia* 12 (1978), 97-121, and *Literary Criticism for New Testament Critics* (Philadelphia: Fortress Press, 1978); John Dominic Crossan, "A Form for Absence: The Markan Creation of Gospel," *Semeia* 12 (1978), 41-55.

primary structural element in the book which opens it to this interpretation is its ending without a resurrection appearance. All of these interpreters suppose (I believe rightly) that the work was intended to end without this element which is part of the narrative structure of the other gospels, as against the alternative view that the original, conventional ending has been lost. But other elements in the book, firmly built into its narrative pattern, also point toward the contemporary interpretation, notably the persistent theme of the misunderstanding of Jesus by the disciples, who should understand him best.

Thus a century and a half of work has produced a striking ironic reversal in Marcan studies. First Mark was valued because it was a transparent story, a coherent narrative which could be read in terms of a liberal Christian universe. Then its story-pattern was lost to sight. When the narrative pattern was rediscovered, largely by the use of critical methods devised for studying fiction, what stood out was precisely the lack of transparency, revealed by the questions which Mark puts to those who want clear answers and secure positions.

It is worth noting that Rhoads and Michie, who have written a fine book which summarizes much of the recent work on Mark, explicitly read Mark as fiction.[13] Equally striking, Frank Kermode (who had earlier given attention to the interpretation of apocalyptic symbolism in *The Sense of an Ending*) has written *The Genesis of Secrecy,* an important book on Mark that describes how narrative can have many meanings and still confront the reader with a final obscurity.[14] Kermode takes his point of departure from Mark 4:10-12, in which Jesus says that parables are told to puzzle the hearers; Kermode rebukes biblical scholars for trying to explain this away, and he takes the passage as a model for his whole interpretation of Mark and of narrative generally.

A contrary proposal to that of Kermode is that of Hans Frei. Following the lead of Kähler but restricting his vision strictly to the intended level of the story and bracketing the question of history beyond the story, Frei turns the tables on historical reconstruction and treats the gospel story (he is not specially concerned with Mark) as one which simply car-

---

13. David Rhoads and Donald Michie, *Mark as Story: An Introduction to the Narrative of a Gospel* (Philadelphia: Fortress Press, 1982).

14. Frank Kermode, *The Sense of an Ending: Studies in the Theory of Fiction* (New York: Oxford University Press, 1967); *The Genesis of Secrecy: On the Interpretation of Narrative* (Cambridge, MA: Harvard University Press, 1979).

ries within it its own validity; it could not not be true.[15] Again, we are called to come into the story to understand it.

Kermode's dissection of Mark's coherent narrative into allusive hints is coherent with the humanist's urge not to be locked into any one perspective—*homo sum; humani nil a me alienum puto.* Frei's reaffirmation of narrative coherence "from within" is characteristic of the aim of faith to find a place to stand, a vantage point from which all other reality may be measured—*hie stehe ich, ich kann nicht anders thun.* A new encounter of these long-standing perspectives in terms of our understanding of narrative is a mark of contemporary work in both theology and humanities.

This sketch has been presented as if humanistic scholarship provided the agenda for biblical interpretation. When the humanists were interested in history, Mark was history. When the humanists turned to fiction, Mark became fiction. There is much truth in this. All live in the same world; both humanists and theologians are dealing with the same reality and to a considerable degree are asking the same questions. There is a long history of often uneasy interchange between them. In the present case there have been many gains for biblical interpreters in the shift of sensibility noted above. The pluralistic setting of the more recent period has freed biblical scholars from the older tendency to harmonize the various biblical writings into one single point of view. Mark can be allowed to be only one way of speaking about it.

More profoundly, theologians like others have been learning to confront the negative, the experience of what Crossan calls "absence." One may not wish to go all the way with Kermode's reduction of access to the ultimate reality to a Kafkaesque glimpse of something that eludes us. But Mark is a congenial text for the post-modern theologian because it does indeed avoid "triumphalist" oversimplified promises. It promises that those who suffer and struggle and misunderstand will go on doing these things, for a time. In the midst of that, meaning and God are to be found.

A more methodological factor has been harder for biblical scholars to cope with. They have always felt at home with the will, which came to such prominence in Bultmann's work. Now we see that the broader category is the aesthetic, not the ethical, and that imagination is the proper predecessor of decision. Here the biblical scholars still have much to learn.

---

15. Hans Frei, *The Identity of Jesus Christ: The Hermeneutical Bases of Dogmatic Theology* (Philadelphia: Fortress Press, 1975).

At the same time their texts and their tradition also have much to contribute to the ongoing humanistic discussion. For these texts have been profoundly formative of our whole Western vision, and in the past have repeatedly been reformative of it. Those who deal with the biblical texts will have to learn to appreciate them in the modern pluralistic context; but they will also have to press for a view of the aesthetic that is not mere aestheticism, that does not see only in terms of perception and the grasp of a possible perspective, but sees the human being as social and active among his or her fellow creatures and world, as an ethical being in a word, and called to a mysterious destiny that leads always beyond oneself. We may close by citing Amos Wilder, who in reflecting on the reduction of language to enigmatic disclosures, responds:

> . . . [S]uch loss of confidence in language as commonly understood contrasts with the biblical use of speech. Here, in all operations of naming and imaging, language charts the way between truth and fantasy (also called "vanity"). In its dialogic aspect as communication, the biblical word similarly establishes personal reality and exposes the alienations and evasions of the self.[16]

From this point of view, what is called a crisis in the humanities is seen in the narrower range of questions which are asked in the more recent scholarship which concentrates on internal relations within the text and avoids the older question of "what is there." Those of us who have worked in the Graduate Institute of the Liberal Arts [at Emory University] have been warned against the limits of specialization by Gregor Sebba, and encouraged to take a broader view by Charles T. Lester, for many years.[17] If what Wilder speaks of as biblical speech is to remain a living language in our time and is to speak critically to our alienations and evasions, the referential questions about reality will have to be addressed, as well as the questions of narrative coherence. To do this in a fashion adequate to the world we honestly experience is the task that lies beyond "Mark as fiction." It will not be possible to reenter the narrative world of the nineteenth century, in which the aim was to find a single story, for the unifying factor, the end, is rightly seen as problematic in our time. But the experience of life as a story, and one in which reality and, in religious terms, God, are actually encountered and known as real, is not thereby

---

16. Wilder, *Jesus' Parables and the War of Myths,* 17-18.

17. [This essay was orignally published in a volume honoring Gregor Sebba and Charles T. Lester, and sponsored by the Graduate Institute of the Liberal Arts at Emory University.]

eliminated. But it will be a story which continually transcends itself, rather than heading to a single unifying end. Though Mark is cast in the traditional form, moving toward a decisive end, its actual claims on the reader make it a valuable clue toward entering this new style of story.

- 7 -

The Infinite

Erosion of the Traditional Western View of the Infinite

In much of our culture, the "infinite" is a problematic notion, and one that threatens the forward movement of life which takes place through definite and limited moments into the future. Since hope can flourish only in the latter setting, it is important to examine the place of the infinite in the theology and in the imagination of our culture.

"There is but one only living and true God, who is infinite in being and perfection, . . . immutable, immense, eternal, incomprehensible, almighty, most wise, most holy, . . . most absolute . . . .God . . . is alone in and unto himself all-sufficient, not standing in need of any creatures which he hath made" (The Westminster Confession of Faith). The majestic prose of the seventeenth century articulates the form of the infinite that has been the central one in shaping our imagination. Here the infinite is partly defined negatively (immutable, incomprehensible), but it is given positive character as an infinite extension of a group of experienced qualities that are of highest value (almighty, most wise, most holy). The reach away from the human toward infinity is mysterious through the negative aspect of infinity, its opposition to whatever is limited, and its incomprehensibility. But the movement toward infinity is ordered by the fact that the beginning point of the reach is at least partly known. Wisdom, holiness, etc., are affirmed as really experienced in human life. The infinite is not just a negative or mysterious reality, despite the presence also of negative qualifications. Rather, the pressure or weight of the infinite is felt precisely by the fact that it is an infinite expansion of something fragmentarily known in our own experience. Against my wisdom,

---

From *A House for Hope: A Study in Process and Biblical Thought* (Philadelphia: Westminster Press, 1972), 56-74.

God's wisdom! Against my goodness, God's goodness! The immense power of this way of relating to the infinite can be seen especially in Protestantism. Guilt and creativeness alike are stimulated by the pressure of the infinite. People feel guilty because they fall so far short of the infinite, and at the same time they may be pricked forward by the claim of the unfulfilled reach of the infinite qualities they already partly know. The tension between guilt and creativeness, so clear in the history, for instance, of American culture, arises from the incongruity between the finite creature and the infinite which can scarcely be felt other than as infinite demand. It is no accident that in this piety the saving element, the figure of Christ, is precisely a limitation upon God's infinity, a finite figure. The infinite in itself is all but unbearable.

The Calvinist doctrine of the sovereignty of God is the clearest expression of this way of being grasped by infinity. If God is infinite in power and glory, nothing can stand in God's way. The consequences were worked out with stunning consistency. Despite the over-rationalistic form of the supralapsarian-infralapsarian debates and of the controversies over the freedom of the will, this whole style of faith was at bottom driven by an intense sense of wonder and mystery, a sense of the illimitable mystery of God. In studies of American culture, it is the merit of Perry Miller's work on the Puritans and on Jonathan Edwards that he perceived this vital sense of mystery, a mystery surprisingly conferring dignity on human life, behind the formidable and now unfamiliar intellectual expressions through which it came to words. But the combination of fire and penetration in a thinker such as Jonathan Edwards brings to light precisely the problem of God's infinity conceived as the infinite extension of what we experience as good—the problem of competition between God and human beings. If God is all-powerful, what is left for us? Edwards' honest answer was: No freedom of the will, for God's power runs completely through the sequence of causal determination, which exhaustively shapes human actions. This was the only way he could preserve without loophole the infiniteness of the God he adored.

Edwards, like other Calvinists, was persuaded that such a view left sufficient dignity for human beings, and it is better recognized today that in its vital period the Calvinist tradition was an immensely productive stimulus to creativeness. But the onesided and unrelenting stress on the infinite power and glory of God has led to a progressive rejection of this whole mode of imagining the infinite, whether through the course of perceiving the demonic quality of such a sovereign infinity (Melville), or through the course of brushing aside the whole seriousness of the question of ultimate mystery (Franklin).

Parenthetically, I should add that it is surprising that this rigorous and sober view of wonder has not become the center of a theological revival today. When there is so prevailing a determinism in many scientific fields, there could well be a renewed, modern vision of the sovereignty of God in a universe where human consciousness is strictly an epiphenomenon, a by-product of the things that really act. Is the lack of such a theology a sign of a failure of courage? Personally, I should be very much inclined to explore this alternative if I were not committed to the contrasting process view with its basic assumption of freedom and, within limits, indeterminacy.

A deterministic view of God's sovereignty has often been an intense stimulus to creativeness. But we are now in a period of strong reaction against the style of faith which is grounded on the infinite majesty of God, a reaction incidentally testified to by the fact that hardly any of the sympathetic and penetrating studies of the Puritan culture which so valiantly wrestled with the infinite God come from authors who have any commitment to this kind of faith. The reaction against the infinite so conceived arose from a sense of its repressiveness, its threat to freedom. A straight line runs from prophets of the repressiveness of God such as Blake and Melville to the "death of God" theology of today and to the less extreme perspective expressed by the slogans, "human beings on their own," and "human beings come of age." Apart from this line of theological development, it must not be forgotten that an immensely important consequence of God's infinity conceived as an infinite extension of qualities highly valued by human beings has been the stimulation of human competition with God. Milton's Satan and Melville's Ahab remind us of the force of rebellious competition which the infinite God provoked. The overwhelming conclusion has been that despite their common term, a valued quality, the infinite and the finite so conceived are simply incompatible. If God competes with what human beings do, God can do it so much better that the human beings lose significance; or, put the other way around, they can be their own finite selves with dignity only by getting rid of the infinite—and the infinite on the horizon may tempt them to exceed their finitude and reach for infinity themselves. Not only so, but a focus on the infinite may lead to a loss of focus on the definite in the creative act.

The Infinite as the Indefinite

But the rejection of the infinite as the infinite extension of known values has not expelled the infinite from modern consciousness. There have been many who have tried to establish a purely finite and relative view of things, but the lure of the infinite has forcefully reasserted itself. In many different ways people have been trying to revisualize the infinite in a form older than the rejected form: to return to the ancient perception of the infinite as the indefinite. This was the way in which the infinite was first introduced into our thought by the Greeks. For Aristotle, for instance, the infinite was potential rather than actual, and indeterminate, and as such it could not be known, for knowledge requires form. Since Aristotle associated God with form and with perfection, and since the infinite by escaping form was neither perfect nor actual, for him infinity was not an attribute of God. It was the contact between the Greek effort to clarify the meaning of infinity and the Christian tradition in which the transcendent God was known as having definite qualities related to human ones that brought about the shift from the infinite as infinite potential to the form of infinity against which we are still reacting. Though the modern search has little direct contact, for the most part, with the earlier formulation of the infinite as the indefinite, much of the modern imagination has been rediscovering a vision of the indefinite infinite as the mystery beyond the concrete and formed reality which we experience. Thus a resurgence of an essentially archaic form of the infinite is under way. For beyond the abstract thought of the Greeks lies the archaic intuition of a primordial unformed totality out of which the actually existing world emerges.

The clearest form of the rediscovery of the indefinite infinite comes in the search to appropriate Eastern forms of understanding. Emerson, who inherited Edwards' sense of wonder, moved away from Edwards' version of the infinite toward an indefinite infinite which he was able to grasp partly because of the newly available Hindu thought. Since Emerson's time the influence of the East has become progressively stronger, and a battery of recent thinkers such as Alan Watts, Arnold Toynbee, F. C. S. Northrop, and Aldous Huxley have explored the ways of relating Western culture to an infinite which is undifferentiated and all-inclusive, and which relativizes the concrete manifestations of reality or regards them as illusion. Others have found something similar in the mystical tradition of the West; thus Richard Rubenstein draws on the negative mysticism of Isaac Luria, a Spanish Jew of the sixteenth century. Here the ultimate focus of mystery is Holy Nothingness, No-Thing-Ness, the undifferentiated, transcending indefinite from which all concrete manifestations emerge and to which they return.

But the sense of an infinite indefiniteness is far more pervasive, and appears also quite apart from any reliance upon a religious or ontological tradition. In fact, the whole thesis that the modern world is secular and has lost the sacred needs to be strongly qualified by seeing that the sense of mystery before the indefinite is a widely present modern phenomenon, often not recognized either by its authors or those who respond to them as an expression of wonder, often inarticulate or despairing but nonetheless significant as one of the central expressions of the sense of wonder in our time. Modern writers have explored all the available avenues to try to show that life is lived without moorings, that it has no unity, and that it simply is what it is, unrelated to any setting or framework of meaning. But the background of such a vision is the indefinite or chaotic disorder out of which and against which life is lived, and in this background mystery resides. Thus Nathan Scott comments on some French writers:

> The tradition, in other words, that extends from the great *poètes maudits* of the mid-nineteenth century through Mallarmé and Valéry to Pierre Reverdy and the Surrealists André Breton and Louis Aragon is a tradition whose aim it has been to liberate the mind from the fragmentation and illusoriness of reality, in order that it might somehow gain an entry into the dark and primitive depths of Being itself: its goal is that cosmic point where all the scattered leaves of life are into one volume bound, where substance and accidents, and their modes, are all fused together into one blazing flame . . . . And in his *Second Manifeste*, André Breton declared: "Everything suggests the belief that there is a certain point of the mind where life and death, the real and the imaginary, the past and the future, the communicable and the incommunicable, the high and the low are no longer perceived as contradictions. It would be vain to look for any motive in surrealist activity other than the hope of determining that point."[1]

It proved most difficult to bring to expression the vision of the infinite point of unity, where there are no more contrasts between life and death, past and future; and the later history of this French tradition has been the story of a literature of despair, not of hope, and a story that is almost entirely devoid of anything that we can recognize as sacred or

1. Quoted in Nathan A. Scott, Jr., "The Recent Journey Into the Zone of Zero: The Example of Beckett and His Despair of Literature," *The Centennial Review* VI, 151, reprinted in *Craters of the Spirit* (Corpus Books, 1968), 165.

wonderful. But whether one looks at the intricate, indefinitely extended detail of surface in Robbe-Grillet, or at the unbearably extended description of detail in Beckett's novels, it is not amiss to see here a negative, or perhaps shadow, form of the infinite. The definite (and in both writers mentioned, as in Kafka, definite detail is of the essence of their style) is not longer related to anything, so that the infinite reappears in the form of the indefinite totality, a totality of zero. Modern literature is full, as Beckett says of the things that happen to Watt, of "incidents of great formal brilliance and of indeterminable purport," incidents of which it can be said "that a thing that was nothing had happened, with the utmost formal distinctness."[2] The pervasive sense of an indefinite infinity as the backdrop against which the fragmentary concrete appears is seen not just in one line of literary development but very widely in recent literature. It would be foolish to "baptize" it into the circle of the negative sacred of Buddhism or Isaac Luria. But it would be equally foolish to pass over the lure of the indefinite, the desolate, unending unrelated expanse that is the only mystery still perceptible to so many today. There may be a hint in its very infinity that this indefiniteness is somehow "commanding."

At any rate it is clear that the shift from infinity conceived as the infinite extension of known qualities to the infinity of indefiniteness has not been a shift conducive to hope. For hope, despite its unpredictable character, thrives when it has a "place," and the lack of place for the human being and the human world is the central thrust of this whole wing of modern sensibility. Yet the complexity of the situation and the vigor of at least some remnants of hope can be seen in the very persistence of the beaten-down protagonists in these works. Thus, Beckett can be treated as a writer of pure despair, a man with a vision that not only begins but stays at zero, as he is interpreted in the brilliant essay of Nathan Scott cited above. But this view overlooks the stubborn way in which the figures carry on in his stories, despite their lack of place. And Beckett himself, apparently, puts a high value on this second reading of his work.

Does the imagination, cut loose from the infinite on which it was brought up by Western Christianity, have to remain on the zero point, the dead center of a world infinitely random and indefinite? One way forward is to give indefiniteness the ultimate meaning of the primordial reality, and we noted above that this is often done by drawing on Eastern forms of understanding. We may expect further fruitful explorations of

2. Samuel Beckett, *Watt* (New York: Grove Press, 1959), 74, 76.

this theme. Another solution is to grasp this dark situation in an eschatological framework and view it as the dawning of a total reversal, a view to which we now turn.

The Infinite as the End

No one has worked more seriously at conceiving the infinite or totality as the End than Thomas J. J. Altizer, and we refer to his work here rather than to Wolfhart Pannenberg or others who are more familiar as theologians of the End because Altizer's work is directed specifically at the situation that we have sketched above, a situation in which the significance of the concrete tends to be absorbed into one or another form of indefiniteness. Directly sensed as a situation of loss of meaning, this radical unsettling of all perspectives is given a reverse significance by Altizer through the theme "Descent into Hell."[3] Drawing on the eschatological tradition, Altizer holds that total redemption takes place through total reversal, and a key feature of this reversal will be (or, is, to the extent that it is already real) the loss both of personal identity and (for the Christian) of all sense of the particular identity of the Christian faith. Transcendence is here associated with form and hence with repression, and the movement toward the future is a movement toward radical, total immanence. Altizer has much in common with those who try to give meaning to the experience of alienation, disorientation, and loss of transcendence by returning to a primordial undifferentiated infinity, as it is known in Eastern religion. But this Eastern vision, in its usual form, he sees as a return to the beginning and therefore a flight from history, rather than as an acceptance of history and a movement into the future. The West, with its sense of the Fall and history, must be brought together with the East and its sense of the primordial undifferentiated infinity. They can be brought together, Altizer holds, by viewing history in a radically Hegelian-apocalyptic manner in which the Western structural pattern is given Eastern content. The Buddhist nirvana reflects the pre-Fall undifferentiated unity which the West can no longer experience. And the End will be, not a return to this beginning but nonetheless an embodiment of a movement out of it which includes it in a new form. The End is radical, total immanence which not only leaves behind the transcendent God who has come to function as repression, but also leaves behind the separate centers

3. Thomas J. J. Altizer, *The Descent Into Hell: A Study of the Radical Reversal of Christian Consciousness* (Philadelphia: J. B. Lippincott: 1970).

of consciousness which have been so grotesquely exaggerated in the Western style of consciousness.

Much of this may sound quite gnostic to some readers, but Altizer is striving precisely to reverse the gnostic flight from this world to a higher reality. "Just as Buddhist love is unreal if it appears by way of the actuality and reality of the world," he remarks, "so Christian love is unreal if it appears apart from the brute reality of the full historical actuality of a fallen world."[4] Further, in contrast to a widely held view, Altizer says that love is not acceptance of the other. It is rather an attack upon all distance that creates and also alienates the other, an attack upon the estrangement of a fallen condition. This eschatological love can only be named Christ and is actually the reality of Christ.

In this serious and powerful vision we have an attempt to pass directly into and through the infinity of indefiniteness that has reappeared in the modern world and has replaced the infinity of experienced quality. There is no returning to the old God who had infinite but definite qualities of goodness and power! For this God is known to be repressive—Altizer has this in common with the sensibility that has rediscovered the indefinite infinity. But unlike most of those who speak for that insight, he resists the motif of return that makes the indefinite meaningful or bearable to thinkers such as Richard Rubenstein, Alan Watts, or Norman O. Brown, all of whom view the indefinite through the experiences of Western or Eastern mysticism. The dawn of meaning in the abyss of vagueness cannot take place through a movement backward. There must be a resolute motion forward, and to this motion corresponds the symbol of the End as total redemption. The End will be an inversion or total reversal of the undifferentiated point of origin, and will at the same time be a total coincidence of opposites. In Hegelian terms,it will be the complete passing of Spirit in itself (transcendent Spirit) into Spirit for itself (immanent Spirit). This reality cannot be known or confronted by flight from history.

This perspective takes with utmost seriousness the need for bringing into coherence the deepest insights of East and West. It is not accidental that Altizer's thought has been deeply stimulated by Orthodox Christianity, which is more open to a theology of the Spirit than is the thought of the West. The effort to bring together East and West, Buddhism and Christianity, must be a prime concern of theology for a

---

4. Ibid., 201.

long time to come. But it appears that at the present time a resolution is premature. The faiths of the East must be recognized as expressing an encounter with ultimate reality as profound as that of the West. But the two perspectives, for the present at least, in the last analysis offer a choice rather than the possibility of a synthesis. At any rate this is the case from the perspective of this essay. Why this is so will become apparent as we make a further examination of the concept of infinity.

In Altizer's thought the concept of infinity appears in the form of the infinite or total End, and the End means the breaking down of all barriers of consciousness, and the union of all consciousness in total immanence. His emphasis on process, and on God's involvement in process, is surely to be welcomed. His focus on love as total loss of distance is more questionable. Taking Christ as his central symbol, Altizer argues astutely from the New Testament as a starting point for his concept of love as total mutual immanence. The questionable thing is precisely the adjective "total." We can illustrate from a powerful vision which makes concrete what seems to be the central thrust of Altizer's vision of loss of distance and of total mutual immanence. John Woolman, the eighteenth-century New Jersey Quaker, records in his journal that at a time when he was about fifty years old he was so sick that he became delirious and could no longer remember his name. "Being then desirous to know who I was, I saw a mass of matter of a dull gloomy color to the South and East and was informed that this mass was human beings in as great misery as they could be, and live, and that I was mixed up with them, and henceforth I might not consider myself as a distinct or separate being." Later he hears an angelic voice, "John Woolman is dead."[5] The interpretation is that he is united with the slaves digging silver in the mines of South America, and his death is the death of his own will. Here is a magnificent expression of the death symbolism so central to Altizer, signifying for Woolman as it does for Altizer the breakdown of barriers between selves ("I might not consider myself a as distinct or separate being"). But can this moment bear the weight of the totality of the End? In Woolman's case he got well and resolved to abstain from the use of silver as a testimony against this suffering with which he found himself united. He resumed his separate focus of existence but with a difference resulting from the momentary interpenetration and loss of distance. It cannot be otherwise. No moment

5. John Woolman, *Journal*, ed. Frederick B. Tolles (New York: Corinth Books, 1961), 214.

can bear the weight of the "all" or be transformed into the all. For differentiation is of the essence of the real. The End considered as an infinite totality is an unstable symbol for precisely this reason; the End symbolizes other things as well as a total or infinite unity. Thus it is questionable whether the effort of Altizer succeeds in making clear a vision fundamentally distinct from the vision of return to the undifferentiated point of beginning which he is striving to go beyond. A vision of the End which does go beyond the undifferentiated will have to make place for some continuing form of distinction, of differentiation. Altizer makes a real effort to uncover a form of faith that will have room for hope, but he does not succeed in clarifying how the End will differ from the primordial beginning.

A Process View of Infinity

Clearly, infinity is in the most powerful sense of the term an attractive concept. In different forms it appears as a central or often the central symbol of the ultimate mystery, or God. But each form in which infinity appears as a total, all-encompassing reality presents insuperable difficulties. If God is infinite in the sense that God is the infinite extension of qualities we experience as good, then God is forced into a competition with human beings which destroys either one or the other. If God is the indefinite infinity of the undifferentiated primordial beginning, the concrete experiences and moments of life are reduced to unreality. If God (or in Altizer's language, Christ) is the total End, then if this can be clarified to be different from the beginning, no other conceptuality than the old tradition of negative theology is open to give it meaning, and the attempt to speak in this way brings in elements which are meaningful as parts of reality but not as the whole, such as the interpretation of love as total loss of distance, which is meaningful only as part of the whole act of love.

Perhaps what is needed is a fresh view of infinity as a religious concept. If we take a pluralistic point of view, we shall be prepared to hold that there simply is no one all-satisfying, unifying all. There is no such reality as an all-comprehending infinity in the sense of the indefinite infinity or the infinite End. The infinity of experienced qualities, despite its rigidities, pointed in the right direction in holding that there are differentiations even in what is infinite. God cannot be all in all since in the nature of things, God is only one of several fundamentally real entities.

Hence a process view of infinity as a religious concept must sort out three functions that have usually been confused: the infinity of possibility (the primordial nature of God); the total unification of reality (the consequent nature of God), and finally, the infinity which was so troublesome to the traditional Christian view, the infinity of perfection of quality. These three are quite distinct; each has a contribution to make to the way in which we are grasped by wonder at God and the world. The pluralistic view, that other realities are just as real as God, is a salutary and liberating antidote to the lure of the all-encompassing infinity or totality. This pluralistic view, as will appear, is much more congenial to hope than any of the other views.

The location of the indefinite infinite, in a process system, is the primordial nature of God. This is the realm of potentiality, the realm of possibilities—"eternal objects," as Whitehead calls them. On the principle that everything, even the unimaginably infinite range of possibilities, must be somewhere, Whitehead posits that possibilities as they become actualized in occasions do not come from nowhere but are offered to the occasion by God from the infinite store of possibilities in God's primordial nature. This function of God, of course, is by no means an exclusively "religious" one; quite to the contrary, all occasions whatever stand in this relation to God's primordial nature, which is a presupposition required to understand the fact that possibilities do not become actual in a merely random way. But the very vastness and inexhaustibility of God's infinite store of possibilities may become the focus of awe, an awe that is fundamentally the same as the awe of the archaic or Eastern person before the primordial undifferentiated infinite.

But there is a difference. For the primordial nature of God as the locus of infinite possibility is not undifferentiated. Interpreters of Whitehead differ on the question of how much ranking or ordering of the possibilities is implied by the fact that all are unified in God's primordial valuation of them.[6] But at any rate it is fundamental to a process perspective that possibilities are not just random, appearing from the infinite and receding into it again. The store of possibilities is the well of novelty rather than the merely undifferentiated ground of being. This can be so, for one thing, because the primordial nature of God is not "all." It functions in relation to other equally real entities, and thus does not swallow

6. William A. Christian, *An Interpretation of Whitehead's Metaphysics* (New Haven: Yale University Press, 1959), 271-277, emphasizes the minimal amount of ordering in God's primordial envisagement of possibilities. John B. Cobb, Jr., *A Christian Natural Theology Based on the Thought of Alfred North Whitehead* (Philadelphia: Westminster Press, 1965), 155-156, speaks of "an indefinite variety of orders."

up reality as the archaic primordial reality does. The very term "primordial" is misleading to those whose vocabulary is shaped by the archaic image. For an ordered range of possibilities (coming to actuality by reason of their relevance to what now is, rather than just randomly) is a central basis of the lure toward real novelty which is so much a part of the now frustrated intuition of our culture, and which is also a central aspect of Whitehead's view of process.

The Whiteheadian perspective makes possible a shift of imaginative focus from a past-oriented primordial undifferentiated totality to a future-oriented realm of unexplored possibilities which come into actuality by reason of their potential of carrying forward the movement to novelty which is actually under way. The lure of the unknown, the lure of the infinite that is not yet, and the lure that the finite moment move beyond itself can all be brought together as the transformation of the archaic lure of the undifferentiated infinite. The primordial nature of God is oriented to the new rather than to the "primordial" in the archaic sense. Thus infinite possibility does not require us to accept a pattern of eternal recurrence or the higher reality of undifferentiated being.

The second aspect of the infinite, the infinite or total unification of reality, is closely related to the first, but, at least as we analyze our experience, it requires to be separated from it. We have to keep on seeing that the older intuition is trustworthy, namely, that there is an infinitely extended unification of reality in God, but we need to learn that God's unification of reality is not a once-for-all totality whether of primordial beginning or final end. Again we touch on the realism of the process perspective, here in respect to time. However deeply shaped time is by our perception of it, time is nonetheless utterly real, and the unification of all things in God is enriched by or, if you will, subject to, time. In other words, infinite unification takes place moment by moment, and does not endure; the totality of God's realization is a serially enriched totality and not a static one. It is something of a puzzle that Western thought has resisted this notion for so long; of course it did so in the name of the eminence or greatness of God. "God is all-sufficient unto himself," in the words of the Westminster confession. On a process view God is not self-sufficient, but essentially related to all things. God's relatedness is what makes it possible to think of God as a focus of unification.

At this point in rethinking the meaning of infinity we are deeply indebted to Charles Hartshorne, who has seen, perhaps more clearly than any other thinker, the inherent conflict within the concept of infinity with which this chapter started, and who has developed, in the name of sur-relativism or panentheism, a concept of God as the *most* related entity, whose concrete relatedness embraces abstract absoluteness.[7] Hartshorne's phrase for the cumulative, successively enriched infinity is "the self-surpassing surpasser of all." Looking at the question from the angle of perfection and absoluteness rather than infinity, he shows that a God understood as self-surpassing is more perfect than an absolute, unrelated, impassible God. Against the static notion of God's infinite unification, he remarks, "the totality of changes can very well change, by the addition of new changes, previously inactualized."[8]

Time is elusive at best, and there are real obstacles in the view of God as the ever-present unifying point of cumulative reality. Those who wish to follow this point further may read the criticism of Hartshorne by John T. Wilcox, based on time's relativity to standpoint, and the reply by Lewis S. Ford.[9] We leave this problem aside to concentrate on the meaning of this "panentheist" viewpoint for the response of wonder, for we believe that such a cumulatively enriched infinity can provide just that dislocation of the imagination required to allow wonder to enter the multifarious world that so many find depressing. Quite to the contrary of many who find that the absence of a final end in a process view deprives God of the greatness that merits a religious response, we find that the view of God as forward-moving and ever-enriched can become the focus of a renewed sense of wonder, precisely because it makes the unity that religious intuition seeks concrete (if passing) rather than abstract.

Finally, we return to the form of infinity which was central in earlier Western imagination: the infinite extension of known and valued qualities, God as infinitely good. Such an affirmation is essential to faith. Yet in its earlier form it became so threatening that it forced the whole image of God out of consciousness. But once we accept the consequence of a process view, that God is one entity among others, and essentially involved in time and relatedness (God is, in other words, in some respects limited in comparison with the older theism), then the intuition of God's infinite completion of qualities we know and value ceases to be threaten-

7. Charles Hartshorne, *The Divine Relativity* (New Haven: Yale University Press, 1948).

8. Ibid., 84.

9. John T. Wilcox, "A Question from Physics for Certain Theists," *JR* 41 (1961), 293-300; Lewis S. Ford, "Is Process Theism Compatible with Relativity Theory?", *JR* 48 (1968) 124-138.

ing and becomes liberating. Despite the fact that the forms of thought are entirely different, there is a real point of contact here with early Christianity and with some aspects of the contemporary theology of secularization. For the presence of God in suffering, and the suffering of God for and with the world, become comprehensible as they never could in the days of the "impassible" God. As Hartshorne finely says, those who suffer are not "mere external products of an impassive first cause, but integral members of the all sensitive passive aspect or 'consequent nature' of the divine, who suffers in and through all their suffering."[10]

To summarize, Christianity (or Judaism and Christianity, more accurately) introduced into the West an understanding of infinity as not simply indefinite but as a concrete infinity of valued qualities: infinite goodness, holiness, etc. This shift in the image of infinity was the correlative of a shift which made hope a central religious response, because the believer found that his or her concrete existence was of real meaning to God. But this insight, combined with the absoluteness and transcendence of God, showed itself, in the course of many centuries of experience with it, to be a kind of infinity threatening to human existence. God's infinite qualities did not leave any room for human beings to function with dignity. The result has been, either in a mood of despair or one of tranquillity, a shift back again to the infinite as the indefinite on the part of a large segment of sensitive modern people. But if we can so dislocate our imaginations as to break up the image of infinity into three aspects: the infinity of possibility, the concrete infinity of the unity of the moment in God, and the infinite goodness of the related rather than absolute God, there will still be room for the distinctive contribution of the Christian vision, the infinite extension of the concrete qualities known to be best. This dislocation does mean giving up the idea that God is wholly transcendent and self-sufficient. Some think that a God so related to the world is unworthy of awe and wonder, but to the contrary we hold that this perspective will liberate awe and wonder, and hope as well. The alternative route, to return to the archaic sense of the indefinite infinite, is appealing because it draws on ancient perceptions and ancient emotional patterns.

We appeal here to the symbol of the child.[11] Both the stance of hope arising from the freedom of the process perspective and the stance of re-

10. Hartshorne, *The Divine Relativity*, 153.

11. [The symbol of the child is discussed in chapter 1 of the book from which this essay is taken.]

turn to the archaic can be illuminated by this symbol of the child: hope by the child as a symbol of the forward movement of life; the return to the undifferentiated by the adult looking back at the child's world and longing to return to it, or through it to the undifferentiated state that preceded it. Difficult as it is to envision the dismantling and restructuring of the imagination that we call for, and cautious as we must be since there are as yet few signs of response to this vision on the part of those with creative imagination, we nonetheless present this tripartite view of the infinite as profoundly hopeful and liberating. Perhaps it is not too much to suppose that, since the contemporary imagination is largely shaped by possibilities worked out by such thinkers as Hume, Kant, and Hegel, we should not despair that the impact of such thinkers as Whitehead and Hartshorne is not yet great.

Finally, we can relate the response of hope, seen in a process framework, to the structure of experience more clearly. We return again to the two modes of apprehending a mysterious "beyond": the mode of ecstasy, in which time seems suspended, and the mode of hope, in which a future fulfillment is expected. Though each of these is a macroscopic experience, each can be understood from a process point of view as an accentuation of an aspect of the moment of concrescence which is the ultimate unit of experience. Each occasion, viewed from the outside, is an indivisible "droplet" of experience that cannot be analyzed into successive parts. Yet each occasion has an internal structure which we can understand only in terms of primary and supplementary aspects. The final aspect of an actual occasion is its "satisfaction," in which all the elements are unified. It is by stressing the character of an occasion of experience as a movement toward unification in satisfaction that one is led to the primacy of ecstasy or disorientation to time. Here infinity is glimpsed through the dissolution of the links that bind one occasion to another. Such moments represent an immense heightening of the valuation placed upon the occasion of experience, a recognition that its limited unification of the reality available to it is analogous to God's unification of reality. For this reason, there is a tendency to cling to such moments and to imagine that their indefinite prolongation would be the ultimate fulfillment.

Another aspect of the actual occasion is its dynamic character of aiming at a goal. Whitehead was right in seeing that the internal goal of an occasion is not wholly isolated from its expected future. An occasion aims at a satisfaction that will prepare the way for as full a realization as possible of the intensity it seeks in the relevant future as well. It is this aspect of subjective aim, subjective aim not only as functioning in a discrete moment but also reaching toward its relevant future, that supplies the clue to the reach toward infinity in the future. But this is a different kind of infinity, for it is a processive infinity without term. Of course, an aim toward the future does not have to be seen as related to infinite possibility. Most purpose and hope is much more limited, and aims at a specific goal. The infinite possibility of time has in its full weight been a recent discovery in human culture, and it is still so new that we do not quite know what to make of it. People were creative for centuries before they saw that truly creative action presses past its goal toward a beyond, and that the beyond always beckons, no matter what the creative achievement. Our dramatic sense shapes events into stories that come to an end, and this sense also expresses a profound truth that must be taken account of. Yet each end turns out also to be a new beginning.

There are therefore two possibilities for centering experience: the occasion as a detached satisfaction, or the occasion as dynamic and reaching toward a goal. Both have played a role in faith. The former moment has a longer history in religion, while at least in Western history faith has brought the latter more into its consciousness. However varied the evaluation of the Judeo-Christian tradition may be, it would be hard to avoid the conclusion that it has been the principal source of this greater awareness of the dynamic of action and hope toward the future. At the present moment, however, our culture and faith are in reaction against this second emphasis because it came to expression in the rigid form of divine determination of the end. But another reason for this recoil is the difficulty and newness of the notion of infinitely enriched infinity. From the days of archaic religion, with its eternal repetition of what the gods did in the beginning, to the rediscovery of eternal recurrence by Schopenhauer and Nietzsche, the alternative to a goal predetermined by an absolute deity has usually seemed to be the repetition of a limited set of possibilities. One of the immense merits of the Whiteheadian perspective is that it clearly offers a third alternative to what has so often seemed to be the only two choices. This third alternative can provide a new "house" for hope, which is no longer at home in the rigid structure of the predetermined end.

- 8 -

Whitehead and Hermeneutic

A Different Starting Point

Whitehead's concerns were not quite the same as those of thinkers in the hermeneutical tradition. These all believed that humanistic study was threatened by the scientific tradition which, in the nineteenth and twentieth centuries, has repeatedly tried to claim the whole field of humanistic study as its own territory. The close connection between hermeneutics and phenomenology is no accident. For traditional hermeneutics, a deep scrutiny of consciousness must be the avenue to the distinctively human that appears in the text. For the world outside of consciousness seems to have been appropriated by objective, scientific study. The different ways of understanding the hermeneutical process, whether "divination," "reliving the past," or "fusion of horizons," all are efforts to affirm, through a fresh exploration of consciousness, a distinctively humanistic way of study over against the scientific one.

Whitehead, too, of course saw the difference between humanistic and scientific study, but he started from the scientific side in his development, and he remained without the antiscientific bias. His effort was not to defend the human from reductionist, positivistic, and deterministic scientific method, simply accepted as such, but to show how there is a continuum of methods of knowing reality, and to reduce the reductionism, positivism, and determinism of empirical methods by showing that these methods, useful and necessary as they are, are relative in ways that can be understood, and that they can be set in fruitful relation to humanistic ways of study which also have their own integrity.

Analysis of Perception

The place where Whitehead starts in this effort is rather remote from the questions of how to interpret a text. He starts with the theory of per-

---

From *Journal of the American Academy of Religion* 47 (1979), 31-37.

ception. For he saw that the gulf between scientific and humanistic study was above all the result of the work of Kant who believed that he had shown, on the basis of Hume's analysis of perception, that empirical study could not deal with reality, but only with constructions of reality shaped by the mind. To counter this view, Whitehead showed that the error of Hume and Kant was to take clear and distinct ideas or percepts as the model for knowing. Instead, he held, our direct knowledge is indistinct, loaded with feeling, and imprecise, while our clear perceptions are indirect projections upon reality. Whitehead termed these two modes of perception causal efficacy and presentational immediacy respectively. The two modes of perception are connected by "symbolic reference"; that is, the basic perceptual symbols function in both modes of perception, so that our indistinct but direct knowledge by "causal efficacy" is connected (though not infallibly) with our clear perceptions in "presentational immediacy." The net result of this theory is to affirm that we can and do know things about the world as it is, for all the contributions of our minds in shaping our perceptions.[1]

To put it differently, Whitehead shared the modern skepticism about the possibility of a purely rational grasp of reality, but he did not allow this skepticism to become absolute. Nor would he have consented to the extreme theories about the "linguisticality of reality," for all his recognition of the immense power of language to evoke a world of vision. He insisted, as Gerald Janzen puts it, that we experience more than we can know, we know more than we can think, and we think more than we can say.[2] Symbolic reference connects our dim, direct perceptions with the clear world of presentational immediacy, so that we are able to relate and test our clear perceptions against the sheer data of experience.

Language is our most obvious and elaborate symbolic system. For Whitehead, it is an arbitrary system. A statement in language is, by itself, thoroughly indeterminate. But, given a context, a history, a trajectory, it can become an instrument of contact with reality, however fallible. And

---

1. Alfred North Whitehead, *Symbolism: Its Meaning and Effect* (New York: Macmillan, 1927), *passim*; *Process and Reality: An Essay in Cosmology*; corrected edition, ed. David Ray Griffin and Donald W. Sherburne (New York: Free Press, 1978), 168-183.

2. J. Gerald Janzen, "The Old Testament in 'Process' Perspective: Proposal for a Way Forward in Biblical Theology," pp. 480-509 in F. M. Cross, W. E. Lemke, and P.D. Miller, eds., *Magnalia Dei: The Might Acts of God: Essays on the Bible and Archaeology in Memory of G. Ernest Wright* (New York: Doubleday, 1976), 492.

the range of reality in question would include not only the rocks and colors which Whitehead discusses at length in his writings on perception, but also feelings, qualities, ideas, other persons, and the basic elements of reality including God and creativity. The modern sense that these latter realities are at a horizon or limit beyond language is represented in Whitehead's theory by the recognition of the tentative nature of our constructions and the necessity for revision of the ontological scheme, but he was unwilling to exclude any of the elements of reality from at least partial linguistic expression.[3]

Analysis of Concrete Possibilities

The matters usually discussed under the heading of "symbolism" were separated by Whitehead into two parts. "Symbols," as we have just shown, function in perception. Their fundamental function is to link the clear, but error-prone, realm of presentational immediacy to the dim, but direct, perceptions in the mode of causal efficacy. Thus despite his recognition of the purely arbitrary character of many symbols, they are for Whitehead the necessary carriers of information about experience. Clearly his view presupposes that among their other functions, symbols connect the conscious with the unconscious experiences.

That aspect of symbolism which deals with creative imagination rather than with perception, Whitehead deals with not in terms of "symbols," but rather by describing the function of "propositions." In his view, symbols function in the receptive act of perception, but when he came to analyze the creative function of imagination, he chose a different term because he believed that a quite different phase of the process of self-creation was in view. Propositions function in the process of self-creation of an entity, as the instruments through which that entity considers concrete possibilities. Though he adopted the term "proposition" from logic, it should be noted at the outset that most propositions do not function at the conscious level, and that their "interest" is a more basic concern than their "truth."[4]

Thus propositions are prelinguistic, and, for the most part, preconscious. They are "concrete possibilities," taking a subject abstracted from

3. Whitehead, *Symbolism*, 10-13; *Process and Reality*, 11-13, 182-183; *Modes of Thought* (New York: Macmillan, 1938), 31-41.

4. Alfred North Whitehead, *Adventures of Ideas* (New York: Free Press, 1961), 244.

experience and predicating of it some possibilities from the immense range of pure possibility or eternal objects. Propositions have many functions, but the phrase "concrete possibility" indicates that propositions are the indispensable vehicle of imagination which reaches out from that which has already been experienced toward possibilities as yet unrealized, requiring a start in experience for its "flight."

An important aspect of Whitehead's separation of symbolic communication into two parts, symbols and propositions, was his aim to show how there can be an element of freedom in our response to symbolic communication. He did not neglect the massive continuities of human experience which are brought to light, for instance, in the Freudian view of symbols. But he was impatient of any view of humanness which took these massive continuities to be the distinctive and interesting aspects of human existence. It is precisely to open a free space for decision in the process of coming-to-be of a moment of experience that he chose his style of analysis.

A proposition, then, is a proposal, a predication of an abstract possibility or group of possibilities upon an entity already known in experience. It should be noted that a given proposition or proposal may be felt in many ways; the "propositional feeling" or manner in which the proposition is felt is often an important aspect of the new way in which a possibility may be perceived.

As in the discussion of symbols, in the presentation of propositions Whitehead combined an appreciation of the limits of language (for language can never express a proposition precisely) with a confidence that we can analyze "behind" language and are not simply locked into a language-limited universe.[5]

The Text

We may now comment briefly on the reading of a text. To read a text is to encounter a series of groups of propositions. Language being as imprecise as it is, the propositions or concrete possibilities evoked by a text and felt by one reader will never be just the same as those evoked in another. In part the differences will result from the different ways in which suggested propositions are felt, but language may also suggest different propositions to different readers. We can readily see how this is not just a matter of individual differences, since changes in the cultural situation will change the range of possibilities which may be evoked by a text.

---

5. On propositions, see especially *Process and Reality*, 184-207.

Also, successive readings, if they lead to shared interpretation, can cumulatively enrich the range of possibilities which the text can evoke.

Some theories of interpretation speak of the text as if it had an inherent vitality of its own, by which for instance it may interpret the reader. Such views "hypostatize" the text or treat it as if it were a center of activity. As Sherburne points out,[6] Whitehead's theory of propositions serves to indicate that there are indeed reasons for the vigor of our responses to texts. The same can be said for our responses to other aesthetic objects, of course. But rather than attributing to the text a vitality which is not there, we may look to the proposals or propositions elicited by the text.

To understand the reading of a text through the theory of propositions also has the merit of throwing into focus the tension between repetition and novelty in the hearing or reading of a text. Clearly the very nature of language (and of writing) places immediate emphasis upon repetition, upon the renewal of a group of propositions, or a very similar group, which are expressed by the text. At the same time, the sense of the flux of propositions, so that no two readings are the same, cannot only be accounted for in this interpretation, but it can be set in a framework where there is some prospect of making normative judgments about the validity of different readings. For from this point of view one may consider not only the criterion, so strongly highlighted in historical study, of the element of continuity in different readings, but also criteria dealing with the sorts of novelty that emerge in new readings.

The Author

Behind the text there stands the author. Much recent criticism has bracketed the author, and the relation between author, author's intention, and text is a thorny one. At any rate, it is clear from a process perspective that the creative actual occasions from which a text arises are occasions in the experience of the author or authors. There was the locus of the original vision of propositions which was partially embodied in the text. Elusive as the quest is, the author is real and a legitimate focus of inquiry.

---

6. Donald W. Sherburne, *A Whiteheadian Aesthetic* (New Haven: Yale University Press, 1961), 100.

Choice and Inclusiveness

One final comment on the nature of choice in language. Much study of language has attempted to break down the complicated and seemingly qualitative impressions made by language into smaller components which can be handled by "yes or no" choices of alternative decisions. This method can be extended by sketching a "tree" or series of branching paths, a type of logic also useful in computer programming. Thus in the analysis of narrative, a first choice (to leave home, not to leave home) can open a further stage with a second yes or no option following either previous choice. Clearly this style will work only if the tree of possible choices is preset before the actual choices are made. Much linguistic theory works on a very similar assumption, holding that an important function of language systems (*langue*) is to preset the possible choices which can be made in actual concrete speech (*parole*).

A process view would grant that such a procedure can be extremely useful for many purposes, but would inevitably relativize it. Taken as the central model for understanding how language works, the effort to break language acts down to atomic units of "yes" or "no" choices cannot suffice. A process view will understand the matter differently. For while at one level, the handling of constituent bits of information in Whiteheadian thought would coincide with such analysis: the valuation of a given bit of information (prehension) is either "valuation up" or "valuation down,"[7] at a more comprehensive level, the mutual relationships of the bits of information as they are brought into concrescence have to be taken into account. They constitute a harmony, better or worse depending, among other things, on the amount of contrast, which is the whole of the concrescence or new unification of data, as the many become one.[8] Without considering the whole, significant novelty cannot be seen or valued.

Though language does not exactly correspond to this fundamental process of concrescence, it does express it. A full exchange between process thinking and modern studies of language has yet to take place. It will be the case that a hermeneutic which takes both process thought and modern study of language seriously will have to give greater attention than Whitehead did to the constraints which language imposes on the successive unifications of experience which Whitehead termed concrescences.

---

7. Whitehead, *Process and Reality*, 240-241.
8. Ibid., 254-255.

But the useful oversimplification of analysis into successive choices tends to overlook a central aspect of reality itself, the process of self-creation as successive acts of unification.

Thus the act of choice cannot be analyzed into a series, however extended, of "yes or no" decisions, but involves also the synthesizing or constructive unification of a welter of data into as broad a whole as possible. The capacity of an occasion of experience to include in harmonizing contrast as wide a range of data as possible is a primary criterion of value in process thought.

For theological hermeneutic, the importance of this point is that the older hermeneutic of choice, the "either-or" of Kierkegaard and his many successors, could recognize in the reductive linguistic analysis a family resemblance to its own point of view which made it easier to enter into conversation with this "objective" discipline. On the contrary, a process hermeneutic puts in question the whole hermeneutic of decision. Recognizing once more the usefulness of this model for many concrete tasks, a process perspective will set for itself the goal of inclusion, of new light thrown on an old perspective by relating it to a new one, of the novelty of seeing how things belong together that had been experienced as incompatible. Such a perspective does not presuppose that all contrasts can be brought into such creative relationship. Nor does it cancel out the necessity of finding a ground or point of view from which to view the shape of reality and make judgments. But it does set for interpretation a different task from that projected by the hermeneutic of choice.

- 9 -

Openness to the New in Apocalyptic and in Process Theology

"Openness to the new" is a very general pattern of response, and yet one which is not easy to understand. In this article we shall be looking for some structures of response which can be facilitated by apocalyptic and by process thought respectively, and which can illuminate our own situation and what it is to recognize the new and respond to it adequately. The "new" will be taken to include both the new which encounters us and the new actions which, as active subjects, we contribute to the process of life.

There are two ways of coming at the problem. One can ask: what kind of self is resilient enough to confront the new successfully? Or one can ask: what kind of vision of the world is likely to be able to incorporate the new into it? Clearly, these two approaches must converge, since self and world mutually constitute each other. Yet in short-run practical terms, these two lines of inquiry may go in quite conflicting directions. I shall comment briefly on this problem in conclusion, but the present essay will leave the question of the self aside and consider the sort of vision of the world which may be fruitfully open to the new.

The thesis is a simple one: there is an old way of perceiving the world which is sharply challenged today but which still remains the most fruitful and, I believe, the most hopeful option. The world-vision which can receive, and within which we can respond to the new, and ourselves create and work for novelty, is some sort of "narrative vision," in which we see ourselves in the world as part of a story. If we can see the new as, so to speak, an unexpected surprise in the plot of the story, or see our own work as making the story go in a new way, we can be open to it—even though our anticipations are constantly challenged and transformed by the actual unfolding course of events.

From *Process Studies* 3 (1973), 168-178.

What makes the narrative so fruitful as a vehicle for a world-vision is that a narrative vision can be something which we do not simply observe or listen to. We see ourselves as actors in a story; the "view" is not simply something which happens to us, but is also what we do, how we put our impress on the progressing story.

Now, narrative vision or seeing the world in the form of a story is out of fashion in our world. In fiction and drama and film the traditional forms of plot are being pressured out of shape in a way that has never happened since people began to tell stories. In theology, the narrative form of sacred history, as in Lucan theology, is under attack. There are good reasons for these attacks on traditional narrative vision. Nevertheless, we need to give fresh attention to this way of composing reality, for a new formulation of it is necessary if we are to be open to the new. Some attention to the story form in apocalyptic can show us some of the reasons why the narrative form is in trouble, while process theology has some fundamentally useful hints about how we may re-imagine the story, or grasp a new narrative vision of the world, which will enable us to set the new into a meaningful framework and respond to it with hope.

In the story or narrative the past, present, and future are held together in some kind of sequential connection. The heart of narrative is the power of memory to penetrate the future. That is, events still to come are correlated "as if" remembered. It is precisely this ability of narrative not merely to order the past but to run ahead of the present, to give us an expectation, which is the presupposition for the new to be recognized as new, as the surprise that changes the plot, or what Aristotle called the peripety, the unexpected change in fortune. It is only because we expected something else that we recognize the new as new. In a narrative world-vision, then, the future can be something in which there is room for anticipation and spontaneity. In narrative the future does not have to become an object to be manipulated, but rather is an arena for further outreach and participation.

Such a narrative vision can be contrasted with two other options, which are much more popular theologically. One of these is the quest for being. Here, the matter of time and sequence recedes into the background, and one learns to be attentive to being, to why there is something rather than nothing. One thinks of Tillich in whom this motif was in tension with a more temporal perception of ultimate concern, and of Heidegger who has done so much to provide categories for modern theology. Suggestive as this way is, it does not by itself open an avenue to the new or to hope but rather to a world in which the difference between the new and old is irrelevant. The other world-vision which contrasts with narrative vision is that of the moment as carrying the total weight of meaning. Such a vision may indeed be open to the future, but it strongly discounts sequential or developmental tracts of experience, since it claims that the effort to relate moments to each other makes them objects which one strives to control. A genuine narrative vision transcends this dichotomy of freedom in the moment on the one hand, and objectification and effort to control the future on the other. A story sustains the precariousness and openness of the situation until it reaches its end, and does so by virtue of that power of imagination, or what I called memory that looks forward, to envisage a stretch of time as both sequentially related and also developing through human opportunity, intention, decision, and being acted upon.

The problems of narrative form and narrative imagination have not received much attention from philosophers or theologians. Hans Frei is at work upon a book showing how both German idealism and British empiricism turned away from the story form, which has always been so important for Christian faith, to think about other ways of seeing reality.[1] The new linguistic and phenomenological methods of interpretation do deal with narrative, but so far they have not done much to clarify the major narrative visions which are relevant for theology. Thus we shall have to venture some rather broad generalizations. Nevertheless, apocalyptic can show us what some of the roots of the problem are, and process theology can offer some hope for a new grasp of narrative form.

There are many kinds of stories, but for our purpose we need to consider just two. I will call them the little story and the big story. Fundamental to the narrative vision is the "story of my life," the life story or the little story. Despite the chaos and absurdity into which the story has fallen in fiction, we all try to make sense of our lives by seeing them as stories. People have done this as far back as we can see, and they still do it today, however precariously. But the early forms of the life story or the little story were not open to the new. Quite to the contrary, as Mircea Eliade has so skillfully shown us, a major effort of the archaic narrative vision was precisely to exclude the new from the story. A principal function of archaic religion was to wash out or forgive all aberrant new things that

1. [The reference was to Hans Frei, *The Eclipse of Biblical Narrative: A Study in Eighteenth and Nineteenth Century Hermeneutics* (New Haven: Yale University Press, 1974)].

happen in the life stories of archaic people, and to make their lives conform to one story or perhaps to a bundle of stories which cover all the situations that are recognized. Eliade has also documented the extreme persistence of this style of ordering life into a story which is not open to the new, in the rural cultures of Europe right down to the time of his own youth, and not only so, but he brilliantly predicted the resurgence of this kind of life story in the counterculture in a book which he wrote as long ago as the 1940's.[2]

Another aspect of Eliade's work points to the heart of our thesis: he shows the correlation which exists between the life story or the little story, and the cosmogonic story, the big story. In archaic religion each person finds meaning by repeating the creation, or to put it the other way about, people find meaning by projecting the pattern of their own little stories into the great story which explains not only their own little lives but how things are. This correlation between little story and big story, between life story and the story of the universe, is fundamental to the whole storytelling enterprise as a way of giving meaning to human life.

For the Western world, the main alternative to the pattern of repetition is the foundation-story developed in the Hebrew and Christian vision of sequential, successive time, a time of historical struggle and openness, a time which did not wash out the unique, unrepeatable event, but dignified it by giving it its own place in the unrolling process. Without trying to unravel the complexities of this vision, we can turn again to Eliade who has seen the importance of apocalyptic for our topic. The narrative vision in which unique, unrepeatable things do take place is a difficult vision; its power of dignifying the unique event is threatened by the frequent inability of the community which shares this vision to correlate their actual historical experiences with the pattern of meaning provided by the vision. The apocalyptic literature represents just such a crisis of narrative vision. On the one hand, the great Jewish and Christian apocalypses retain the form of dramatic narrative. They recognize the "new," and in particular the future is awaited as the coming of the new. On the other hand, the hope for the end is a confession that the occurrence of new things cannot be tolerated indefinitely.

Thus, ancient apocalyptic brings into focus some of the issues that a narrative vision struggles with today. To see our existence as some kind

2. Mircea Eliade, *Cosmos and History: The Myth of the Eternal Return* (New York: Harper Torchbooks, 1959; French original, 1949).

of coherent story, we have to be able to relate it to a larger story—our "little story" has to be fitted into a "big story" just as archaic people and ancient apocalyptists both saw. It is almost inevitable that the big story should, to some extent, be a mirror of the little story. But this is precisely the central point of the current crisis in narrative vision. The archaic vision offers a fairly clear parallel between microcosm and macrocosm, between the little story of my life and the overall foundational story on which "my" existence as an archaic person rested. But, once the story form is broken open to the new, the parallel between the little story and the big story is thrown into question. Apocalyptic is very instructive for us because it is so strongly torn at this point. The symbol of the end, on the one hand, opens up the life that lives in this vision toward the new, breaking away from repetition. The unique person and moment can be seen as unique because the story does not have to return to a certain point. But on the other hand, the end symbolizes closure, the cessation of the intolerable new, and the little story of the believer's life is subjected to these same tensions that appear in the overall story.

Another way of getting at what is at issue is to say that apocalyptic narrative is instructive for us because it shows the difficulty of working both God and human beings into the same story. The apocalyptic story breaks human life open to the new, but it does not do this for God. The determinism of so many apocalyptic narratives serves to assure the believer that, despite all appearance to the contrary, all these new things that are happening are not out of God's hand. God is still in control, and the new that finally occurs will be fulfillment rather than destruction. But this confident faith that God is in control may serve to stultify or weaken precisely that openness to the new which we called at the start the ability to respond to and interact with the new. Apocalyptic has often stimulated quietism though it can also be the impetus to intense activity. Clearly there is a large sociological component in the choice between these alternatives. But another aspect is precisely the question of how God and human beings can fit into the same story. When God's infinity or totality swallows up human spontaneity, apocalyptic adopts a passive, waiting stance toward the future. This literature comes from people who find life nearly intolerable. Insofar as apocalyptic is open to the new, it is not because its authors "liked" the new, but because they could not tolerate the existing world. The inherited models by which people saw their lives as meaningful were breaking down simply because their lives were not fitting those patterns. The hope for the near end arose among those who were outsiders in society, among those subject to discrimination and persecution. In these circumstances, the eye of apocalyptic faith perhaps paradoxically does not look for a compromise or partial resolution, but looks forward to a total resolution of the conflict. Our imagination requires that stories come to an end, but normally in order that, with the resolution of one particular series of events, the way be cleared for the beginning of a new story. With respect to the life story, this is most obviously the case as one generation follows another. But the projection of this pattern of resolution in an end into the great historical and cosmic story serves the purpose of magnifying the incommensurability of God. The big story, despite its obvious dramatic aspects in the great apocalypses, tends to become, at least in its ending, wholly the story of God, who becomes the all-absorbing totality. God will be all in all, as Paul puts it, the one who brings the story to an end.

Thus the apocalyptic story, with its vision of an all-encompassing end, tends to shift the new from being a surprise in the plot to being a final cessation of new occurrence at all. When the present is almost totally alienated, the narrative vision, it seems, can be endured only temporarily. It is only a short step from this to the breakdown of narrative vision altogether, which happens in gnosticism. In this kind of faith stories will still be told. Gnosticism is full of stories, but these stories have lost the significance of the unique and irreversible event, and instead look, in what happens, for a step-by-step approach to reabsorption in totality. The question of narrative in gnosticism is complex. Instead of analyzing ancient gnosticism, let me quote from a term paper which was submitted recently. In it a young woman named Mary envisages an indefinitely large number of worlds in each of which there exists a Mary. She says: "For each decision I have to make, some other Mary on another earth makes an opposite choice. At the end of our corporate lives all the Marys fuse into their energy sources, the great X out of which everything comes. At that time all the Marys will fuse into one being (not physical) who is complete in every way because she has done all, seen all, known all." In this modern vision, as in ancient gnosticism, the decline of real narrative has gone hand in hand with a blurring of the dialogical or event-character of human existence and of the relation between God and human beings. The end becomes a totality, an infinite inclusiveness, and anticipation of the end blurs the uniqueness of each new occurrence; for everything she does another Mary does the opposite. The great apocalyptic narratives do not go this far, although they prepare the way for this breakdown of narrative by their announcement of the end. Anticipation of the end in which God will be the sole actor discounts the human participation in the present which makes it possible to recognize the present moment as unique. The result is that people cannot be satisfied with finite occurrences and long to lose themselves in the infinite.

The ancient apocalyptic story thus shows a real tension in its narrative vision. On the one hand, it strives to hold things together in a story in which there is dramatic encounter and human participation because the end has not yet been reached. The future is not just a repetition of the past (despite the large element of repetition and return to the origin in apocalyptic stories). The most striking instance of the concrete new taken into an apocalyptic story so that it becomes the peripety or surprise in the plot would be the adaptation of the apocalyptic story by the early Christians to the new which they saw in Christ. They reversed the trend of apocalyptic narrative: instead of thrusting the decisive change out of the plot into the consummation, they brought the symbols of the end into the midst of the crisis of the story by applying them to Jesus. The result was that the early Christians themselves were released for a vigorous participation in the story in which they found themselves. But this would not be the only example, for apocalyptic also served to stimulate the revolutionary action of the Zealots. Both early Christian apocalyptic and Zealot apocalyptic drew on the openness of this form of world-vision to the new, to make possible a meaningful participation of the believers in the big story to which they found that they was contributing as it moved forward to its end. The power to enable participation, so that the new is not only what comes to us but a new reality which we ourselves make as we express our own creativity and purpose, is one of the great functions of narrative vision, and it must be an aspect of any future-oriented vision which is really open to the new.

At the same time, the struggle to avert chaos in ancient apocalyptic pushed it also in the direction of devaluing the concrete new event by absorbing the whole into the final totality. Thus the end threatened to be no more than a reenactment of the primordial, unformed beginning. Apocalyptic was, indeed, one of the principal ways in which a preoccupation with totality or infinity was opened for Western consciousness, and as this preoccupation with infinity developed, its gnostic and mystical forms have been singularly unfriendly to the new and, also, to the narrative or story vision of existence, a point well illustrated by the citation from the term paper quoted above.

Thus the narrative vision, which in archaic religion located men and women in a stable and unchanging story which their little story could repeat, came to be open to the new and unique events and situations in which people struggled with their creativity and their God—a shift particularly clear in the Jewish and Christian visions of existence. But in apocalyptic the effort to affirm God's power in the face of chaotic and unresolved experience threatened the narrative view both by the determinism of apocalyptic stories and more especially by the way in which the infinity of God tended to swallow up all differentiation in the final consummation, a trend which came to be all the more central in gnosticism.

The modern crisis of narrative vision has much in common with the apocalyptic crisis. In both cases there are important sociological aspects, which we bypass to concentrate on possibilities of understanding. The modern crisis of narrative is very different from the ancient one in that we are here dealing with artful stories, with "literature." Without trying to clarify this difference, we will proceed at once to show that the tension between a concrete event as unique and as a decisive bearer of meaning and the infinity in which the definite is overwhelmed is very much an issue today. We could illustrate from stories like Walker Percy's *Love in the Ruins* that are apocalyptic in the narrow sense; these would raise the question, as old as Hebrew prophecy, of the paradoxical tension between threat of inevitable destruction and summons to new, creative action. But even more fundamental for our purposes are writers who are not explicitly concerned with a narrative of the end, but who express the collapse of narrative form. Kafka, for instance, in whose works the characters struggle vainly through some kind of never-understood hindrance for some end which they never reach. Beckett carries this mode of presentation to what are perhaps its limits, in long narratives in which nothing ever happens. A writer more concerned with surface structure, like Robbe-Grillet, makes the same point. The surface detail is almost unbearably complex, but there is no conventional plot. In all of these writers we find, as we read in Beckett's *Watt*, "incidents of great formal brilliance and of indeterminate purport."[3] In all of them, multiplication of detail is the essence of their style. New elements which are infinitely rich and sharp in profile are constantly introduced, but they do not add up.[4]

---

3. Samuel Beckett, *Watt* (New York: Grove Press, 1959), 74.

4. On the apocalyptic motifs in contemporary literature see Frank Kermode, *The Sense of an Ending: Studies in the Theory of Fiction* (New York: Oxford University Press, 1967).

All of these writers are found in modern discussions of the apocalyptic theme, and with good reason. Ancient apocalyptic represented a crisis in which it was a question whether the narrative vision could survive, and now, in the world of imaginative writing, it is equally or even more questionable whether narrative vision can survive. The collapse of what I called the big story has raised the question whether there is any sense in talking about the span of human life as a little story, and with the collapse of the little story it is a severe question whether the new does not become noise rather than information. The superabundance of the new has destroyed its original meaning, and all the detail, if it has a religious meaning, represents not the weight of the definite event, but to the contrary, the reemergence of the indefinite infinite, the infinite field in which everything is the same, which commands the imagination in a directionless time. There is no longer any significance to any particular concrete new thing, but there is significance in the fact that there is so much quantity of the new. The very unmanageableness of the quantity of new things happening or described is the only frame of reference left. Much has happened between the emergence of the sequential narrative vision running through a history which offered genuinely new occasions, and the situation of the writers we have so briefly described. These writers react not only to the political-social breakup of a world, as did the ancient apocalyptists, but also to the intellectual reduction of reality in modern thought. Still, the comparison has weight, since in both cases the loss of narrative vision is a form of loss of anchorage in the world. But in both cases a hard-won and precarious narrative vision is threatened because it is an oversimplification and because it promises more than people can experience in it. And in both cases the loss or threatened loss of narrative vision exposes and brings to the surface an archaic vision, an unformed totality which offers itself instead of the sequential story-like vision.

Let us now consider what light process thought can cast on this situation. Process thought tells us that the fundamental unit of reality is the experience. This insight opens the way to a fresh look at that harsh separation of the world into an outer world in which objects interact inexorably by cause and effect, and an inner world in which we experience ourselves as active agents. Each moment of experience, in the process way of viewing it, as it comes into being, has its freedom (within limits) to create itself. It is genuinely undetermined, within the limits set by the past. Once it has come into being, it becomes a fixed datum, an object, a cause for the events to follow.

Thus in process theology, the fundamental unit is not the story but the occasion. Reality is atomic. The occasions of experience are the ultimately real units. But these infinitely recurring moments of experience are given direction and form; they are not just random. In large part the form is set by the past, but God, as the lure to more intense and massive experience, offers each occasion an aim at its highest potential. The occasion, in turn, may modify the lure to achievement given it by God.

First we note three blind alleys. One might think that one way to rehabilitate the story would be to regard each unit of experience, each occasion, as a microscopic story. But this will not do. Though we virtually have to use narrative language, the language of sequential time, to analyze what we mean by an occasion, we must recognize that the basic unit of experience is not a story which can be analyzed into separate subevents, but a solid unit in its own right, a droplet of time which does not admit further dissection into a story line. Whatever else a narrative is, it is, so to speak, strung together from the separate beads or droplets, the occasions which make it up.

Furthermore, the particular kind of sequential enrichment of experience which is so central for our narrative vision is not necessarily a fundamental characteristic of reality as such. There are occasions which are not sequentially related in any significant way, and although Whitehead did not believe that in the reality we know these occasions could achieve significant intensity, none the less they exist. Though sequential ordering is a prerequisite for the main way of building up significance in the cosmos as we know it, it is not ontologically necessary that things be that way.

In the third place, the final end, and with it the total unified meaning of the whole of experience, that has played so large a role in apocalyptic symbolization, does not have any place in a process system. Though Pannenberg and Teilhard de Chardin, for instance, make much of this aspect of New Testament apocalyptic, the weight and mystery associated with the final end will have to be reinterpreted in a process system. A return to narrative vision via process theology will not give us an end to the "big story" which will, in a process vision, have to be without beginning and end.

What these qualifications mean is that process theology does not open the way of reestablishing one single, unified and to-be-completed story as the framework of existence. Nevertheless, process has been singularly aware of the requirement of being open to the new, and it does offer several important possibilities for a new narrative vision.

In the first place, and I believe that from the point of view of a religious interpretation of narrative this is exceedingly important, process thinking opens the way for a new grasp of infinity or totality as a religious concept. We have seen that in ancient apocalyptic the pressure of the "all" threatened to swallow up the concrete new. Against this infinite field nothing significantly new can happen, as infinity is experienced in many religious forms. But, this does not have to be the way we are grasped by the totality or the infinity that was associated with God. There is, indeed an infinity of possibilities but it does not have to be confronted all at once. Quite to the contrary, the very infinity of possibility provides the inexhaustible source for an unending supply of new possibilities, once we grant that these possibilities are offered to us in some kind of structured way. And the infinite unification of reality, which the apocalyptist longs for in the end, can be recognized as real, in a limited way, in each moment's limited unification in its relevant data, and as an object of religious awe in God's recurrent unification of reality in the divine experience. But this unification in God is never finished; rather it is constantly enriched by the actual experience of the world.[5]

Viewed this way, the infinite is, so to speak, separated into two parts: on the one hand, the infinity of possibility which offers an inexhaustible supply of the new, bit by bit, and on the other, God's infinite unification of experience moment by moment. This way of being open to infinity or totality ceases to be threatening to the new and to hope.

This is an infinite which expresses itself in a narrative vision, not a predetermined narrative nor one which intends to include only a particular kind of people or a particular reality, but a story which is much more open than the old story used to be—a story, indeed, with many strands rather than with one, and a story which is not going to any predetermined place but which is constantly open to the best possibility that is relevant for it. Also, we must add, a many-stranded story which includes the loss, frustration, and tragedy which actually take place and which includes them not only as our experience but as experience shared by God.

In the second place process thinking opens the way to a reactualization in our imagination of human freedom. The correlative of the fact that there is no predetermined end is that there is real freedom, limited though it is; and limited as the choices are which we are able to make, they are

5. I have explored this theme in another setting in *A House for Hope: A Study in Process and Biblical Thought* (Philadelphia: Westminster Press, 1972). [See ch. 7.]

really free and open. Sociological conditions may indeed limit or even often virtually exclude the effective exercise of freedom, but nevertheless it is a constant possibility—contrary to what many think today; thus the "new" can be not only something we encounter but something to which we contribute. This conviction indeed can be powerfully liberating and can contribute to the actualization of possibilities of the exercise of freedom which otherwise would be ignored.

Times of pressure bring to clarity the quest for the infinite grounding of human existence. Much of the current interpretation of apocalyptic, though not often cast in those terms, appropriates it positively precisely because it does expose the believer to the infinite. This interpretation joins in that positive appropriation, but calls for a renewal and reshaping of the forms in which we make imaginative contact with the infinite. Apocalyptic is only a step from, and points toward, forms of perception in which the indefinite infinite swallows up the concrete act or person. Much of the modern imagination comes close to such a vision, though in consciously secular terms and often without quite knowing it. Further, the way of coping with the new which concentrates on building a self with sufficient strength and resiliency to face the new often moves in the same direction; for example, the techniques of meditation which are widely practiced today often function in this way.

Much process thinking has been carried out without much interaction with this field of imaginative exploration. This essay holds that the process perspective may serve to renew and reshape what we take to be imaginative possibilities, so that we may refresh our vision of life as dramatic encounter and story. The new story will be more open and will renounce the powerful image of complete unification as the goal. But the process vision of the "big story" can provide a setting within which the widespread new interest in "my story" can honestly develop in the conviction that my story is not just a private exploration but resonates with the reality within which we find ourselves. Thus the new, both as what we expect and as what we set for a goal, will not have to be thought of as either illusory or ephemeral. The people who have gotten things done have almost always had a narrative vision of self-understanding. Process thought can undergird such a vision even in the complexities and uncertainties of today.[6]

---

6. An earlier version of this essay was presented as the Ernest Cadman Colwell lecture at the School of Theology at Claremont, in March, 1972.

- 10 -

Christology in Scripture and Experience The Case of Process Theology

The role of Scripture as a norm for experience has always been a difficult problem for liberal theologies. By their strong emphasis on a "highest" form of experience, these theologies have tended to look away from a past originating point toward a systematic classification of present forms of experience. When they do turn to the past, liberal Christian theologies have tended to concentrate on the figure of Jesus rather than on Scripture as a whole, but their concentration on Jesus has tended to "liberate" Jesus from the Scripture so as to see him as the model of a perennial possibility. By their strong confidence that the vision of faith may become actual in the world, liberal theologies have turned to a human figure and to personal growth, and away from the "judgmental" aspect of Scriptural norms.

All these aspects of liberal theology were subjected to severe scrutiny in the theological debates of the past two generations. The work of theology is now carried on in a post-modern culture which brings home to us the polymorphous or amorphous qualities of experience, so that it is not easy to speak of a highest form of experience. The study of the Bible has fragmented the figure of Jesus or made this figure difficult of access. And the situation in our world has brought home the gap between the vision of faith and the opportunities for making it actual; in particular, the emphasis on the play of chance in so many aspects of the contemporary way of perceiving the world challenges the earlier liberal hope that rational models could set directions for action.

From *Scripture in History and Theology: Essays in Honor of J. Coert Rylaarsdam*, ed. Arthur L. Merrill and Thomas W. Overholt (Pittsburgh: Pickwick Press, 1976), 343-355.

This paper is written from within a perspective of liberal theology and specifically as an exploration of process christologies. It will examine the christologies of John B. Cobb, Jr. and Schubert M. Ogden as responses to the situation sketched above, and will then explore the relation of christology to Scripture from the vantage point of some questions posed by J. Coert Rylaarsdam about tensions within the Scripture itself. Thus it will appear that the issues with which we are grappling are not unique to liberal theology, but are modern representatives of issues which were already part of the make-up of the earliest christological reflection.

Rylaarsdam himself has expressed (in conversation with the author) a severe doubt that a process interpretation of the New Testament can be viable, though he has been much more sympathetic to process interpretation of the Hebrew Scriptures. The problem which he sees in the New Testament is that Christ is such a fixed point, such an absolute, that it is difficult to see how this fixed point can be incorporated into a pattern of process.

Cobb is keenly aware of this problem.[1] On the one hand, he opens a vision of Christ or the logos as creative transformation, so that Christian faith does not have a fixed essence, but is characterized (when it is true to itself) precisely by its opening us to new forms of life; faith is a matter of attending to the "call forward" in each particular situation.[2] In this way Cobb takes a position in a long-continuing discussion within liberal historical study about the difficulty of discovering an essence of Christianity. But he avoids the historical relativism that so often attends the denial of essence by developing a definite criterion of value with which to scrutinize change: creative transformation. What Jesus incarnated was the logos of a process of continual self-surpassing which contradicts the effort to define a stable essence. It should be said that by his careful correlation of creative transformation with love, Cobb finds an element of contact between the stability which Christians have usually tried to find in their faith and the movement of creative transformation. He rightly says that love itself constantly requires us to question established frameworks of judgment. It is creative transformation as love which is Cobb's equivalent of the highest form of experience which has been a mark of liberal theology. His version goes far to overcome the "triumphalism" of much

1. John B. Cobb, Jr., *Christ in a Pluralistic Age* (Philadelphia: Westminster Press, 1975).

2. See also John B. Cobb, Jr., *God and the World* (Philadelphia: Westminster Press, 1969).

liberal theology, for though he does not give up the effort to rank types of experience, he holds that there is more than one line of development, so that there is not one highest form of experience.

Cobb also stands in the liberal tradition with its emphasis on the historical Jesus. He grounds his own interest in Jesus in the Whiteheadian conviction that important changes arise from actual events; the new presence of God which the early Christians experienced "was somewhere"; was fully incarnated in the selfhood of Jesus. Jesus' decisions were made in so full an attention to the concrete will of God for each occasion that the sense of tension between the self and the call of God which we commonly experience was overcome; Jesus' "I" was "co-constituted by the incarnate Logos."[3] From this new selfhood sprang Jesus' own sense of authority, and still today it is our confidence in the transcendence by Jesus of our ordinary struggle to respond to God's will which opens our attention to his words and deeds, and delivers us from the quest for self-salvation which would dominate us if we responded to him only for the pragmatic reason that paying serious heed to his words had good results in our own development. Thus his theory of Jesus' uniqueness is a central moment in Cobb's christology, expressing the primacy of grace in the experience of Christ.

At the same time, the new fluid understanding of the logos as creative transformation provides the background for Cobb's approach to the question of making the vision of faith actual. It is no longer a question of the extent to which a pre-established pattern of the Kingdom of God can be realized in human experience or social life. His recognition that each new achievement of a more complex order brings with it the possibility of greater evil as well as greater good signals the full recognition of the precariousness of human existence. But Cobb refuses to fall into the stance of irony or that of resignation, which so often characterize the post-modern consciousness. Like the older liberal theologians, he holds that one of the valid tests of any theological perspective is its potential for changing behavior. The link between creative transformation as the meaning of Christ and the changing of behavior is a twofold one: on the one hand, this view of Christ opens the way for full commitment to ventures where Christ is not explicitly named; and on the other hand, creative transformation as the logos opens the door to hope, to the hope that the relevant future can be different. Seeing that "the world produced by

3. Cobb, *Christ*, 144.

the older notion of the credible is in shambles, . . ."[4] he calls for a more venturesome and pluralistic exercise of the imagination to open new possibilities of existence. "What exists does not fully determine what will be"; our hope for the future is based on its partial undeterminedness.[5] Thus Cobb meets the new cultural perception of rootlessness and chance by an appeal to the power of Christ as the power of the future, as the dimension that can still give direction to our choices and actions.

Cobb's christological positions are directly related to the theses of the older liberalism; he has modified these in the framework of process theology to take account of the less rational, pluralistic world that we perceive today. Ogden follows a different path, developing his christology from a perspective of liberalism modified by the neo-Reformation critique of liberalism.[6]

As a basis for his christology, Ogden establishes that the question about God is "at bottom, the existential question about the ultimate meaning of our own existence."[7] Ogden does not mean to eliminate language about God. What he does affirm is that the path to the recognition of Christ is identified theologically by finding that there is for humans ultimately *an* existential question with, in faith, *an* answer. In other words, the liberal quest for a highest form of existence has been reformulated in terms of the Heideggerian analysis of existence. Heidegger's understanding of authentic existence offers a less speculative, more existential way of understanding what it is that faith in Christ responds to. Though he speaks with approval of Cobb's exploration of a possible mutual enrichment of Christianity and Buddhism,[8] Ogden does not develop a pluralistic view of types of authentic existence as Cobb does. Rather he is concerned to separate the existential and the speculative ways of grasping life, so that the distinctiveness of faith and of the Christ to whom faith responds may be sharply separated from theoretical knowledge; an old Reformation theme.

The originating point of faith is also handled very differently by Ogden. He sharply dissents from Cobb's effort to describe Jesus' personal

---

4. Ibid., 181.

5. Ibid., 182-183.

6. Schubert M. Ogden, "The Point of Christology," *JR* 55 (1975), 375-395; *The Reality of God* (New York: Harper & Row, 1966).

7. Ogden, "The Point of Christology," 377.

8. Schubert M. Ogden, "Christology Reconsidered: John Cobb's 'Christ in a Pluralistic Age,'" *Process Studies* 6 (1976), 118.

response to God. He marshals the evidence for the difficulties of speaking of Jesus' own experience, and insists that the New Testament makes no positive claims about the historical Jesus. Rather than affirming anything about Jesus' existence, the New Testament "takes" Jesus' existence and personal commitment as an assumption on the basis of which it makes its proper assertions about faith. Should these assumptions actually be unfounded, this conclusion would no more disconfirm New Testament faith than would a metaphysical theory be disconfirmed by the discovery that one of the presumed empirical facts was not true, on the basis of which the theory had been constructed. For Ogden, here following a major trend of modern Reformation theology, faith is not grounded in the message of Jesus but in the message about Jesus.

Though the forms in which this message is presented are extremely varied,[9] it is essentially one message, in which "man's authentic possibility of self-understanding" is re-presented.[10] This message is essentially the Pauline-Augustinian-Lutheran message of judgment, acceptance, and love. Christ is the predicate by which you and I are definitively interpreted. This means that statements about Christ are at bottom statements about God, since God is "the ultimate reality in which the norms of existence have their ground and end."[11] One sees at once that the point of contact with Cobb's treatment is the centrality of God's love to both. But Ogden develops this central insight in terms of a fixed structure of human existence and in terms of a message about Christ, the early forms of which serve as a constant norm for the church's reflection.[12]

If we turn to the third motif which we cited as characteristic of liberal theology, the confidence that the message of Christ can be made actual, Ogden again displays a modified liberalism. He insists that application is one of the essential aspects of the whole movement of theology, and emphasizes this point by following a traditional division of theology in which "practical theology" is one of the three branches of theology (along with historical and systematic theologies), and by stressing the ethical and social dimensions of practical theology.[13] But it is noteworthy that in describing the task of practical theology he mentions first the "limitations"

9. Schubert M. Ogden, "What Is Theology?," *JR* 52 (1972), 22-40, esp. 24.
10. Ogden, "The Point of Christology," 382.
11. Ibid., 378.
12. Ibid., 380.
13. Ogden, "What Is Theology," 24.

that thinking faith must identify as it moves into action.[14] He is very reluctant to submit faith to the traditional liberal empirical test, for he sees a sharp disjunction between empirical and existential statements, but above all he is eager to preserve the privacy of faith between a person and God, a relationship which is not to be measured by someone else or even by the person himself or herself, but to be known only to God.[15] This concern to separate faith from that which can be empirically tested by observation—again a Reformation motif—is so strong with Ogden that it prevents him from dealing more directly with the question of the expected impact of faith in Christ.

Each of these Christologies displays a tension between the effort to perceive Christ in ways that are continuous with the rest of experience, and the effort to affirm the uniqueness of Christ. We can clarify what is at issue in this tension by referring to Rylaarsdam's presentation of the two covenants as sources of christological symbolism.[16] Neither Cobb nor Ogden gives much attention to the roots of their christologies in the Hebrew Scriptures; both are more interested in discussions that arose later in the church. But the contrast between the symbolism of the covenant with Israel and that of the covenant with David was a constitutive factor in the early christologies, and the elements which were in tension then are, many of them, still apparent in these contemporary christological reflections.

In Rylaarsdam's presentation, the covenant with Israel was historical, relative, and mutual. It promised nothing beyond what could be given in this spatio-temporal world, and, equally important, its promises were joined to requirements; grace and demand were inextricably interwoven. This covenant has been the predominant organizing center of Jewish faith. The covenant with David, in contrast, was static rather than historical; it was absolute, and its absoluteness forced those who used its symbolism to project a future beyond this historical world, where its promises could be realized. It focused on an individual and his line rather than upon a people. Most important, the promise to David was understood as absolute in such a way that the reciprocal interplay of promise and responsibility was not a part of this covenant. In Rylaarsdam's inter-

14. Ibid.

15. Ogden, "Christology Reconsidered," 118-22; "What Is Theology," 36-37.

16. J. Coert Rylaarsdam, "The Two Covenants and the Dilemmas of Christology," *Journal of Ecumenical Studies* 9 (1972), 249-270.

pretation, the covenant with David provided the major occasion for the development of apocalyptic. Though Christians used covenant-with-Israel symbolism, they drew predominantly from the symbolism of the covenant with David and its apocalyptic developments to find categories in which to express the absoluteness of the coming of Christ which was central to the early Christian faith.

We do not need to commit ourselves to the details of Rylaarsdam's thesis about the narrow connections between the covenant with David and apocalyptic (which may indeed have developed from much more diffuse and complex factors) to see how useful and important his typology is for understanding the dynamics of christological symbolism. He notes that while the early church and classical christologies were strongly "Davidic," modern theology has striven to eliminate the Davidic symbolism and to develop christologies that in effect use covenant-with-Israel symbolism. Process theology would be an example of this reformulation; its rejection of supernaturalism and its explication of reality in terms of events is highly coordinate with the covenant-with-Israel symbolism as Rylaarsdam sets it forth.

We shall concentrate on the elements or equivalents of covenant-with-David symbolism in the authors we are studying. Factors in the covenant with David which are relevant to the christologies under discussion are: the focus of the promise on a person rather than on a people; the consequent limitation of the locus where transcendence is perceived to elements associated with that person; a universalistic claim (arising from the royal symbolism); a sense of the totality or finality of revelation, which cannot be surpassed, though it can and must be completed in the future; and a definitiveness of grace which tends to thrust responsibility into the background.

Cobb's recasting of the meaning of Christ to be creative transformation shows many analogies to the historical-processive covenant with Israel as Rylaarsdam sketches it, and Cobb's concept of the interplay of grace and responsibility (with grace primary) is closer to that of the covenant with Israel than to the absoluteness of the promise to David. The "Davidic" elements that appear in Cobb's christology are particularly two. First, his emphasis on the unique personal constitution of Jesus, which corresponds to the Davidic theme of the divine representative, the king, as the bearer of salvation, and second, his conviction that, once the logos is perceived in Christ, all forms of creative transformation can be seen to be coherent with what is revealed in Jesus. Cobb has set these convictions in a highly processive framework, in which Christian faith can cling to no fixed forms.

In the case of Ogden, the absoluteness of the Davidic symbolism shows itself in the assertion that "nothing is more striking about the New Testament witnesses to Jesus the Christ than the extent to which they emphatically place Jesus on the *divine*, rather than the human, side of the God-man relationship."[17] Of course, for Ogden this is the Christ who is re-presented in the Christian message. The existentialist reading of this message by Ogden only strengthens its claim to be decisive of any and all human existence, for the kerygma is *the* answer to *the* human question—a stance typical of a universal religion which Christianity became, and used Davidic symbolism to do so. Ogden's insistence on *the* question and *the* answer is his way of resisting the pluralism and relativism of contemporary culture.

This brief sketch has well substantiated Rylaarsdam's suggestion of the usefulness of the Israel and Davidic covenant symbolisms as a way of identifying problematic areas in christology. He is right both that modern christologies have moved strongly toward categories that are coherent with the covenant with Israel, and also that they cannot eliminate the Davidic type of symbolism altogether.

The way forward in christology will also be determined largely by how one understands and deals with the tension between the two symbolic complexes. My own path in christology will be the resolutely liberal one of constantly questioning the "Davidic" elements in the conviction that they can be transformed without being eliminated, to make them more appropriate to the pluralistic situation in which faith must understand itself—a theme strongly articulated by Cobb. Ogden's effort to maintain central Reformation emphases is gained at the price of restricting the flow of Christian reflection, by his insistence on an existential/speculative dichotomy which does not correspond to the experience of reflection as I understand it. Faith must be more self-reflective than I understand him to allow it to be; that is, it must be able to question the very forms in which it appears. Ogden's desire to affirm the enduring oneness of the representation of Christ represents a concern that I share; but I cannot recognize this oneness in the actual diversity of the proclamations. I believe that we must think of early Christianity and of Christianity in general as constituted by the coming-together of a variety of commitments.

17. Ogden, "The Point of Christology," 388.

No one of these remains constantly in the focus of all the forms of faith. Rather, reflection about the different styles of Christian faith will lead us to construct a grid with various squares filled in for various forms of faith. This will be true even for the very earliest stages, for the notion of a uniform early Christianity is not supported by the sources. Normative judgments will be judgments about various clusters of commitments rather than judgments about the effectiveness of realization of a single essence.

Further, Ogden's unquestioning acceptance of the claim of faith to be the decisive answer to the human question also needs to be scrutinized by faith itself. This claim is part of the structure of a universal religion; we need to ask what it means to be moved beyond the stage of the universal religion. As we pass into a situation where genuine encounter with other faiths is possible in a way never before actual in Christian history, faith must reformulate its unreflective understanding of its own absoluteness, in the hope for a more comprehensive faith yet to come.

Thus, a further exploration of the more speculative methods followed by Cobb holds the greater promise. But here, too, it is precisely the most "Davidic" elements which are the most questionable. To understand the logos as creative transformation is a major advance in christological thinking. But creative transformation comes into our field of experience from a complex set of sources. One might think that Plato, moving from his early theory of ideas toward his later view of the quest for truth as a dialectic movement often without final conclusion, has been a model of creative transformation for many modern as well as ancient theologians, parallel to Jesus. Cobb would not question the variety of the sources through which we may encounter creative transformation. The question is whether the different types of creative transformation can be seen as coherent, as one logos. I would doubt this, and would hold that the convergence of different movements of creative transformation has to be regarded as a hope, a part of eschatology—an essential part of Christian hope even though it will, probably, never be fully realized.

Secondly, Jesus' selfhood as co-constituted by the logos is a questionable thesis. We need to recognize that the Jesus to whom we respond in faith is a "constructed" figure, constructed in the imagination of believers. Elements contributing to the construction of this figure are the power of symbols from the Hebrew Scriptures and from the Hellenistic world, the experiences of early Christians, and our own experiences, as well as the impact of the selfhood of Jesus himself, made manifest through his words and deeds. We can indeed know something about Jesus, and that knowledge, for all its tentativeness, is relevant to faith. A part of the basis for our trust is his commitment to God and to his task. But we cannot rigorously distinguish his sense of vocation from that of others who understood themselves to be authoritative representatives of God, by making the distinction that Jesus was responding fully to the call of God, while others were exaggerating their responsiveness. Rather, it is the setting in which he acted and spoke and was perceived that enabled the first Christians, and enables us, to fuse his person with the symbols drawn from the two covenants and elsewhere and to see in him the full representation of God and the fulfillment of our hopes.

We have seen that the various forms of process theology considered here take seriously the tension between the historical-mutual-processive symbolism originally mediated by the covenant with Israel, and the absolute-personal-universal symbolism of the covenant with David. Putting the stress on the former type, in various ways they recognize the necessity for some equivalent of the latter. Since the strongest statements of the Davidic themes occur in the Psalms, and the highest christologies of early Christianity in hymnic passages in the New Testament, the tension we have been studying is an instance of the problem of poetic language versus discursive language. So far this way into our problem has not been much explored by process theologies, which have tended to be weighted toward discursive, rational thought. Cobb's exploration of Christ as an "image" is an opening into this further line of exploration.

Finally, what light has our sketch of process christologies cast on our original question about the relation between Scripture and experience? Rylaarsdam has shown that in contrast to some earlier versions of Scripture as a norm, it is precisely the tensions within the Scripture that have made it fruitful in deepening our understanding of new issues. Both Cobb and Ogden take Scripture very seriously as a norm. Ogden thinks of it as in some sense, at the existential level of interpretation after the legendary elements have been discounted, a fixed norm. He takes the view that the community of the church simply finds it to be the case that "the New Testament contains the original as well as the finally normative witness of Christian faith."[18] Cobb follows the path of seeking for an explanation of how it is that the early witness can still be a shaping power. His view of

---

18. Ibid., 380; "What Is Theology," 29-30.

Jesus' person is developed largely to meet this question.[19] Neither theologian is much concerned with the outer limits of the canon; these theologies will be adequate for those who find the heart of the question of Scripture to be the finding of a center of the Scripture. It is the merit of Rylaarsdam's essay to have taken this starting-point presupposed by most liberal theology, and shown how important for the clarification of it large reaches of the Scripture actually are.

19. Cobb, *Christ*, 136-146.

- 11 -

Recent Hermeneutics and Process Thought

I

Contemporary hermeneutics offers a varied picture, but one of its central strands is the analysis of linguistic constructions apart from their dimension of reference. Thus Frank Kermode can say,

> All modern interpretation that is not merely an effort at "recognition" involves some effort to divorce meaning and truth. This accounts for both the splendors and the miseries of the art. Insofar as we can treat a text as not referring to what is outside or beyond it, we more easily understand that it has internal relationships independent of the coding procedure by which we may find it transparent upon a known world. We see why it has latent mysteries, intermittent radiances. But in acquiring this privilege, the interpreters lose the possibility of consensus and of access to a single truth as the heart of the thing....some such position is the starting point of all such hermeneutics except those which are consciously reactionary.[1]

Kermode's statement, carefully elaborated in a whole book on narrative choosing the Gospel of Mark as a central example, turns away from a text's reference in order to emphasize the plurality of meanings conveyed by a text, the free play of the imagination in encountering a text, and the need for separating oneself from established interpretation in order to hear a text freshly and freely. There is nothing casual about his taking this position; such interpretation, he tells us, is "henceforth linked to loss and disappointment, so that most of us will find the task too hard, or simply repugnant, and then abandoning meaning, we slip back into the old comfortable fictions of transparency, the single sense, the truth."[2]

Kermode's work nicely sums up the shift from the old to the new hermeneutics since several central changes of attention all appear in it: (1)

From *Process Studies* 12 (1982), 65-76.

1. Frank Kermode, *The Genesis of Secrecy: On the Interpretation of Narrative* (Cambridge, MA: Harvard University Press, 1979), 122f.

2. Ibid., 123.

a shift from the ethical to the aesthetic as the locus through or beyond which the transcendent is known or quested for; (2) a rejection of both empirical and transcendent truth in favor of an inner exploration, an exploration which often centers on language but which may have a broader phenomenological base; and (3) a dismantling of the intuitive assumption that narrative fundamentally makes sense.

The quest for "truth" in Christian thought and interpretation is one of the principal aspects of the hermeneutics of the past against which the current trend is reacting. If traditional philosophical theology was given methodological confidence by a sense that coherent relations exist in reality, traditional religious hermeneutics was given methodological confidence by a particular form of this sense of coherent relations—the sense that there is a narrative shape to reality, that narrative has ontological reality. It is clear, however, that a radical reconsideration of the meaning of narrative lies at the heart of Kermode's hermeneutic. His last chapter is entitled "The Unfollowable World": narrative in a superficial sense is followable; we go with it, but when we reflect on how it is put together and on its possible multiple meanings, we conclude that any connection between a story told and the reality beyond the story is so tenuous that the world is, indeed, "unfollowable."

Philosophers of religion might try to transplant narrative content into non-narrative statements, which are or may be subject to types of tests which are difficult or impossible to apply directly to narrative. Important as this task is in assessing the current crisis of the narrative sense, it will be set aside here in favor of the narrative structure itself, since the other two hermeneutical questions—about the relation between the aesthetic and the ethical, and about the relation between the inner structure of language or experience and reference to a world relating to them—are closely bound to the interpretation of narrative.

We may begin by reminding ourselves that a severe questioning, indeed a virtual rejection of the traditional relation between narrative and faith, was a central trait of Bultmann's existentialist hermeneutics. Bultmann's lack of interest in the Hebrew Scriptures as story, his reduction of the narrative element in the New Testament, and his effort to reinterpret what was left, are well known. In large measure he followed this course because it appeared to him that experienced sequences could only be interpreted in the cause-and-effect pattern of natural science, a pattern which evacuated human existence of meaning. Thus the gap between coherent sequences and meaning appeared at a different point in

Bultmann's thought from that seen by Kermode, but Bultmann's perspective comes from a movement of thought which lays a groundwork for the latter.

Bultmann saw clearly that the past contributed to the present by efficient causation; he interpreted this contribution as a confining one, and opposed to it the moment of decision. Instead of the traditional narrative sense, in which anticipation, recollection, and decision interact to give direction, in Bultmann's perspective significance is collapsed into the moment. Openness to the future, it is true, is opposed to the effort to know and control the future; but openness to the future involves the renunciation of the sense of direction. Bultmann's principles of interpretation represent a powerful reassertion of the centrality of the ethical as the route toward the transcendent. But his version of the ethical was not a rational ethic; it was a spontaneous moment of decision.

One move in post-Bultmannian hermeneutic has been to follow his dismantling of the narrative sense in order to find an authentic element in it, but to search as well for a more aesthetic and less ethical way of characterizing the freedom of the present. For one thing, Bultmann's pressing seriousness in the face of decision could be maintained because for him decision was focused confrontation, with all the energies of the self concentrated on responsiveness to the mystery of the death and resurrection of Christ. (His view was, of course, modeled in analogy and contrast to Heidegger's seriousness of confrontation with existence toward death).[3] Later interpreters have moved away from centered confrontation to a wider appreciation of the multifariousness of existence, so that there is no one center for confrontation; this move results in an interpretation of the moment as a moment of play among a rich variety of alternatives. Crossan among interpreters of the New Testament is a clear representative of this style of interpretation.[4]

For the Christian theologian, this move raises a serious question about the traditional assumption that faith has a center. In addition, as the philosopher of religion will note, it produces a situation which may be described as one in which Kant's interpretation of the limits of our knowl-

---

3. Cf. Rudolf Bultmann, "The Historicity of Man and Faith," pp. 92-110 in *Existence and Faith: Shorter Writings of Rudolf Bultmann*, ed. Schubert M. Ogden (New York: Meridian, 1960).

4. John Dominic Crossan, *Raid on the Articulate: Comic Eschatology in Borges and Jesus* (New York: Harper & Row, 1976); *The Dark Interval: Towards a Theology of Story* (Niles, IL: Argus, 1975).

edge of reality is still regarded as valid, while Kant's sense of the seriousness of the moral claim is eroded.

But hermeneutic thinking has also taken another direction, a direction of effort to recover the narrative sense. Among the various proposals along this line, it is useful to note that of Hans Frei, because his work puts special stress on a point that links narrative and the ethical dimension, namely, the role of narrative vision in identity formation. Frei's treatment of this theme, Barthian in derivation, concentrates on the identity description of Jesus Christ in the Gospels. But his acute analysis of the ways in which identity is described is of great significance for the general question of the role of narrative as well.

Frei notes, as have many others, that "moral responsibility is a prime relating factor between a person's past, present, and future."[5] His model of identity description as narrative includes two types: intention-action description, which answers the question, What is a person like?, and self-manifestation description, which deals with the continuity, Who is the person?[6] What links these two types of description is the very different analysis which Frei offers, in comparison to Bultmann, of the moment of self-constitution of a person's identity. For Frei, who has his eye fixed on moral responsibility in time, identity requires what he calls a "total integration of the self by itself."[7] "A person is what and who he is just by the way he holds all these things [the elements of selfhood] together and orders them."[8] Frei's formulation may undervalue the social elements of selfhood by his insistence that the self is integrated by itself, but this not a necessary consequence of his insights. The move from "moment of decision" to "moment of integration" offers a conceptuality for retaining the narrative sense of life and at the same time the centrality of the ethical in self description, both of which are excluded or rather sharply limited by the move from existentialist decision to the moment of play among a variety of options.

The contrast between Kermode and Frei seems at first sight to offer us a choice between the two sorts of approach to the transcendent, and thus to two different sets of presuppositions to bring to texts that deal with the transcendent. Frei, like Bultmann, represents the traditional view that the transcendent is centrally encountered beyond the ethical, though he

5. Hans W. Frei, *The Identity of Jesus Christ: The Hermeneutical Bases of Dogmatic Theology* (Philadelphia: Fortress Press, 1975), 40.

6. Ibid., 44.

7. Ibid., 40.

8. Ibid., 41.

presents the ethical in a different way. Kermode moves toward the aesthetic as the vehicle beyond which one may glimpse the transcendent. But though these moves can be and often are presented as alternatives, requiring a choice, I urge that we find a framework comprehensive enough to include both possibilities and to set them in relation to each other. Primarily this means rethinking the ethical dimension to give it a ground more closely affiliated to the aesthetic than has been common at least in theological ethics. I find suggestions made by John B. Cobb, Jr., and Charles H. Reynolds exceedingly helpful here.[9] Their work can open the way for a fresh appropriation of the ethical dimension as a possible vehicle for the transcendent, freed from many of the factors which have repelled the modern artists and critics who have sought another, an aesthetic vehicle for their language about what is ultimate. But, as noted above, I do not see this move as a "return." Those who have asserted the centrality of the aesthetic are, in a sense, right, since they have recognized that imagination, risk, and self-creation are central factors in the human, factors that have often been obscured both by rigorously moralistic ethics and by rigorously logical ethical speculation.[10]

Nevertheless, if it is correct that a fresh perception of the vitality and creative possibility of the ethical dimension is an important ingredient in a more adequate hermeneutic, the reference above to a process ethics is a demonstration of the importance of speculative philosophy for con-

---

9. I refer especially to Reynolds' contribution to *John Cobb's Theology in Process,* where he proposes a "somatic ethics." We may note Reynolds' emphasis on the aesthetic imagination and on the world as thoroughly social existence (118) as elements which can reshape those factors in the ethical demand which have repelled many modern interpreters. Cobb and Reynolds both recognize the fact that from the point of view of process philosophy, there still are problems in differentiating the ethical lure or claim from the broader aesthetic one; see esp. John B. Cobb Jr., *A Christian Natural Theology Based on the Thought of Alfred North Whitehead* (Philadelphia: Westminster Press, 1965), ch. 3; and Charles N. Reynolds, "Somatic Ethics: Joy and Adventure in the Embodied Moral Life," pp. 116-132 in *John Cobb's Theology in Process,* ed. David R. Griffin and Thomas J. J. Altizer. (Philadelphia: Westminster Press, 1977).

10. I do not claim that process thought is the only possible path toward a more inclusive and more realistic vision. The work of Amos N. Wilder (not uninfluenced by process thought, it is worth noting) can serve as powerful example of a parallel path; see Amos N. Wilder, *Eschatology and Ethics in the Teaching of Jesus*; revised ed. (New York: Harper & Row, 1950); *Kerygma, Eschatology, and Social Ethics* (Philadelphia: Fortress Press, 1966); and *Theopoetic: Theology and the Religious Imagination* (Philadelphia: Fortress Press, 1967). I sketched Wilder's work briefly in "Amos Niven Wilder: Poet and Scholar," *Semeia* 12 (1978), 1-11.

temporary cultural interpretation.[11] Thus speculative philosophy is called upon to make it possible for the interpreter of religious texts both to do justice to their ethical dimension (I believe that the broader context suggested here will be an enabling factor in this), and to make it possible for the interpreter to see how the symbolic or metaphorical language of religious texts can be saying something about the structure of reality.

We cannot here discuss the background of both recent literary criticism and recent linguistics which has made them largely turn away from the question of referential truth to concentrate on internal systems of coherence. Nor am I intending to be critical of reductionist models of language which bracket out the question of reference, so long as it is understood that such models are incomplete. Instead I wish to comment briefly on one point where process thought can help interpreters to see why and how they can connect the internal structures of language with their referential dimension as part of their interpretive task. I am referring to Whitehead's thought about symbols and propositions, which can provide a foundation for an integration of internal coherence and external reference.

Current discussion of symbolism is divided between those who regard the symbol as an arbitrary sign and those who hold that the symbol participates in the reality which it expresses. Phenomenological interpretation of symbols can be regarded as an attempt submit the second of these views to a rigorous methodology. It shares the Kantian restriction of symbol to phenomena but strives to retain a sense of the whole communicated by the symbol against the analysis of it into bits of information, as in some types of structuralist interpretation. Thus Ricoeur offers us the "symbol" in which we can still participate, the "myth" which interprets the symbol by locating it in an imaginative world (or rather, a series of imaginative worlds) in which we can no longer directly live, though neither can we live without some such orientation, and "thought" which is

11. The point is all the clearer if we note a comment of Cobb about why he turned toward developing a process ethic. In his formative period, he says, "the dominant philosophical mood emptied the 'ought' of all serious meaning, through various forms of non-cognitivism." (*Christian Natural Theology*, 181). A process ethics will be one which holds together the ethical dimension and knowledge of the world rather than narrowing the ethical question as much modern theory has done. This point is all the more important since the earlier ethical direction of much religious hermeneutic was strongly cognitive, while a great deal of the current aesthetic hermeneutic is noncognitive, as is well illustrated by the quotation above from Kermode.

critical of myth at the same time that it needs symbolic experience from which to arise.[12]

II

This sketch shows a background for current discussion of symbols which is also shared by Whitehead, though his main effort was directed to a different front. Most interpreters of the symbolic sort of communication stand broadly in a Kantian tradition, but Whitehead's effort was to overcome the Humean scepticism and the Kantian dichotomy between phenomenal and noumenal, and thus to bring scientific thought and humanistic understanding, including religious understanding, into a comprehensive frame of discourse where they could interact.

Whitehead's theory of symbols plays an important role in his revision of the epistemological tradition. He separated what in other schools is broadly the topic of symbolism into two parts; his theory of symbols, which deals with important aspects of perception, and his theory of propositions, which deals with the use of perception in the total act of self-realization or self-creation.

Whitehead's discussion of symbols is shaped to confront and overcome the Humean scepticism about perception which is an important ingredient in the Kantian dichotomy mentioned above. Thus "symbol" has a much more restricted meaning in Whitehead than in, for instance, Ricoeur. Whitehead's primary illustrations come from the realm of the perception of spatial configurations. Symbols connect the clear but indirect and constructed perceptions in the mode of presentational immediacy with the dim but direct perceptions of that same spatial area in the mode of causal efficacy. Whitehead's symbol has something in common with Tillich, who holds that a symbol participates in the reality which it expresses. For Whitehead, also, the symbol has something in common with what it symbolizes. A common eternal object as well as a common location connect the data given in the two modes of perception. There is always a possibility of error in relating the two modes, but these common elements make possible a real knowledge of the data on the part of the perceiving occasion—a key point in overcoming the Kantian division between phenomenal and noumenal. ". . . [I]n fact, our process of self-construction for the achievement of unified experience produces a

12. Paul Ricoeur, *The Symbolism of Evil* (Boston: Beacon Press, 1967).

new product, in which percepta in one mode, and percepta in the other mode, are synthesized into one subjective feeling."[13]

Whitehead believed that the model thus established would also suffice for symbols of personal and social significance, which he discussed briefly in the concluding pages of *Symbolism*.[14] Such symbols would combine the clearly-perceived object (in presentational immediacy) not only with the dim prehensions of its location and qualities given in causal efficacy, but also with inherited feelings of valuation—a given subjective form—which are adventitious. Thus symbols in this broader sense do participate in the "power" of the things they symbolize in the sense that they communicate the appropriate feelings about them; but this power to communicate is socially constructed, and such symbols change and indeed within limits may be changed.

Whitehead had great interest in the connection between the large unconscious aspects of experience and the much more restricted conscious aspects. But he endeavored to give a description of experience in very broad terms, and showed little interest in the limiting configurations of the unconscious which shape experience in specific ways in Freudian or Jungian analysis of the unconscious. There is no necessary conflict between Whitehead's general description and a system which posits firmly-fixed limiting structures in the unconscious. However, Whitehead's choice of fairly superficial symbols (ceremonial garments, etc.) is a sign of his interest in the changeability and social construction of symbols. He would have agreed with Tillich that powerful symbols come into existence and die, and also that they may be reinvigorated. He would not have agreed with Tillich that one cannot invent a symbol.[15]

The more complex symbol involves reference and hence knowledge, as does the symbol which simply connects the two modes of perception. But this more complex symbolic power arises from an arbitrary association of subjective forms of prehensions. Whitehead illustrates three stages of indirectness in the perception of this sort of symbolic meaning. In the

---

13. Alfred North Whitehead, *Process and Reality*; corrected edition, ed. David R. Griffin and Donald W. Sherburne (New York: Free Press, 1978), 179; See Donald W. Sherburne, *A Whiteheadian Aesthetic* (New Haven: Yale University Press, 1961), 86.

14. Alfred North Whitehead, *Symbolism: Its Meaning and Effect* (New York: Capricorn Books, 1959), ch. 3.

15. On Tillich's view, see *inter alia* Paul Tillich, "The Meaning and Justification of Religious Symbols," pp. 3-11 in Sidney Hook, ed., *Religious Experience and Truth* (New York: New York University Press, 1961).

first, the subjective form is directly given by the complex object perceived; a mother's cheerfulness is felt directly by a baby; the appearance of the mother is qualified by this form, which is felt conformally by the baby. In the second, more diffuse relationship, the environment is felt in a way appropriate to the survival of the particular species responding. Whitehead means that the selection and organization of the percepta and the subjective feelings associated with them are such that, "We have perceived what well-conditioned individuals of our own type would perceive under those circumstances."[16] The third type of relation is the pre-eminently symbolic one, and here it is clear that the association between "Appearance" (a perceived symbol) and "Reality" (that to which the symbol refers) are established arbitrarily or culturally.

> A set of adventitious circumstances has brought about this connection between those Appearances and those Realities as prehended in the experiences of those percipient. In their own natures the Appearances throw no light upon the Realities, nor do the Realities upon the Appearances, except in the experiences of a set of peculiarly conditioned percipient. Languages and their meanings are examples of this third type of truth.[17]

Thus the symbols which are important for the larger issues of human existence are the vaguest in their correlation with the givenness of experience. It is evident from this sketch that Whitehead's view makes symbols fully open to "deconstruction," a deconstruction which he himself carried out in a certain way in his analysis of the process of concrescence of an actual entity. But by rooting the more complex symbols in an epistemological theory which makes clear that these complex perceptions arise from simpler symbols which communicate information about the world being perceived, he laid the groundwork for an interpretation of symbols which will probe their referential dimension of truth. He drew the conclusion, not that this sort of communication is not capable of truth value, but that it is deeply in need of rational criticism.

A further and distinctive aspect of Whitehead's analysis is his separating the theory of symbols from the theory of propositions. The result is to offer a clear model of how human (or subhuman) freedom reacts to symbolic communication. The imaginative and creative dimensions of

---

16. Alfred North Whitehead, *Adventures of Ideas* (New York: Free Press, 1961), 317.

17. Ibid., 318f.

"symbolism" appear in Whitehead's thought under the rubric of the theory of propositions, in contrast to symbols which appear in the context of prehension.

The background of Whitehead's theory of propositions was laid in his early mathematical writings, in which he posited that every proposition is "about" something; it has a real subject. This is also the view of *Principia Mathematica*; the abstractions of mathematics require a starting-point in experience.[18] For Whitehead, thinking is more than a linguistic act. The issue was debated between Russell and Meinong, where discussion centered on the status of nonexistent objects in propositions. In his 1905 essay "On Denoting," Russell held that:

> when there is anything with which we do not have immediate acquaintance, but only definition by denoting phrases, then the propositions in which this thing is introduced by means of a denoting phrase do not really contain this thing as constituent, but contain instead the constituents expressed by the several words of the denoting phrase. Thus in every proposition that we can apprehend (i.e., not only in those whose truth or falsehood we can judge of, but in all that we can think about), all the constituents are really entities with which we have immediate acquaintance. . . . In such a case, we know the properties of a thing without having acquaintance with the thing itself, and without consequently, knowing any single proposition of which the thing itself is a constituent.[19]

The phenomenological tradition followed the line represented by Meinong, obliterating the distinction between propositions derived from experienced data and imaginative constructions. Whitehead agreed with the early Russell in affirming that every proposition has as its logical subject a definite item of experience and hence it can, in principle, be checked for truth or falsehood (even though this procedure is often in fact impossible to carry out). For Whitehead, like the logicians, a proposition is a prelinguistic reality. Yet he moved toward a larger sphere of significance for propositions by making their primary role to be as lures for feeling in the process of self-creation of an entity.

This move it is which puts Whitehead's work on propositions in touch with other discussions of symbols. But it should not be forgotten

---

18. Alfred North Whitehead, *A Treatise on Universal Algebra* (New York: Hafner, 1960), 112f., and *Principia Mathematica* (Cambridge: Cambridge University Press, 1925), 191; see Michael L. Harrington, *Whitehead's Theory of Propositions,* Unpublished Ph.D. Dissertation, Emory University, 1972, 16-26.

19. Bertrand Russell, *Essays in Analysis,* ed. Douglas Lackey (New York: George Braziller, 1973), 119.

that the logical analysis of propositions lies in the background, implying that a proposition is not simply a statement, but rather that a statement may well require to be analyzed into a bundle of propositions, which must derive from actual experience as far as their logical subjects are concerned. Thus the proposition combines imaginative freedom with grounding in reality; just as in the theory of symbols, the way is open to relate propositional expression to referential testing.

As briefly noted above, an important aspect of Whitehead's separation of "symbolic communication" into two parts, symbols and propositions, was his aim to show how there can be an element of freedom in our response to symbolic communication. He did not neglect the massive continuities of human experience which are brought to light, for instance, in the Freudian view of symbols. But he was impatient with any view of humanness which thought that these massive continuities were the distinctive and interesting aspects of human existence. It is precisely to open a free space for decision or what we have called above "self-integration" between the perception of a symbol and the placing of it in a unified moment of experience that he chose his style of analysis. Many other styles of analysis emphasize the constraints. Both emphases are needed. But it is important to remember the dimension of freedom, the dimension of self-creation in response to symbolic communication, which is brought into focus by Whitehead's theory of propositions.

The theory of propositions thus emphasizes the aspect of the potentiality of symbolic language. Such language is always pointing beyond itself. Propositional feelings lure an occasion toward novelty. Though a proposition is neutral in itself, and can be felt in many ways, it is the principal vehicle by which new possibilities are presented in concrescing occasions.

To recognize the role of the proposition, the proposal or lure, in the self-construction of an entity is a fundamental step in rediscovering the reality of the narrative sense. Indebted as we are to linguistic analyses of narrative, and fully as we recognize the constraints which language and its traditions impose upon our imaginations, we should be able to recognize also the component of self-composition toward a lure for the future as an essential part of existence, a process thinker would say of all existence, but in any case fundamental for human existence, diverse as are the ways in which the process can be actualized in different cultures. The narrative process and the narrative experience are inextricably linguistic, but the interweaving of the linguistic with other components of reality is not of such a nature that we cannot know something about its non-narrative components, nor need we ascribe all narrative movement to linguistic factors.

Whitehead's view makes room for the modification and enrichment of symbolic communication by critical thought and even speculative philosophy. His is of course not the only discussion of language which takes the dimension of reference seriously. But no one else has analyzed the two dimensions of symbolic communication, reception and imaginative consideration in relation to an emerging self-constitution, as Whitehead did.

III

An adequate hermeneutic will obviously have to deal with large scale symbolic structures (of which "myths" are a central example) as well as with the small-scale symbolic structures which are among the building blocks of our perception of reality in Whitehead's thought. The great challenge of modern hermeneutics is how it is possible to make connections between the smaller pieces and the whole, whether, in other words, the deconstructed symbolic meaning can be put together again to convey meaning to the critical thinker.

Adequately to discuss this problem would require another paper. I can only suggest that a process perspective will try to contribute on this front through its conviction that the Whiteheadian ontological categories, which arose in a context of ontological deconstruction and reconstruction quite analogous to the linguistic deconstruction and reconstruction now under way, can provide a framework within which, however imperfectly, a reconstruction of a vision of the whole can take place, precisely because they constitute a form of deconstruction which, unlike Peer Gynt's onion, reaches a level of contact with a definite reality on the basis of which one can rebuild.

The narrative models which have emphasized the arbitrariness of narrative sequences or the moment of disclosure as a rupture of expected sequence have been extremely helpful in bringing into the focus of attention and in interpreting certain aspects of the meaning communicated by texts. They have pointed to the centrality of the unexpected and of disruption in the process of life, both if one is to be honest about life and if one is to be reminded of the mysterious and ultimate claims of God or being. What these models uncover is not to be discarded. And we cannot return to the unreflective confidence in narrative sequence which characterized a good deal of the interpretive perspective of an earlier period.

But the process categories proposed above can set the unexpected aspect of experience fruitfully into interaction with the continuities, the memories, the expectations that played so large a role in the older style of seeing. The model of reality as a series of experiences, each with its uniqueness and freedom, but each interwoven in a web of sequences (or "stories") opens the way to affirm that continuities and meaningfully composed sequences also offer the possibility of disclosure. The process model in turn offers a built-in criticism of closed visions and of inevitable endings, for there can be no ending wholly determined in advance. But the effort to compose narrative meaning is one central manifestation of a fundamental process of reality, the process of concrescences in relation, and it is to be remembered that concrescence holds in contrast a range of data and possibilities, and at its best, as wide a range as possible.

Thus process thought is badly misunderstood if it is taken as another version of fixed, single truth. The process conceptuality itself is part of the process and is in process. And the past or the text is always known perspectivally, in the context of a new process of self-constitution. But process thought strongly maintains the dialectic between perception and reality instead of dissolving it in favor of the imaginatively created world as more extreme forms of post-modern thought do. From a process perspective, since on the small scale we can assert that we really are talking about reality, we can hope to develop more adequate criteria for judgment about the larger scale symbolic systems. In particular, the process model can enter into discussion of the nature of narrative very readily, since it implies a kind of underlying "narrative" quality to reality itself, though some of the features of narrative (notably the "end") are not part of the ontology of process.[20]

The importance of this aim may be emphasized by asking in conclusion what is at stake in the narrative problem? Many things, of course, and we have to choose what is central. If we say, with Paul Ricoeur and with Johann Baptist Metz, that the issue we cannot allow to escape is the untold story of those who suffer, then the importance of the interaction

20. See chapters 8 and 9 of this volume and William A. Beardslee, "Narrative Form in the New Testament and in Process Theology," *Encounter* 36 (1975), 301-315.

between language and experience is apparent.[21] In more general terms, we must note the following quotation from Amos N. Wilder:

> The final question as to any representation, phantasy, graph, emblem, rune or utterance is that of *reference,* referentiality, the ground of communication. But this test which older epochs have called "truth" would set in motion again all the tropisms, all the impulses toward coherence and survival, of the species from the beginning, moral and cognitive as well as imaginative.[22]

It is important to note that Wilder, like Whitehead, associates truth with the selection of experience toward coherence and survival; note Wilder again: "The dividing line between the real and the unreal, meaning and mania, must ultimately be determined by some line with human health and survival, some fiber or filament in consciousness which relates us to the older and plenitude of being. Our grasp of this as occidentals is inevitably mediated to us through many confusions 'by our tradition.'"[23]

Wilder is calling for a healing of the rupture between tradition and imagination. Our contention is that a more adequate philosophical approach, showing how imagination and experience fruitfully enrich each other, can be a central ingredient in healing that rupture.

---

21. See Paul Ricoeur, "Narrative and Hermeneutics," pp. 37-56 in *Religion and the Humanities* (Research Triangle Park, NC: National Humanities Center), 1981; Johannes Baptist Metz, "The Future *ex Memoriae Passionis*," pp. 117-131 in *Hope and the Future of Man,* ed. Ewert H. Cousins (Philadelphia: Fortress Press, 1972); a slightly different version of Metz's essay is found in Johannes B. Metz, ed., *New Questions on God*; "Concilium" 76 (New York: Herder and Herder, 1972), 9-25; William A. Beardslee, "Response to Ricoeur's 'Narrative and Hermeneutics.'" *Religion and the Humanities*, 57-69.

22. Amos N. Wilder. "Post-Modern Reality and the Problem of Meaning," *Man and World* 13 (1980), 322.

23. Ibid., 313.

- 12 -

Scripture and Philosophy

Scripture and philosophy were for a long time regarded as two stable sources of knowledge which stood in a kind of uneasy balance. Scripture disclosed the special truths of the Christian faith, or at least provided a basis from which they were to be deduced, while philosophy presented in clear and rigorous form what could be known to all on the basis of their common humanity. The uneasiness of the balance between these two sources of human knowledge sprang from tension over the question of how much of our knowledge is open to all, and how much is derived from specifically Christian roots.

This traditional way of setting the question of the relation between Scripture and philosophy is still meaningful. Our vision of the world is shaped by the concrete stream of historical influences in which we stand; for Christians, the Bible is the foundational factor in that stream, or rather, testifies to the foundational history. And it is also true that we are aware of our simple humanness. Though there is no way to be "universally human," the move toward a vision of reality that is accessible to all on the basis of their humanness is a necessary, if never fully successful, effort. Philosophy represents this effort on its most general level.

We could, then, discuss the relationship between Scripture and philosophy using this traditional framework. But now the situation in which we try to establish the meaning of Scripture and that of philosophy is radically different from that in which the traditional view arose. In contrast to those who worked out the classic formulation, we know that neither Scripture nor philosophy is a stable entity. It seems that, of the two, Scripture is the more stable, since it has relatively fixed boundaries. There are persistent questions about, say, the role of the Apocrypha in the canon, and the importance of newly-discovered non-canonical docu-

---

From *Listening: Journal of Religion and Culture* 21 (1983), 115-121.

ments like the Gospel of Thomas for our access to the story which Scripture tells. But these are details. The fluidity of Scripture as it is now perceived arises from the perspective of modern hermeneutics. Increasingly we hear it said that while the text is fixed, the meanings that it communicates are derived as much from the reader as from the text, and are extremely variable. How do we relate our reading of the Scriptural text to the readings of the great interpreters of earlier generations?

In the case of philosophy, the question of stability is even more acute. Though the great classical philosophical texts continue to be read, new ones are always being written. These may, and in fact do, interpret the task of philosophy in terms which are sharply at variance with its traditional role of interpreter of our vision of reality. Typically, modern philosophy understands itself as critical of the language in which discourse is carried on, and the older concern for ontology or metaphysics is often set aside.

What are we to make of the way in which Scripture and philosophy will not stay put as they used to be supposed to do? Our first comment is that one (not the only one, but one significant) source of the instability is Scripture itself. That our existence is a flow of experiences, concretely situated in a history; that our encounter with God does not take place in terms of truths about God but in terms of our actions and those of God; that we do not ever have a finished, stable position from which we could establish a permanently valid vision of the whole—these are insights that an attentive reading of the Bible can give. The modern sense of historicality and of the relativity of our knowledge to our situation has many sources, but we must not forget that one such fundamental source is the biblical tradition itself. In the Bible, the principal way in which the encounter of God with human beings is presented is in the form of a story. The truth which the story makes known is relative to the situation in which it comes to human beings. God, too, is involved in the passage of time and is deeply affected, even changed, by what happens.

At the same time, the great variety of the encounters between God and human beings, and the great variety of human situations that we find in the Bible, are far from communicating that sense of directionless self-enclosure within one's immediate situation that is often taken to be the typically modern understanding of what the relativity of our situations means. We can only briefly review the history of the interplay between the older faith in stable truths separately disclosed or partly shared by the biblical revelation and general human knowledge, and the dynamic but relative understanding of knowledge as historical which has partly biblical roots. For the relation between Scripture and philosophy, the key figures are Kant and Hegel.

Kant believed that he had established the failure of the older style of philosophy according to which reality could be rationally grasped through mental forms which correspond to it and in which the existence of God could be rationally demonstrated. For Kant, the world as it appears to us is a product of our perceptual and cognitive activities; thus, ultimate reality is forever hidden from us, and the classical "proofs" of the existence of God have no rational foundation. This critical view of knowledge as limited to phenomena (what appears, as against what is there independent of its appearance), and in which God is a "regulative idea" (Kant), is the great watershed of modern thought.

Hegel responded to Kant's work precisely by questioning the latter's distinction between phenomena and reality and his concomitant ahistorical standpoint, and by turning to the dynamic and changing way of perceiving that is characteristic of the Bible, from which Hegel drew heavily in working out his view. But, Hegel located the dynamic processes of change within consciousness, so that existence is a continual process of consciousness reaching out and finding itself in what it encounters, and continually being changed thereby. The universal form of this process is the movement by which the Absolute overcomes its self-alienation in the finitude of the world. For Hegel, God is involved in the history of God's own self-alienation into the world and God's ultimate self-reconciliation in a final consummation. Human history reflects the stages of this process of divine self-alienation and reconciliation—a history that lives in human consciousness.

These brief notes will indicate that Kant and Hegel left a new situation for their successors. They set the agenda for a great part of the philosophical thought that followed them. We must quickly move to the present day and see how two very different thinkers use this heritage to interpret our situation and our understanding of Scripture and philosophy. The two are Thomas J. J. Altizer and Charles Altieri.

Thomas J. J. Altizer holds the biblical and the philosophical traditions very close together, and he radicalizes their implications. In the biblical tradition, it is apocalyptic that furnishes him his principal clues, for he believes that it brings the tensions in the biblical tradition into such sharp opposition that they can be resolved only by total reversal. Hegel, on the philosophical side, offers a model of this reversal in a God involved in history who passes into God's opposite. In his earlier work, Altizer presented Western history in terms of the death of God. Though he continues to employ this radical motif, his current work, as in *History as Apocalypse*, concentrates on the emergence, and apocalyptic abolition of, interior self-consciousness, traced in the history of the Christian epic form. The God figure stimulated self-consciousness in ways which Paul and Augustine exemplify. The tensions between God and the human which the growing self-consciousness brought about led to a movement of which Blake is the turning-point and Joyce the culmination, and in which the rejection of God fuses with loss of self-consciousness. This gives rise to total immanence. Speaking of Joyce, Altizer writes, "Moreover, the bread and the wine are now real in the actual words and languages of the *Wake [Finnegan's Wake]*, words whose very scatology, ribaldry, and blasphemy sacramentally embody the real presence of 'Life,' and do so because love and life are now brutally and immediately present. This immediate presence is the transcendental annulment of the substance of death, for death now becomes life itself."[1] Altizer is careful to distinguish this eschatological coincidence of opposites from the primordial myth of the eternal return, though he notes that one could not come to his understanding of Western history without reflecting on Buddhism.[2]

It is difficult to imagine a stronger contrast to the traditional way of relating Scripture to philosophy than what we find in Altizer. Here the two are fused and turned to the end, not of establishing a vision of truth, but of overturning our accustomed stabilities and asking us to learn to appreciate the spiritual significance of nihilism. What looks like, and is, the end of all established values, becomes, if we can affirm it, the revelation of that presence which traditional faith had been able to worship only as absent, as transcendent. In Altizer, history does not merely destabilize tradition, it kills it in order that it may come to life in its opposite.[3]

If Altizer represents the radical fusion of Scripture and philosophy, Charles Altieri represents the effort to distance them. Like Altizer, Altieri is a kind of radical Hegelian; but, instead of envisaging the Absolute's self-transformation into immanence, Altieri offers a vision without an

1. Thomas J. J. Altizer, *History as Apocalypse* (Albany: State University of New York Press, 1985), 253.

2. Ibid., 2 and 252.

3. I have discussed Altizer's earlier work in "Dialectic or Duality," pp. 58-67 in John B. Cobb, Jr., ed., *The Theology of Altizer: Critique and Response* (Philadelphia: Westminster Press, 1970).

absolute. His thought is important for our study even though he is not interested in the question of the interpretation of Scripture, but of literature generally.[4] His importance lies in showing how, in a world seemingly without reference points to values and meanings beyond human experience, and in which Hegel's confidence in an absolute has receded, one may nevertheless affirm human values and the humanistic tradition. Altieri's concrete literary analysis is derived from Wittgenstein's understanding of meaning as used in "language games." He gives density and also "recoverability" to literary meaning by focusing on literature as a form of action. This procedure enables us to distinguish between internal relations of the relevant action, which have their recognizable integrity (intensional action), and the external relations which we impose on or read into the work. While probabilistic, such analyses do give knowledge, knowledge of actions in which we recognize ourselves; that is, poten tialities within ourselves.

The ability to recognize intentional action presupposes a grammar, or interrelated pattern, which gives meaning to a particular action by locating it. Literature is thus not directly referential, but it provides us with terms which can be transferred to referential propositions.[5] One way in which Altieri deals with the transitoriness which has been so much stressed in recent thought is to observe that the problems with which literary works deal are not perennial. Nevertheless, we do not have to have the same problem to understand these works because the strategies and attitudes *are* perennial.

Our knowledge of the human situation is bound to be circular, but this circularity is not vicious. By entering into the complexities of our tradition we are enabled to resist ideological temptations and the notion that we are mechanistically determined. Furthermore, this kind of thinking, which is self-reflexive (in thinking about literature we are thinking about and discovering ourselves), helps us to see thinking itself as a power, and to relate to others. In a word, we are creating ourselves, and, at the same time, learning to evaluate the creation.

Here we have a powerful restatement of the humanistic tradition worked out in the face of the many reductive trends that are at work within it. In a way that is reminiscent of Cardinal Newman, Altieri reminds

---

4. Charles Altieri, *Act and Quality: A Theory of Literary Meaning and Humanistic Understanding* (Amherst: University of Massachusetts Press, 1981).

5. Ibid., 278.

us that humanistically educated people will not necessarily respond to the actual ethical challenges of life more effectively than others, but they will have the equipment to see the potentialities of the actual situations of life.

The unifying factor in this whole process of self-creation and self-discovery Hegel called Spirit (the Absolute). In contrast to Hegel, for Altieri the operation of the Spirit in human existence and culture does not presuppose or disclose an absolute which could be described in religious language as God. There is no overarching teleology. But the strength of his model is shown, for instance, in his alternative to the deconstructive understanding of cultural sequences as displacements or misreadings (e.g., Derrida). Of the critical line from Milton to Wordsworth to Arnold to Eliot, which may be read in a deconstructive way, he observes, "We can view each poet as turning to his predecessor's terms for dramatizing significant qualities of the psyche, and then as imposing on them a performance displaying the seriousness of another perspective—on the implicit grounds that the latter perspective at once accounts for the other's power and adapts it to a richer or different sense of situation."[6] A key term here is "seriousness," for it is a major thrust of Altieri's work to show how to take the human person and her or his cultural achievements seriously.

We must not fault Altieri for not being a theologian! He is, after all, a philosophically-minded literary critic. He represents a wide spectrum of such interpreters in resolutely focusing on human culture, and seeing the Bible as an important monument of our heritage. From this point of view, what is lasting in the Bible will be the human responses and the structures of culture which they imply.

One cannot help being struck by the fact that these two very different responses to our current situation, both cast in post-Kant-and-Hegel terms, are at one in rejecting the dominating lordship of God which was a central aspect of the older Christian faith, including the older Christian humanism. In Altizer's case, Scripture and philosophy are turned to showing that faith in such a God was a temporary phase in the history of the human mind, an alienating phase which is overcome in the total immanence represented by Christ. In Altieri's case, following a more traditional line in our culture, God has simply been lost or left aside, since the operations of the human psyche and the structures which are disclosed in culture seem adequate to account for what needs to be understood. At the

6. Ibid., 317.

same time, "Spirit" is an important image to both of them, a point to which I shall return.

In the face of such opposite transformations of traditional faith, one may well be tempted to follow the path of Karl Barth, and try to show that the life and faith that spring from the Scriptures do not need philosophy. This approach arose in the face of a cultural collapse in order to show that faith derived from roots other than those which the culture offered. Such a theology still has meaning and power in the face of our continuing cultural collapse. A vigorous contemporary version is represented by Hans Frei.[7]

Instead, I propose as more fruitful the effort to do over the work that Kant and Hegel and their successors have done, not in the spirit of a retreat from the consequences of modernity, but with the claim that a more comprehensive framework than their heritage affords is possible. Of course, we must start with experience and the phenomena of experience. But the consequence does not have to be the unbridgeable gap between the phenomena experienced by the human mind and the underlying reality that is supposed in the Kantian tradition examined above. The key thinker here is Alfred North Whitehead, whose criticism of the presuppositions about experience that have dominated modern critical philosophy opened the way to a new vision of all reality as occasions of experience.[8] Within such a process philosophy, one can deal with the complexities of human life and culture without isolating these from the world of less complex experience to which, after all, we are intimately interrelated. We do not have to assume that all meaningful patterns are the creation of the human mind, since all experience, and the data which give rise to it, are value-laden. This wider world of experience is not directly accessible to our conscious inspection; it comes to us through the, at best, only dimly-conscious route of what Whitehead called "causal efficacy." But with care it can be interpreted within the categories of conscious thought. A further strength of this perspective is that it enables us to take seriously and reinterpret the traditional religious category, "God," without imputing to this term the features of dominating power that have made it unacceptable to so many, including both of the thinkers we discussed above. From the process point of view, the element of persuasive lure toward

7. Hans Frei, *The Identity of Jesus Christ: The Hermeneutical Bases of Dogmatic Theology* (Philadelphia: Fortress Press, 1975).

8. Alfred North Whitehead, *Process and Reality*; corrected edition; ed. David R. Griffin and Donald W. Sherburne, (New York: Free Press, 1978).

more complex achievement that is ever-present, though often unrecognized, is God.[9]

Such a philosophy may be used to interpret a wide range of stances within our culture. It will be useful not only to those who accept Jewish or Christian Scripture as foundational. Rather, in any perspective it will be able to recognize in the manifestations of "Spirit" more than the creativity of the human mind or the supportive "grammars" of cultural patterns. These latter will continue to need the rigorous attention that they receive, for instance, from Altieri. But we can affirm that the process point of view will make it easier to move from Altieri's extremely helpful study of literary works as "actions," from action as a semantic category, to action as the effort to take responsibility for our world and to contribute to the changing of it, once we see that the life of the mind is not isolated from the larger world of experience. Then Scripture, even viewed simply as a cultural document, can freshly be seen as a liberating book in the social sense, a testimony to the lure of the "Spirit" to overcome oppression.

A similar enlargement of perspective is possible when we reflect on the problems of history that are so central to Thomas Altizer. His passionate commitment to the finding of a perspective from which to live fully both with awareness of our past and with sensitivity to what is perceived to be a nihilistic situation can only elicit our warmest admiration. He helps us see how critical is our spiritual and cultural situation. But again, his dialectic of opposites may not correspond very well to the whole reality with which we have to deal. There are ways of holding in creative contrast some of the tensions which Altizer presents, and of finding new finite meanings in them rather than looking for total reversal. We concur in Altizer's judgment that the transcendent, absolute God did stimulate a competing sense of self-consciousness, and that this *totally* transcendent God is no longer viable. But there are many other resources in the biblical tradition besides those elements that point toward the radical transcendence of God. This latter is, in fact, a very one-sided reading of the Bible. Correspondingly, Altizer is quite right that the self of the heightened interiority of consciousness is outmoded. But rather than displacing it by moving into the marginal tradition of nihilism, we need to link to and develop traditions of interrelatedness and interdependence. The Bible is a rich resource, among other sources, to which to turn for these. From

9. See the helpful discussion in John B. Cobb, Jr., *God and the World* (Philadelphia: Westminster Press, 1969).

a process philosophy point of view, the interrelatedness of human life can be seen in a wider framework of total interrelatedness.[10]

There are other philosophical approaches which can clarify the framework within which Scripture is interpreted, of course. This one has the merit of calling for a thorough re-working of our basic framework of thought while at the same time making possible a greater openness to the continuing function of the tradition of the past than is the case in some other approaches. In particular, the line that flows from the biblical foundation, which is alive in the Jewish and Christian communities, can continue to provide an orienting perspective to those who stand within it, without making the imperialistic claims that once were common, at least in Christian circles. Since the Spirit is at work in all of life, we do not need to claim a single line of access to its work. In fact, the biblical tradition itself calls for its own reinterpretation or transformation, and the process perspective can aid us to do this, and help us to see that the adaptation of this tradition to a richer or different context, to which Altieri pointed in a literary setting, need not be a random shifting, but can be a response to the Spirit which is at work in everything.

---

10. See Charles Birch and John B. Cobb, Jr., *The Liberation of Life: From the Cell to the Community* (Cambridge: Cambridge University Press, 1981).

- 13 -

Men in the Post-Patriarchal World

One of the great questions of our day is the question whether and to what extent there is a public sphere. It used to be taken for granted that there is a public sphere—an ambience of shared values and meaning within which new ideas and competing projects could be discussed and decided upon. The primary impetus to the disassembling of the public sphere came from the unmasking of its ideological elements, so that the public sphere has come to be discredited because it is seen to serve only the interests of some powers in the society. Yet the first major critics of the public sphere, the Marxists, proposed replacing the bourgeois public sphere with a new, truly valid, public sphere of their own.

The Marxist critique of ideology opened the way to successive waves of distrust of the public sphere, articulated by voices which were excluded or distorted by the accepted world of values and meanings. Thus an Afro-American theologian like Cornel West can celebrate the loss of an embracing framework of meaning, since this loss opens the way for excluded voices to be heard.[1] He shows, for instance, how the claim of general application for modern Western standards of human beauty was actually parochial and ideological.[2]

Similarly, feminists have deconstructed the public sphere which excluded women's experiences and values. Many of the most discerning of feminists have concentrated on making women's experience meaningful to *women*, with little concern for whether or not the feminist vision is a

---

Previously unpublished. An earlier version was prepared as a response to Nancy Howell's paper, "Imaging Post-Patriarchy," for a conference on Post-Patriarchy at the Center for Process Studies, Claremont, California in March, 1987.

1. See "Postmodernity and Afro-America," *Art Papers* 10 (1986), 54.

2. Cornel West, *Prophesy Deliverance: An Afro-American Revolutionary Christianity* (Philadelphia: Westminster Press, 1982), 53-57.

public one, that is, whether it expresses a vision of a world, a cluster of values, which have meaning beyond their meaning for women.

It is also the case that much of the rhetoric of feminism has been chosen, often with great skill and imagination, to function to shatter the assumption that widely accepted values and practices are truly general. I think that I need not give examples.

There are strong reasons for the erosion of the public sphere, and probably there are few sectors of contemporary writing in which suspicion of the public sphere is more evident than it is in feminist writing. Many who write from this vantage point believe that it is their task to bring into focus the need for separateness, for a distinctively women's sphere, rather than to correlate the perspectives of women with those of men.

Yet many of those who fight for an end to patriarchy are at the same time drawn toward recovering the sense of connectedness which is seen by many to be characteristic of the way in which women understand the human situation.[3] The initial move will be to press for connections among women, but the recognition of connectedness leads naturally toward reopening the question of the public sphere. Nancy Howell's paper, "Imaging Post-Patriarchy," ably sketches the reasons for the decay of a public sphere (though she does not use this terminology). At the same time, she looks forward to the re-establishment of a public sphere through the "mingling of female visions arising from sisterhood and male visions arising from man's experience and his relations with the sisterhood."[4]

There are many men who find it difficult to understand the need for the establishment of a separate community, a sisterhood, which excludes them. Indeed, Christian images of caring have often been interpreted in a patriarchal way to imply that women do not need an autonomous realm of their own, since they are adequately cared for by men. Many men have not yet become aware, or are only coming to be aware, of the social system of stereotypical values which puts men in an advantageous position, and of the need for women to establish a strong position from which they may enter the world on equal terms. Thus for many women and men the immediate task may be the task of separation, of the conscious recognition of the need to break the old patterns. Yet the need for a public sphere is

3. Carol Gilligan, *In a Different Voice: Psychological Theory and Women's Development* (Cambridge, MA: Harvard University Press, 1982).

4. Nancy Howell, "Imaging Post-Patriarchy," unpublished paper, 5.

inescapable, and it is encouraging that women and men are able to see this even in the midst of the task of breaking the old forms.

This post-patriarchal re-visioning will not come easily. Men will have, not to submit to, but to engage in the deconstruction of our imaginative patterns. In part this task will be best achieved by the changing of social and political structures. But correlative with this political task is the need to recast imaginative patterns, images which shape our approach to political action. An example is the powerful re-visioning of the world which we can read in Catherine Keller's recent book.[5] In such re-visioning it is natural that the established male images are treated negatively, but along with a sharp critique there is also the need for taking men's experiences seriously, and to me this means not treating the deconstructed visions as mere husks, but going back to them to see what in them can still speak to us once we have at least partially liberated ourselves from them.

Let me give an example from Catherine Keller's treatment of Homer. Her critique of the self which forms itself by forging its independent journey, grounded only in the perennial possibility of returning to the sustaining source, the woman, is an extremely powerful one, and her use of the Odysseus story to illustrate it is a strong reading of the *Odyssey*. Here Odysseus represents the typical male hero, discovering himself by separation and self-assertion, expressing or reaching for a transcendence which has no immanence. As Keller puts it, "Odysseus' vigorous mobility, requiring the immobilization of the woman, is not a movement of feeling and transformation, but the project of an ego to master itself and the world. His movement thus fortifies his inner immobility through its external adventure: a motion of ego, not soul, demanding the denial of emotion."[6] Correspondingly, Penelope, bound to home and to her desperate struggle to hold off the suitors, manifests a fidelity which lay "not in any integrity of self but in waiting for her man's return, keeping herself defined purely in terms of his identity"; she is "rewarded only by his return."[7] The power of these images is shown by their resonance in the lives of men today, some of whom Keller cites in the course of her discussion.

---

5. Catherine Keller, *From a Broken Web: Separation, Sexism, and Self* (Boston: Beacon Press, 1986).

6. Ibid., 221.

7. Ibid., 30.

But Keller recognizes that the image of the seemingly powerful independent male is not as perspicuous as it appears. It is not only that Odysseus requires Penelope; without the possibility of return to her, his lengthy adventures, including adventures with other women, would not cohere. More than that, there is an undeveloped connectedness or relationality in the very project of the journey or adventure. Naturally the relatedness of male bonding, evident from the *Iliad* to the locker room, is not favorably regarded by feminists. But from the point of view, shall we say, of a more traditional reading of Homer, the Homeric poems do indeed provide, on the surface level of the narrative, the imagery of the strong and independent, in fact, violent and destructive self. Yet even in the terms of the poetic structure of the *Iliad* itself, the independence and fierce competitiveness are woven into a recognition of human connectedness. When we come to the climactic scene at the end, where Priam comes to plead with Achilles for the return of Hector's body, the deepest message, the "real" message, is "we are all related." "Think back, god-like Achilles, and remember your father, an old man as I am, on the deadly threshold of age."[8] Achilles, who incidentally knows full well that he will never see his father again, and who struggles lest his wrath break out, does grant Priam's request and insists that the two eat together before the latter returns to Troy to give proper burial to Hector. In a fifth-century black-figured Attic amphora Priam is shown in an attitude of supplication before Achilles, who is reclining on a table spread with the food the two will shortly eat—while under the table lies the corpse of Hector, who thus in a sense takes part in the communion.[9]

What is wrong with this scene, so to speak, is not separateness—though the communion is indeed precarious, fragile, and temporary—but that their interrelatedness is discovered only under the aspect of pity, of shared human feeling which does not change the action. They have to go through all they have gone through, and will go through to the bitter end of the destruction of Troy, to bring their interrelatedness to expression. And nothing in their recognition of their interconnection will change the course of events—except, of course, that within that framework it did make a great deal of difference that Hector received a proper burial. Pity is a long way from active love, but it can open the way to

8. *Iliad* 24.486-487, tr. Rush Rehm in *Emory Magazine* 63, 1 (March, 1987), 16.

9. The amphora, attributed to the Rycroft painter, is figured in *Emory Magazine* 63, 1 (March, 1987), 15.

loving action more readily than has often been seen by those who associate pity only with weakness and inaction.

So, what I am suggesting is that here is already relatedness, but it is an interrelatedness that is locked up; it is not free to act. The challenge of a meeting of these two readings of Homer would be, I should think, not only to challenge the self-enclosed, dominating, phallic mode of male selfhood to which Catherine Keller addresses her reading, but for women and men to explore together how to release and creatively transform the relational elements that are already there in men's experience, and powerfully if painfully set forth in this wonderful, almost unbearable scene at the close of the *Iliad*, so that they may more effectively be actualized in praxis.

Thus this man's reading of Homer brings to light the emphasis on limits and constraints rather than the (obvious and necessary to be dealt with) emphasis on unilateral power. Women have been so intent on resisting the limits which patriarchal culture has set for them that they do not always see how sharply limited are the contours of men's experience. Surely, despite the soaring attempts to reach the limits of human possibility which we see in the culture of Greece, the final word of the traditionally central expressions of Greek culture is: "know yourself; you are nothing more than a human being." No doubt men have to learn to re-imagine limits, but the dialog between women and men may well have some of its hardest passages in dealing with this question of limits.

This same theme will appear as we move to the strictly theological sphere and discuss together those dominative, male images of the divine which are so penetratingly analyzed by Sallie McFague and Catherine Keller.[10] McFague and Keller emphasize the domination and control that are symbolized by the masculine deity, which are particularly apparent as such images are heard by women. After this critique, we cannot return to these metaphors and employ them as we used to do. But such images were also intended to convey to the human being a sense of limit. "Thus far shalt thou go, and no farther." Women have rightly been protesting the limits which they experience as set on them. But life intrinsically is lived within limits, and the male metaphors for God speak of the acceptance of limit, and thus might enter fruitfully into discussion with the feminist vision which is sometimes expressed as "having it all."

---

10. Sallie McFague, *Models of God: Theology for an Ecological, Nuclear Age* (Philadelphia: Fortress Press, 1987); Catherine Keller, *From a Broken Web.*

It is my conviction that a process or Whiteheadian framework, which sees the possibility of holding what first seem like contrary options in creative tension, so that a new whole may emerge which includes elements of both contrasting possibilities, is eminently suited as an approach to the kind of post-patriarchal discussion which might be appropriate as a way of following up on the illustrations which I have sketched. At the same time, I recall Hartshorne once remarking about a certain theologian, now dead, that he was the only person he knew who could accept all four positions on an issue about which only two positions were possible. I am not suggesting that we can have it all in the sense of having the present and the future too. There is real giving up, real dying, in moving ahead.

With some hesitation I apply these remarks about the reshaping of our encompassing vision to the re-visioning of a post-patriarchal academia. On this point I profoundly feel the need to listen to women. At the same time, some possibilities in academia express the recognition of relatedness that one may expect will be a major contribution of the input of women. What will be different about a post-patriarchal academia? I believe that insofar as academic institutions move beyond patriarchy, they will move beyond the traditional organization of scholarly work into narrowly-defined disciplines. Feminist insights will reinforce and expand the perception of the sterility and irresponsibility of much academic specialization.

The inertia of academia is legendary. Yet there are very hopeful signs. In many fields it is easier for a competent woman to find a position than it is for a competent man. This is only a transitional situation, and I realize that a big part of the issue is the definition of competence. I would suggest, in line with the emphasis that many thoughtful feminists make on variety, that it is wrongheaded to expect all feminists to do the same sort of thing. It is essential for there to be scholars who force new questions and new ways of envisioning reality on us. But there are, and will be, feminist scholars whose professional work does not show a highly visible feminist profile. Yet some of these scholars may be, and in fact are, among those who are most helpful to women students in encouraging them to believe in their own powers and to venture forward in the scholarly realm.

It is also possible to work collaboratively in academia, though it is often frustrating to do so; and it is possible to work across disciplinary boundaries, to move beyond the frameworks which one has already learned to use, and to spend time aiding and encouraging one another's work. These motifs may often be in the shadow in academia, but they do exist there, and it is possible to work and succeed by emphasizing them.

True enough, it may be that as a teacher or student follows such paths, she or he may be coopted by the system—a danger to which Nancy Howell refers in her paper.[11] But the reason for taking the risk is obvious—academia needs the post-patriarchal input, both from women and from men. There are good reasons why not everyone is an academic, but schools and universities are still focal points for influence on our public life, and it is there more than anywhere else that a new and more viable public sphere will emerge, if it does. I believe that this is a major question for our time, since unless there can be, even if only partially recognized, a public sphere, then the criteria by which decisions among competing possibilities are made will be simply criteria of power.

11. Nancy Howell, "Imaging Post-Patriarchy," 1-2.

- 14 -

Ethics and Hermeneutics

Ethical Presuppositions in Hermeneutics

The focus of New Testament hermeneutics on the conditions of understanding has meant that the ethical presuppositions of interpretation have usually not been closely examined. But as one reads recent New Testament interpretation, one cannot avoid being struck by the contrast between the ethical vision that shaped the earlier and still largely dominant styles of hermeneutics, and the very different understanding, or understandings, of ethics that more recent work presupposes. In hermeneutics, ethical presuppositions function both in the process of interpretation and in the pattern of meaning that the interpreter finds in the text. To clarify these ethical dimensions of hermeneutics, we shall begin with the familiar distinction between deontological ethics, the ethics of the irreducible "ought," and teleological ethics, the ethics of action to achieve a goal. In the course of our study we shall try to show that this traditional classification used in philosophical ethics is inadequate, despite its great influence on hermeneutics.

The emphasis of this paper will be on ethical patterns discerned in New Testament texts, although the two aspects of hermeneutics, the process and the result, deeply interact. This emphasis is chosen in part because Elisabeth Schüssler Fiorenza has recently reopened the question of ethics in the process of interpretation with a forceful questioning of scholarly detachment as the central ethical criterion for methodology.[1]

From Deontological to Teleological Ethics

Most older New Testament interpretation viewed the texts and culture of the past with the assumption that the human person is called to

---

From *Text and Logos: The Humanistic Interpretation of the New Testament: Essays in Honor of Hendrikus W. Boers*, ed. Theodore W. Jennings, Jr. (Atlanta: Scholars Press, 1990), 15-32.

1. Elisabeth Schüssler Fiorenza, "The Ethics of Interpretation," *JBL* 107

respond with a sense of obligation in a universe in which general moral (and religious) rules set a firm framework for choice. This view is classically illustrated by Adolf Jülicher's great work on the parables of Jesus.[2] Indeed, the ethical presuppositions which have dominated New Testament hermeneutics until recently have had a predominantly Kantian cast—assuming (1) that an irreducible sense of obligation is the distinctively human trait, and (2) that the sense of obligation can be clarified and applied by following consistently that aspect of it which leads toward generalizing or universalizing the claims in which it is expressed. Though responsibility was of course exercised in a social setting which defined most of the problems of choice, the clarification of ethical choices led toward principles rather than toward reflection about the social constitution of the self. And because principles were usually formulated in terms of the individual choosing self, the notion of social justice which lay behind the sense of obligation received little scrutiny.

If these ethical presuppositions have been little discussed, that is because most parties to the debates about biblical hermeneutics shared this kind of perspective. The New Testament texts were read with an eye to how grace transformed obligation, and to the question, how one sets the limits to the "acceptable" expressions of responsibility/faith within the diversity of early Christianity. As one moves from the time of Jülicher to the work of his successors in the early twentieth century, confidence in the existence of an ethical framework within which one exercised choices was steadily eroded, but the structure of human existence as responding to a sense of obligation was seldom questioned.

In more recent work, the ethical universalism presupposed in earlier hermeneutic discussion has been thrown into question by the increasing recognition that we must deal much more seriously with the pluralism of early Christianity than the older hermeneutics used to do, at the same time working in the setting of the pluralism of the societies in which the interpreters live. This change has meant that scholars have begun to question the adequacy of the central criterion of how believers responded to the "ought" and its transformation in faith. Other ways of setting ethical questions, often clearly focused on fulfillment rather than on obligation, are being reexamined as "acceptable" aspects of early Christianity.

(1988), 3-17.

2. Adolf Jülicher, *Die Gleichnisreden Jesu*; 2 vols. (Leipzig: J. C. B. Mohr, 1899).

Equally important for the relation between ethics and hermeneutics has been a shift from an emphasis on obligation to a focus on aesthetic perception as the distinctive trait which is in focus as the interpreter works with New Testament texts. This shift was expressed in the lively movement of New Testament literary criticism. But the aesthetic clue to interpretation is in turn being superseded, or at least supplemented, by a return to strongly ethical interpretation of early Christian texts, but now with much more attention to the variety of their ethical claims, and to the social network within which these claims are developed and expressed. The aims and goals of the various groups in early Christianity are taken as central interpretive clues. Simply put, we see a shift from deontological to teleological ethics in New Testament interpretation. To examine this shift is the purpose of this paper.

Ethics of Decision: Bultmann's Hermeneutics

Bultmann's hermeneutics can serve as a starting point for this discussion, since Bultmann's work displays the deontological presuppositions of traditional hermeneutics so clearly, and since his work has been so widely influential.

Bultmann gave renewed life to the rigor of historical method by joining it to a phenomenological analysis of human existence. Historical study presupposes an unbroken chain of causation. But the historian must also "translate" to his or her own culture the existential meaning of the lives of the actors in history.[3] Neither aspect of the interpreter's methodology has any place for divine action, but it is clear that the faith which sees the described event (say, the resurrection of Jesus) as an act of God is understood as a transformation of the act of decision which was originally shaped by a deontological ethical vision.[4]

This "dialectical" hermeneutics, in which a given event both is and is not a witness to the divine presence, proved liberating to scholars, who were able to pursue the rigor of both historical and phenomenological research while reserving the question of divine action or faith. It has been a lasting tradition. Much attention has been given to the freedom for faith which was seen to result from this move. Less obvious, but more impor-

---

3. Rudolf Bultmann, "Is Exegesis Without Presuppositions Possible?", pp. 289-296 in *Existence and Faith: Shorter Writings of Rudolf Bultmann*. tr. and ed. Schubert M. Ogden (New York: Living Age Books, 1960), 291-293.

4. Rudolf Bultmann, "The Meaning of God as Acting," pp. 60-85 in *Jesus Christ and Mythology* (New York: Scribner's, 1958).

tant for our purpose, is the strong sense of obligation to the rules of scholarly research, the strong deontological component in the rigorous separation between research and faith. In this way the ethics of the "ought" has had a strong community-creating function. Scholars of widely-differing commitments join in the common task of research. We shall see later that this apparently universalizing ethical thrust of scholarly distanciation has recently been challenged as unconsciously ideological.

The conviction that a transformation of the "ought" is at the center of Christian existence is fundamental for Bultmann's New Testament interpretation. On the one hand, this model makes intelligible the break with the "law" of Judaism, as well as casting light on the degeneration of Christianity into legalism in the post-apostolic period.[5] On the other hand, it serves as a criterion for excluding forms of self-understanding, such as gnosticism, which did not take seriously the decisional nature of human existence.[6]

We may note that Bultmann explicitly rejects a teleological ethic as a suitable framework for New Testament interpretation; specifically he had in mind an idealistic form of teleological ethics, rather than the utilitarian form of this ethic which has been so prominent in Anglo-American thought. Utilitarianism would no doubt have seemed to him even less appropriate.[7]

While the whole concept of "the imperative" that, in interplay with the indicative, is so constitutive of Bultmann's New Testament theology, is indeed drawn from New Testament texts, classically those of Paul, the imperative that Bultmann heard was a very Kantian one, as is shown by the universalizing tendency that goes hand in hand with the imperative's concreteness of call to decision. This tendency is shown in the implication that there is only one form of authentic existence.[8] At the same time, the insistence that what is significant is an individual person's decision means that political decisions can only be of second rank. Despite his insistence that biblical texts are to be interpreted in the same way as any other liter-

---

5. Rudolf Bultmann, *Theology of the New Testament*, 2 vols.; tr. Kendrick Grobel (New York: Scribner's, 1951-55.), 1, 259-269; 2, 218-231.

6. Ibid., 1, 345-351.

7. Rudolf Bultmann,"Das christliche Gebot der Nächstenliebe," pp. 229-244 in *Glauben und Verstehen*, 1 (Tübingen: J. C. B. Mohr, 1958).

8. Rudolf Bultmann, "The Historicity of Man and Faith," pp. 92-110 in *Existence and Faith*.

ature,[9] these texts are to be interpreted in terms of their proper understanding of existence, and as this interpretation proceeds, it discloses a normative center which is given by the transformation of the "ought" by grace.

Thus, though Bultmann recognized the path into interpretation through aesthetic perception,[10] the deepest key is the serious encounter with a style of existence, and this means serious choice. An aesthetic approach seemed too much a matter of "looking on," while the aesthetic elements tended to appear as decorative details.[11] There was little place in Bultmann's hermeneutics for the entry into interpretation through "play" that appears, for instance, in Gadamer.

Bultmann's ethical clues to interpretation, then, arise from deontological ethics, but the basis of this ethics in social life (rules that make the common life possible) is strongly deemphasized. Even when the person is led into encounter with another, in *agape*, this relation does not arise out of internal relations with the other, but out of love's own spontaneity. A presupposition which lies behind the "ought" of this vision is a very traditional view of distributive justice—"rendering to each his or her due." The assumption is that there is a fixed quantity to be distributed. Though this definition comes from the Greek tradition, with its strong teleological thrust, it was also used to interpret the imperative of the "law." The understanding of justice as the giving of appropriate shares to separate individuals has a strongly patriarchal cast. Someone is dealing out to individual persons what they deserve. Such a patriarchal and individualistic view of justice has deeply affected the whole Protestant view of justice under the law. It is precisely the rigidity of this concept of justice which requires the transformation of the "ought" in faith and love, but the transformation only grudgingly makes room, if at all, for the teleological, goal-oriented aspects of life, or for an intrinsic relationality of beings.

Transition: Gadamer's Hermeneutics

The hermeneutics of Hans-Georg Gadamer can serve to illustrate a transition in approach that has also taken place beyond the explicit in-

9. Rudolf Bultmann, "The Problem of Hermeneutics," pp. 234-261 in *Essays Philosophical and Theological*, tr. James C. G. Grieg (London: SCM Press, 1951), 256.

10. Ibid., 248-250.

11. See also Robert C. Tannehill, *The Sword of His Mouth: Forceful and Imaginative Language in Synoptic Sayings* (Philadelphia: Fortress Press and Missoula: Scholars Press, 1975), 8.

fluence of his work. His hermeneutics is often treated as a further development along lines pioneered by Bultmann.[12] This is not incorrect, but the ethical implications of interpretation are very different in Gadamer. It would not be wrong to regard the move from Bultmann to Gadamer as an instance of a very widespread shift in twentieth-century sensibility which can be described as a transition from a situation in which Kant's second critique defined the problems to be wrestled with, to one where the problems are set by the third critique.[13]

Gadamer notes that before the modern period, "common sense" did indeed imply a common moral context for decision-making, and he calls attention to the persistence of this theme in some religious hermeneutics; but he also shows how the mainstream of European thought moved away from this presupposition in the direction of a rationalistic individualism.[14] But he does not attempt to reconstitute an ethical basis for hermeneutics, turning instead to base his work squarely on the aesthetic dimension which Bultmann had skirted. His perceptive discussion of "common sense" is immediately followed by a treatment of (aesthetic) "judgment" (*Urteilskraft*).[15]

The contrast with Bultmann can be seen in Gadamer's taking "play" as a central hermeneutical clue.[16] Here we deal with the construction of a possible world, or, better, the construction of a variety of worlds, and the role of self-presentation in play contrasts with the self-in-decision model of Bultmann. Gadamer's central image of "fusion of horizons" also cuts very differently from Bultmann's hermeneutics. Although the latter was indeed a skilled interpreter of a wide variety of styles of existence, Bultmann's decisional emphasis tended to develop an interpretation in which one pattern excluded another. The goal of fusion of horizons, on the contrary, implies expansion of vision, and contrasting tensions within the fused horizons, rather than decision among competing options. The strong emphasis on "application" in Gadamer does not contradict this thrust of his

12. As by Richard E. Palmer, *Hermeneutics: Interpretation Theory in Schleiermacher, Dilthey, Heidegger, and Gadamer* (Evanston: Northwestern University Press, 1969), 48-52.

13. The emphasis on decision in Heidegger's *Sein und Zeit*, which is reflected in Bultmann's work, contrasts similarly with the focus on poetry and aesthetics in the later Heidegger, whose work was important for Gadamer.

14. Hans-Georg Gadamer, *Truth and Method*, tr. Garrett Barden and John Cumming (New York: Seabury Press, 1975), 19-29.

15. Ibid., 29-33.

16. Ibid., 91-99.

work; it is precisely in applying the broader humanistic understanding that the expansion of vision will take place. Finally, we may note how Gadamer, virtually at the end of his great work, explicates the universal aspect of hermeneutics with a reference to Plato's vision in which the key concept is beauty, and the beautiful is "fused" with the highest good.[17]

Gadamer's work is paradigmatic of a widespread focus on aesthetic vision in hermeneutics, including New Testament hermeneutics. Much of the vigorous work in New Testament literary criticism, whether or not it has been carried out specifically with reference to Gadamer, is consonant with the emphases noted above. In this style of interpretation the intention is to be open to as wide a range of options as possible, including ethical options. The implication is that there is a wide range of authentic forms of human existence, in which quite varied ethical patterns function. Gadamer's work has been criticized as still too narrowly focused on the Western tradition to carry out this intention.[18] Nevertheless, the direction of his interpretation, and of this type of interpretation generally, is to encompass, to use Gadamer's term, by fusion of horizons, multiple possibilities of being human. The action-oriented ethics of transformation, to which we shall shortly turn, is often impatient with this aesthetic turn in hermeneutics, but it has none the less played an important role in turning away from a universalizing deontological ethic toward the recognition of multiple aims for an ethics of goal-oriented action.

Further, this hermeneutics takes more seriously the human person and society as creative, as actors. Gadamer's use of Plato shows that his style of interpretation will be far more open to a positive evaluation of *eros* than was the hermeneutics which preceded it. As against a view of love which starts with disconnected realities and understands *agape* as the unilateral creation of a relationship, the perspective from which Gadamer works supposes that already existing relations and impulses provide a basis from which understanding can grow.

Ethical reflection is not highlighted in Gadamer's work. Nevertheless, we can note several implications of his perspective for the place of ethics in hermeneutics. In the first place, aesthetic perception is the central category, and ethics, however it is understood, will be drawn closer to aesthetics. Further, it will be easier to make the move from aesthetics to

---

17. Ibid., 435-447.

18. John D'Arcy May, *Meaning, Consensus, and Dialogue in Buddhist-Christian Communication: A Study in Constructive Meaning* (Berne: Peter Lang, 1984), 255.

ethics if a teleological ethics, perhaps emphasizing the "fitting," is the framework, rather than the traditional ethics of the "ought."

Second, Gadamer's model of dialogical interchange among a variety of positions is open toward a greater pluralism of ethical positions than was the case with Bultmann's hermeneutics. It is true that, though there is no "center" in Gadamer's vision, he does work within what he understands to be a connected flow of the Western tradition. His position has been criticized for its inability to offer a critical perspective on the present.[19] In this latter point we see the claim of ethics in hermeneutics reasserting itself. There is validity in this criticism, yet the greater openness of what is here termed an aesthetic hermeneutics has been, both specifically in the case of Gadamer, and more broadly in literary interpretation generally, a significant step toward a reopening of the question of ethical variety in early Christianity.

Finally, though the issue of justice is also not a focal one in Gadamer's work, the implication of his image of the fusion of horizons for justice is that of breaking away from the "zero sum game" model of rendering to each her or his due. A truly fused horizon is an enlarged world of new possibilities. We shall see that in the field of justice precisely this sort of new vision is needed. The aesthetic hermeneutical perspective itself did not develop into a hermeneutics of transformation, but it has provided a setting in which dialogue between traditional hermeneutics and that kind of interpretation is more easily possible.

Ethics of Transformation
The Hermeneutics of Elisabeth Schüssler Fiorenza

Hermeneutics of action has not been unknown in earlier New Testament interpretation.[20] Resistance to action-oriented interpretation which advanced the specific dogmatic or social aims of the institutional church generated the scholarly distanciation which characterized nineteenth-century historiography, and which is still a strong element in contemporary hermeneutics. The resistance to action-oriented interpretation is still strong. But the hermeneutics of transformation is pressing the point that the seeming neutrality of this traditional scholarly posture conceals its

19. Elisbeth Schüssler Fiorenza, *Bread Not Stone: The Challenge of Feminist Biblical Interpretation* (Boston: Beacon Press, 1984), 132-135.

20. For instance, a large part of Walter Rauschenbusch's *Christianity and the Social Crisis* (New York: Macmillan, 1907) consists of biblical exegesis.

ideological function of supporting an establishment, and fails in its objective of sustaining a community of scholars, since it excludes those who work from other perspectives.

On this point there is much convergence among Latin American, Afro-American, and feminist theologies. These theologies also move in the direction (though not all draw this conclusion) of reversing the assumption of traditional biblical interpretation, that the primary locus of divine action is to be seen in the biblical past. They affirm that divine action in the present, in the struggle for the liberation of the oppressed, is the starting-point for biblical interpretation. From the point of view of traditional hermeneutics, this starting-point can be seen as a particular preunderstanding. But the claim is a still stronger one than that. For the faith that, if divine action is significant anywhere, it must be so in the actual struggle of the oppressed, is incompatible with dialectical theology's closed world of historical causation. The claim entails reopening the question of the way in which God acts in the world, and demands the development of scholarly tools which can bring together the two worlds, the world of faith which sees God at work, and the world of social analysis which studies how human societies behave. It is because one can speak of God's action in the present that one can go back to the Bible and re-read it as a book of liberation.[21]

We shall explore the hermeneutics of liberation through the work of Elisabeth Schüssler Fiorenza, since she has addressed the issue of interpretation theory explicitly. The positions noted above are explicit in her work.[22] She rejects the "neo-orthodox" attempt to find a way of "divorcing the language and text of the Bible from its patriarchal conditions,"[23] that is, of finding a general theological statement which would transcend the androcentric character of the actual Bible. Though she is more sympathetic to the "sociology of knowledge" model of Mary Daly, she holds that Daly has not sufficiently taken account of the historical character of human existence, which requires that women join themselves with the

21. To say this is not to overlook the very positive response of many dialectical theologians to various forms of liberation theology. But it is to affirm that a theology will be crippled which both affirms the present action of the divine, and rigorously separates that action from scholarly analysis.

22. Elisabeth Schüssler Fiorenza, *In Memory of Her: A Feminist Theological Reconstruction of Christian Origins* (New York: Crossroad, 1983); *Bread Not Stone*; "The Ethics of Interpretation."

23. *In Memory of Her*, 21.

women, oppressed as they usually were, of the Bible. What is required is to reclaim this past, by subverting the history which conceals it.[24]

Her aim is a critical hermeneutics of emancipation. "Liberation theologians must abandon the hermeneutic-contextual paradigm of biblical interpretation, and construct within the context of a critical theology of liberation a new interpretive paradigm that has as its aim emancipatory praxis."[25] This critical hermeneutics, which is critical both of traditional readings of the Bible and of its own presuppositions, arises from a concrete social location, the community of women engaged in the struggle for liberation. One of its central aims is re-reading of New Testament texts to recover the teleological ethic, the aims at the creation of community, of the almost-forgotten early Christian women.[26]

Such a hermeneutics squarely puts the final emphasis on engagement rather than on scholarly distance. Scholarly distance still has its place, in the "ethics of historical reading," which doubly relativizes the ancient text and the present situation of the reader.[27] In this way the "modern" achievements of "scientific" historiography are incorporated into the "post-modern" relational and transformational vision of the author. But in its final stage, interpretation is a battle against established powers. Schüssler Fiorenza observes, "Feminist biblical scholarship has its roots not in the academy but in the social movements for the emancipation of slaves and of freeborn women."[28] The "ethics of accountability" is a political ethic which is aware of the pragmatic impact of one's work, and aims for responsible social effects. The conflictual imagery must not deflect our attention from the strong emphasis on relatedness. An authentic style of existence cannot be described by showing how a self is structured, or how it confronts reality, but must focus on social relations, however perverted these may be. The social, related character of human existence is a basic presupposition. And the consequence for ethics is a strong emphasis on teleological ethics. The ends for which action is undertaken are what is to be judged ethically.

A struggle against injustice could be conceived in terms of traditional distributive justice, as a claim for a share in what has been denied. This is certainly a motif in most liberation theologies including that of Elisabeth

24. Ibid., 31.
25. *Bread Not Stone*, 63.
26. *In Memory of Her*, passim.
27. "The Ethics of Interpretation," 14.
28. Ibid., 7.

Schüssler Fiorenza. But it is important to note that her interpretation also implies a far more relational and reconstructive image of justice. It is by no means implied that if women win men will always lose. And though the actual present circumstances compel a thorough commitment to the ecclesia of women, from this vantage point one can also see the church of women and men, not as a utopian ideal but as an actual reality which can emerge as the androcentric character of the church is overcome.[29]

Ethics and Hermeneutics

At the risk of some oversimplification, we have sketched a shift from the widespread presupposition of New Testament hermeneutics that ethics is rooted in an irreducible "ought," to a goal-oriented, transformative ethic of political responsibility. Acceptance in the guild of the latter is far from wholehearted, but there are many signs that this is the creative direction in the ethical aspect of interpretation. But the new direction would be terribly impoverished if it were taken to imply the abandonment of either rigorous historical discipline or a dialogical, contextual hermeneutics. All three forms of interpretation are required, if the New Testament is to recover its ability to speak to the issues which the community of the church and also the wider human community bring to it.

If interpreters of the New Testament give a somewhat uncertain sound about the shape of their ethical commitment, that is a reflection of a very widespread confusion in ethical thinking today. We cannot here survey the field of ethics (even if the present author were competent to do so), but we shall try to offer some directions toward greater clarity, and sketch a proposal which should make it easier for different points to view to communicate. Among the issues we can note the following. The connection between ethics and faith is problematic, not only because ethical standards are seen to be relative to particular social settings, but also because many hold that moral action is so inextricably connected with the use of power that it cannot be a gateway to the ultimate mystery. Thus Peter Sloterdijk closes his exhaustive *Critique of Cynical Reason* with the slender hope for a basis for life in "another reason than the activist one."[30] Perception of the use of ethical standards as expressions of power has placed a question over the whole project of traditional reasoning about

29. *Bread Not Stone*, ch. 1.

30. Peter Sloterdijk, *Kritik der zynischen Vernunft*; 2 vols. (Frankfurt: Suhrkamp, 1983), 2, 952.

ethics.[31] The erosion of an ethical consensus, which may seem dismaying to representatives of traditional positions, is often welcomed by those who speak for excluded groups, that have found traditional ethics repressive.[32] Another factor in the decline of established ethical traditions is the conviction among many professional ethicists that ethical statements are non-cognitive. Some claim that ethical discourse consists of a group of non-communicating language games.[33] In spite of these daunting problems, there still is profound ethical commitment on the part of many who have no way of making it intelligible.

To sort out these issues would carry us far beyond the scope of this paper. We can, however, seek to sketch a framework in which the original cleft between deontological and teleological ethical styles can be more adequately bridged. This can serve as an approach to some of the wider questions.

Deontology does not offer the self-evident claim that it used to do, or at least was thought to make. And the "ought" is so often perceived as a power claim that many are skeptical about universal ethical claims. Yet the ethics of the "ought" is far from exhausted. Despite our classifying the ethics of liberation as teleological, marked deontological elements do appear in it, especially in the claim of loyalty for the group. And the radical pluralist Jean-François Lyotard closes his conversation on ethics with an outright deontological command: "[Justice] . . . prohibits terror, that is, the blackmail of death toward one's partners . . . ."[34] We will expect that the claim of response to an "ought" will continue to be a part of the language of ethics.

This paper has shown the vitality of teleological ethics in theologies of liberation. This type of ethics suffers from the opposite difficulty from deontology. The ethical claim of a goal all too easily becomes the interest of a particular party. We need to recognize that a universal position is never available to us, and to take seriously the situatedness of any ethical formulation, but along with that particularism there needs to be a reach

---

31. This issue is discussed by Jurgen Habermas, "The Genealogical Writing of History: On Some Aporias in Foucault's Theory of Power," *Canadian Journal of Political and Social Theory/Revue canadienne de théorie politique et sociale*, 10 (1986), 1-9.

32. Schüssler Fiorenza, *Bread Not Stone*, chap. 4.

33. Jean-François Lyotard and Jean-Loup Thébaud, *Just Gaming*, tr. Wlad Godzich; Afterword by Samuel Weber, tr. Brian Massumi (Minneapolis: University of Minnesota Press, 1985).

34. Ibid., 100.

toward a wider situatedness, and a willingness to allow one's position to be transformed toward a deeper recognition of other claims.

An important resource for reconstructing ethical discourse is found in the work of H. Richard Niebuhr, who proposed that both of the classical approaches be subsumed in a more comprehensive ethical image—that of the "responsible self."[35] Niebuhr showed how the concrete image of responsibility can function more comprehensively than either of the traditional alternatives. It implies an interactive, related person and humanity; all action is response; it is interpreted response; and it takes place in a situation of social solidarity.[36] Without examining Niebuhr's book in detail, we can note how the ethics of interpreted response in social solidarity frees one from the abstractness of rules in the ethics of "ought," while at the same time the aspect of social relatedness serves as a constraint to the choice of limited goals.[37]

Niebuhr's model recognizes the pluralistic, non-centered ethical world in which we find ourselves. It is coherent with the view that values are not simply imputed to objects by the human mind, but are inherent in reality—an issue too complex to unfold here. At the same time, through its monotheism, it maintains that there is an inclusive standpoint, even though this is never fully available to us. Such an affirmation of pluralism as well as an ultimate inclusive standpoint will be a powerful tool in interpreting New Testament texts. Catherine Keller has sharply criticized Niebuhr for that aspect of his monotheism in which he presents the self as unified only by its relation to a unilateral divine influence which establishes unity in the flux of life. She calls for a "multiple integrity."[38] We agree with Keller that we encounter the divine in and not in opposition to the multiple and often conflicting strands of relationship which elicit our commitment. But that even stronger emphasis on pluralism does not negate the role of a unifying standpoint toward which we can, at least sometimes, in real measure approximate. Keller's caveat is an important reminder that this approximation is not the only goal of ethical reflection.

---

35. H. Richard Niebuhr, *The Responsible Self: An Essay in Christian Moral Philosophy* (San Francisco: Harper & Row, 1978).

36. Ibid., 61-66.

37. Niebuhr's ethical thought is highly compatible with the ethics that arises from Whiteheadian or process thought, which can serve as a general framework in which to develop ethics. See Daniel W. Metzler, *Essay on Whiteheadian Ethics*; Dissertation, Emory University (Ann Arbor: University Microfilms, 1988), esp. 311-317.

38. Catherine Keller, *From a Broken Web: Separation, Sexism, and Self* (Boston: Beacon Press, 1986), 181.

If it be objected that this language is too private, too dependent on a particular commitment, the response is that public discourse always consists in conversation from particular standpoints. The image of the responsible self-in-relation, acting always in a particular social context, yet related to a universal standpoint, the standpoint of God, can very fruitfully enter in conversation with those who do not understand themselves as relating ethics to faith, through the affinity of the Niebuhr-process model to the model of the ethics of the ideal observer, a well-established ethical tradition which itself recognizes the difficulty of simple universals.[39]

Those of us who were trained in the universalism of deontological ethics may readily suppose that the goal of conversation among ethical positions is to find elements in common, convergences toward which a consensus can be built. This move is a valid one, but it is not the only one, and often is not the most important one, in an ethics of response in social relatedness. Equally important is the recognition of enduring differences, and the search for ways of respecting these. The deeper goal, not always to be attained, but to be striven for, is not the uncovering of commonalities but the transformation of conversing positions so that each may hold in tension its initial insights with elements at first perceived as incompatible, from the other position.

It is especially at this point that aesthetic hermeneutics and hermeneutics of liberation can fruitfully interact. For both work to understand and release the creative possibilities of the human. Each can easily be impatient with the other, since one emphasizes sympathetic understanding, and the other action. While each posture is a fully justified one, neither is self-sufficient. We noted above that those who speak for excluded groups are suspicious of overall ethical perspectives, because these support established powers. Similarly, the aesthetic hermeneutics of the humanistic tradition is suspicious of what appears to be the too limited perspective of the ethics of action. But both appreciate human creativity or *eros* in ways that the older hermeneutics did not, and this common, though differently developed, ground gives them both a stake in a continuing conversation.[40] This dialogue will show that while the desire to use power does shape ethical discourse, it can be transcended since it does

---

39. See Metzler, *Essay*, 309-310; 321-323.

40. The interplay of these styles of essentially humanistic interpretation points to the shared concerns of this essay with the work of my honored colleague, Hendrikus Boers. [This essay first appeared in a volume honoring Professor Boers.]

not totally control such discourse, and it will also show that a deeper humanistic understanding is unfinished if it does not lead to action.

The ethical framework here proposed will honor human creativeness more fully than much traditional ethics has done. A theme in New Testament interpretation in which this emphasis will be apparent is the understanding of love. Most treatments of love in the New Testament are suspicious of *eros*, and see *agape* to be the legitimate New Testament form of love. There is good reason in the texts for this tradition. But a fuller consideration of the dynamics of the New Testament communities calls for a wider view. Charles Reynolds remarks, "A full and robust theory of love...needs the attractive, luring, binding indeterminate and driving vitality of eros together with the steadfast, determinate, and equal-regarding characteristics of agape."[41] An interpretation of New Testament texts about love which recognizes the interaction and, often, struggle, out of which the texts arose can do justice to the centrality of both of these styles of love in early Christianity.

Finally, we have noted above that a fresh vision of justice is a major need in ethical thinking, and that recent moves in hermeneutics are places where one can see a new way of thinking about justice emerging. Particularly in the tradition of the ethics of the "ought," a distributive conception of justice has been the rule, and this view has all too often implied that justice consists simply in some authority dividing up a given amount of what is desired. This starting-point has heightened the incompatibility of justice and love, as well as increasing the interpreter's suspicion of human creative capacities, which so easily deform the rules of justice. We have shown that both Gadamer's dialogical hermeneutics and the feminist hermeneutics of Schüssler Fiorenza open the way to a more relational understanding of justice. In this kind of justice, participation and consideration of aim function not only in distribution but in the whole network of social relations, and the creation of new possibilities can be an aspect of justice. A commentator on *Economic Justice for All*, the Pastoral Letter of the Roman Catholic Bishops of the United States on the economy, interprets their view in this way: "Participation at all levels must be improved before justice in terms of both individual freedom and social

41. Charles H. Reynolds, "Somatic Ethics: Joy and Adventure in the Embodied Moral Life," pp. 116-132 in *John Cobb's Theology in Process*, ed. David Ray Griffin and Thomas J. J. Altizer (Philadelphia: The Westminster Press, 1977), 120.

equity can be realized."[42] An important distinction is that participatory justice can consider rearranging the structures so the social issue will not always be the distribution of an already fixed amount. Further exploration of a relational, participatory view of justice will be a central task of ethical thinking about the New Testament, for at important points New Testament texts point toward just this concept of justice, and where they do not, they can more fruitfully be criticized from this point of view than by working from traditional distributive justice.

Behind the ethical uncertainties which we noted above lies the intractable, disruptive terror of our time. The deeper issue is not the technicalities of ethical theory, but the question whether any ethical framework can enable women and men to live with moral integrity in our disordered world. The preceding reflections are not offered as easy solutions, but as a proposal for freeing the resources of the New Testament so that they may more fully be available to contribute to that task. The path sketched above envisages not a single uniform community of interpreters, but conversation among communities: uninstructed readers and scholars, humanists and activists. In such conversation the rigidities of each position can be questioned, yet each can speak, and frankly. This path will move away from the rigid image of hermeneutics as "translation," which presupposes a fixed element to be re-expressed. It will contribute to the formation of a hermeneutics that can fully recognize the strangeness of the text, which offers no "pure" disclosure, and yet can release the ethical power that successive generations have found in an encounter with the New Testament.

---

42. Carol Johnston, "Learning Reformed Theology from the Roman Catholics: The U. S. Pastoral Letter on the Economy," pp. 203-215 in *Reformed Faith and Economics*, ed. Robert L. Stivers (Lanham, MD: University Presses of America, 1989), 213. I am also indebted to an unpublished paper of Carol Johnston for analysis of the contrast between distributive and participatory justice.

15

Christ in the Post-Modern Age

Our present age, or the one into which we are moving, is increasingly being called the "post-modern age." In itself this is a negative term, which sets our perception of the world over against an earlier one that we are leaving behind. Thus "post-modern" is shaped in good measure by what we think of as "modern" or (to introduce a term widely used in literary and cultural criticism) "modernist."

I distinguish two senses of "post-modern," which are related to two senses of "modern" or "modernist." In the broader sense the "modern age" refers to the period begun by Galileo, Descartes, and Newton, a period which continued into the nineteenth-century rationalism and scientism which are still so influential today. In the narrower sense, the "modernist" period was a period of artistic and cultural activity early in the twentieth century. In the broader sense, "post-modern" means the movement beyond the scientistic modernism which we have called modernism in its wider meaning. In the narrower sense, "post-modern" means the movements in art and literature which react to or move beyond the "modernist" movement in the culture of the early part of this century.

The two "post-modernisms" share a strong awareness that ours is a pluralistic world, and one with many centers. The new vision arising in the post-modern world is perhaps above all a vision that can take account of our new awareness of pluralism and the problematic nature of the center.

Nevertheless, the two types of post-modernism are strikingly different. The modern age in the first sense was characterized by a reductionist interpretation of much of our culture's effort to interpret human creativity and express a relation to the transcendent. Its single most per-

---

From *Varieties of Postmodern Theology*, by David R. Griffin, William A. Beardslee, and Joe Holland (Albany: State University of New York Press, 1989), 63-80.

vasive factor was a deterministic model of reality ("Newtonian science") which was used to interpret phenomena ranging from physics to sociology, psychology, and religion.

In the broader sense, then, the "post-modern" development is the process of breaking away from the determinism of the modern worldview. Post-modern thought and imagination can be seen in such diverse figures as the existentialists (but see also the next paragraph) and philosophers like Alfred North Whitehead and Charles Hartshorne, as well as in the pioneers of post-Newtonian physics. Most of the essays in the series (this one included) in which this volume appears [in its original publication] will be exploring varied aspects of the more open vision of the world that is made possible and encouraged by post-modern thinking and imagination in this sense.

But "post-modern" also is the description of a different, though not completely unrelated, style of thought and imagination, deriving from the developments beyond the "modernist" movement in art and literature. There is considerable disagreement about how to understand "modernism," but we can say that the modernist movement in art and literature in the early part of this century represented an effort to make a sharp break with inherited cultural patterns, and to think and imagine bold new reconstructions of the shape of the world. Traditional visions were broken down and reassembled in new ways. But the great modernist artists were still working on the assumption that human creativity could evoke a vision of the whole, even though they thought of their work in much more subjective terms than had most artists and writers of an earlier time. The modernist period—the time of Eliot, Yeats, and Pound, the time when existentialist and Marxist thought were dominant in continental thought—has set the background from which the second type of "post-modernism," which I call "severe post-modernism," has developed. This post-modernism is marked by the abandonment of the quest for a vision of the whole. Usually great emphasis is placed upon the nature of understanding as "interpretation," that is, the view that there is no standpoint outside the flow of history and experience, so that all writing is interpretation of earlier writing. The social and ethical judgments of this kind of post-modernism are marked by the political-social disillusionment of Europe, and this post-modernism is as much a search for a new sociological grasp of our situation as it is a philosophical description of it.

My topic in this essay is how to speak of Christ in the post-modern age. To ask this question assumes that the word we hear from Christ is not a timeless one, but that our hearing and the expression of the word of Christ are both blocked and empowered by the concrete and changing circumstances in which we live. If this is so, it is of great importance to assess the limitations and the possibilities of our world, so as to see what new ways of understanding and expressing our faith can arise from the dialogue between faith and the world. Our path in this exploration will be to turn first to a strong presentation of the severe post-modern vision as it is sketched by Jean François Lyotard in *The Post-Modern Condition.*[1] Then we shall see how the broader type of post-modernism, oriented by faith, may enter into dialogue with this severe post-modernism; finally we shall consider the implications of this study for speaking of Christ.

Lyotard's Severe Post-Modern Vision

Lyotard concentrates on a single aspect of our situation, as is shown by his subtitle, *A Report on Knowledge*. He makes a good deal of the shift of knowledge, and also of power, into actual computerized information systems, but above all these serve as his metaphor for the wider human situation. They offer Lyotard (who follows the lead of a group of social scientists) a powerful way of re-imagining human existence. As over against the centered self, which was a focus of creative energy and whose expressions were the great cultural products (a view particularly associated with Romanticism, but which continued still into much modernism), Lyotard offers us the image of the person as a node in a complex network of information exchanges. There is no way to be an isolated self. But, equally important, as this author sees it, different exchanges are carried on under the rules of different "language games," so that the consistency of the self is eroded away. Lyotard reminds us that language analysis has not been able satisfactorily to relate different language games, in particular, denotative games which describe situations and prescriptive games which set norms. Direction and norms were formerly set by orienting narratives which did not have to be completely analyzed. But neither individual nor social life is any longer organized around a foundational narrative, Lyotard tells us, and most people no longer even have a nostalgia for one of the old orienting stories which set the self and society in a history or a tradition.

1. Jean-François Lyotard, *The Post-Modern Condition: A Report on Knowledge*, tr. Geoff Bennington and Brian Massumi; "Theory and History of Literature," 10 (Minneapolis: University of Minnesota Press, 1984).

What is disconcerting about this image of the person as a node in a non-centered web of exchanges of information is that the network or social-technological system has its own momentum. According to cybernetic theory, it works to increase its own efficiency of operation—in technical language, its own "performativity." It is almost a lost cause to try to impose some other goal upon the network itself.

It is clear that Lyotard's world is both a post-Marxist and a post-existentialist world. The disillusionment with narrative is a disillusionment of the West European world with the secular kingdom of God in Marxism, which seemed to so many in that world to be the only viable version of a forward-moving global narrative. A loss of hope resulting from the failure of radical protest movements in France in the 1960's, especially the failure of the radical student movement, on the one hand, and the narrow bureaucratization of life in Eastern Europe on the other, are powerful factors leading such a figure as Lyotard to move away from narrative to a directionless view of human existence. However, these distinctively European factors need to be set over against the fact that *we* are the ones whom Lyotard is describing in his information society. Much of his social analysis comes from American sociologists, especially Talcott Parsons, with his view of society as a self-regulating system; and in general one is struck by how widely Lyotard has studied and reflected upon society in the United States, and how extensively he has drawn upon American thinking.[2]

To Lyotard this is not a despairing picture, however. In two different ways he indicates the cracks of openness that exist in the web of relationships that constitute the person. In an appendix to the English translation, dealing with the work of the artist, Lyotard comes to the defense of the avant-garde. Their task, he says, is "not to supply reality but to invent allusions to the conceivable which cannot be presented."[3] This conceptuality is drawn from Kant's description of the sublime. As applied by Lyotard, it suggests that what is known, what can be presented, is already thereby evacuated of any decisive significance. Yet there is a "more" that cannot be presented, though it can be conceived that there is such. The work of art does not (nowadays) aim to be beautiful, but to raise the question, "Is it art?", that is, "Does this presentation

2. We cannot here compare Lyotard's work with that of French deconstructionists like Jacques Derrida or American thinkers like Richard Rorty.

3. Lyotard, op. cit., 81.

raise the question of the unpresentable?" Transposed into the key of the aesthetic, we see here an old debate about the possibility of knowing God. The artist does not work in any trajectory or narrative (for instance, by the use of traditional symbols), but tries to disclose what cannot be disclosed, and to give (in line with Kant's analysis of the sublime) both pain and pleasure in the combined presentation of presence and absence. He or she does this, of course, in the mode of shock or irreverence.

Lyotard's other opening into freedom appears in his consideration of scientific knowledge. Not having space to report this in detail, I only call attention to a few aspects of his analysis. In contrast to positivistic conceptions of science which do away with narrative symbolism altogether, Lyotard restores narrative to scientific method in the "short story" of scientific discovery. The new knowledge, which is the only thing of interest, is found by breaking the rules of the existing language game of the particular area of science in question. Freedom of knowledge and new discovery are made possible by what Lyotard calls "parology." In traditional logic, parology is reasoning falsely unconsciously, in contrast to sophism which is reasoning falsely with intent to deceive. But in Lyotard's post-modern vision, parology acquires a slightly different nuance, in that it is breaking the rules of the game (thus reasoning falsely) in order to open up a new possibility. But let us be clear that in Lyotard's framework we are not talking about a more adequate understanding of reality—an overall understanding of reality is what this post-modernism gives up. Opening up a new possibility is purely a matter of renewing the game, of keeping things from falling into a sheer state of repetition or entropy. The human creative impulse can be asserted only in these modest ways, Lyotard believes, under conditions of modern knowledge.[4]

What place could there be for Christ in this information world, in which there cannot be any centered selves, in which living consists in making moves or plays in a network of language games that are not clearly related to one another, and in which one finds oneself both con-

---

4. It should be added that Lyotard also recognizes the place for less focused expressions of creativity and freedom, in part at least in response to the sharply-profiled forms sketched in the text of this paper. Thus, in *Newsweek*, April 22, 1985, in connection with an art exhibit which he planned at the Pompidou Center in Paris, Lyotard observed, "We wanted to show that the world is not evolving toward greater clarity and simplicity, but rather toward a new degree complexity of in which the individual may feel very lost but in which he can in fact become more free" (p. 80). It is worth noting that here Lyotard employs narrative language ("evolving") of a sort, which could open up a further range of dialogue.

stituted by and confined within a network which has its own impetus toward strikingly non-human efficiency, and in which the only significant creativity is declared to be found in breaking the conventions, whether of art or science?

Three Possible Responses by Christian Faith

Let me mention three ways in which Christian faith might respond to such a situation. One way would be to recognize and accept the adequacy of the type of social and (shall we say) spiritual description of the post-modern world which is offered to us by Lyotard (and he is only one very articulate speaker for a perspective that is widely shared). If one accepts this view, then the question is whether the total picture can be interpreted in such a way as to disclose the contemporary meaning of Christ. This is the path followed by Mark C. Taylor in his *Erring*.[5] Christ as word brings us into language games, and the non-presence of reality in language leads us to the *trace* rather than to presence, to the deferring of meaning which is never found, but which is never completely not found either. Taylor, like Lyotard, rejects conventional narrative and replaces it, as the title of his book suggests, with "erring," which means both wandering and, like Lyotard's parology, transgressing, breaking the established patterns in the directionless movement of life. Such a theology would be a theological critique of culture, not a church theology, since the special meaning of a historical community of faith would have been erased by the absorption of "Christ" into the whole.

A contrasting approach was used by Karl Barth in an earlier cultural and religious crisis of meaning. Barth's situation was different from what confronts us now, because he was contending with those who precisely did see meaning, rather than the lack of it, in the dominant culture.[6] Barth contended that faith proclaimed a *different* meaning—it was not subject to or discovered in the contemporary perceptions of cultural meaning, but sprang from a different dynamic and had its own integrity. This response has its difficulties, and cannot be entirely consistently carried through,

---

5. Mark C. Taylor, *Erring: A Postmodern A/Theology*, (Chicago: University of Chicago Press, 1984). Taylor's work is in part a theological application of the work of Jacques Derrida, and is analyzed by David R. Griffin in David R. Griffin *et al.*, *Varieties of Postmodern Theology* (Albany: State University of New York Press, 1989), ch. 3.

6. Karl Barth, *The Epistle to the Romans*, tr. Edwyn C. Hoskyns (London: Oxford University Press, 1933).

because faith has no purchase over against culture which is not in turn influenced by culture. None the less, it would be wrong to regard this as a nostalgic or purely conservative reaction. Rather, it presupposes that the cultural crisis opens the way for a fresh disclosure of the power of Christ, and that the biblical tradition has, in its own form, sufficient consistency to stand on its own over against the culture. Hans Frei's affirmation of *The Identity of Jesus Christ*, a strong restatement of a theology that places both Christ and the believer in a story, is a good contemporary version of this response.[7]

You will have guessed that I am choosing a third response, which I think of not so much as in between these other two as on the third angle of a triangle—a response in which we see ourselves as deeply shaped by the post-modern world, and try to enter imaginatively into the interpretation of it offered by such writers as Lyotard, and yet affirm ourselves as finding our identity conferred by the history of our faith. A conversation arising from this kind of tension, I believe, promises the most creative possibilities for faith.

A Broader Post-Modern Vision

If we embark on this course, we shall have to adopt a position that has already tried to take account of many of the shifts in perspective sketched above. That is, we shall be working also from a post-modern perspective, but from that broader post-modernism to which I referred earlier. The specific perspective adopted here is dependent upon the vision of Alfred North Whitehead, and is exemplified excellently in *The Liberation of Life*, by Charles Birch and John B. Cobb, Jr.[8] This broader post-modernism accepts the decay of the modern vision, with its substantial, single-storied self and its imperialistic single-narrative history. But it does not believe that this decay means the arbitrariness of every kind of identity-conveying narrative structure for the self and the cosmos. This type of post-modernism suggests a post-modern *worldview*. We shall try to enter into dialogue with what I call severe post-modernism from the point of view of this broader post-modernism.

---

7. Hans Frei, *The Identity of Jesus Christ: The Hermeneutical Bases of Dogmatic Theology* (Philadelphia: Fortress Press, 1975).

8. Charles Birch and John B. Cobb, Jr., *The Liberation of Life: From the Cell to the Community* (Cambridge: Cambridge University Press, 1981).

Our first comment is that the reflections of Lyotard help us to clarify much of what we already knew and believed. Particularly the movement away from the self as a stable, centered focus of creativity, the self of our Romantic and modernist pictures of the creative process, toward the self as a focus of exchanges, a self which exists only in a relational network, is a helpful move with which we should wish to join. A positive aspect of this move is the effort to defuse the desire for domination which is so easily a central meaning of the centered self. At the same time, the role of continuing commitments has to be honored also, and this is easier to do if one sees that the formulation of personal existence purely in terms of linguistic exchanges—language games—overlooks the wider interactive aspects of existence in a network of exchanges. As well as commitments, truth also can have meaning in this kind of post-modern world. Even though it is never available to us in a final and finished form, it is as much a concern of the process of interaction as is the play and modification of the rules of the game on which so many post-moderns concentrate.

In other words, we can legitimately affirm a larger world than the severe version of the post-modern vision allows. A principal question, in inspecting the view of life and reality which we sketched as the severe post-modern vision, is: From where does the creativity come that is manifest, albeit only in a few privileged ways, in this post-modern vision? Even after we accept the assumption that neither life nor the world as a whole operates from or moves toward a single center, but is multi-centered, still the question arises: How does it happen that these centers—"nodes of communication" as we called them—do not simply *relay* the data that they receive, but *modify* these, sometimes in strikingly creative ways? The post-modern problem is not the one that was central to many in the modernist period, which was the problem of how we deal with the mechanical, deterministic perception of reality. Rather, the post-modern problem is that there are *many* centers of creativity, often at odds with one another. This is masked by Lyotard's treatment because he sees creativity so restricted by the cybernetic network that it can only be expressed in ways that are "outrageous." Nevertheless, we find a common ground with him in pointing to striking cases of creativity to alert us to the distinctively human.

By its very nature the outrageous is something that we resist. Yet we must recognize that it is one of the authentic exemplifications of creativity. But not the only one! The power that such post-modernism sees at work in this restricted way is far more pervasively at work. If this fact is not widely recognized, that is because, on the one hand, so much of the humanist wing of post-modernism is still under the influence of a deterministic view of nature and is not open to seeing creativity at work beyond the boundaries of the human; and on the other hand, because so much post-modern thought is unable to see creativity at work in any structured form. Structure and authority have come to be so thoroughly blended that these thinkers fail to find any creativity except in the outrageous, in the effort to break or to resist structure—with the result that they overlook the presence of creativity in many other more gradual or even more gentle ways.

Further, recognizing many foci of creativity does not have to imply the renunciation of orienting narrative. We have to remember that there is quite a history here. Already the existentialists abolished the orienting narrative, but they retained the centered self. With no kind of coherence through time remaining, there is no context in which the more gradual or more gentle forms of creativity can have significance.

Here the severe post-moderns are too preoccupied with the breakup of the old single-thread story to contemplate the possibilities of another kind of story. A story can be open, multiplex, and indeterminate. It is true that this kind of narrative vision does not correspond to the way in which we have ordinarily told stories. But there is much pervasive evidence, from quite different directions, pointing to this new way of thinking of story, and hence the story of our world as a whole. Even Lyotard has his mini-narratives of scientific discovery, and his hidden narrative of the quest for justice. And such widely diverse fields as biological evolution and the history of human religion can best be interpreted in this way, as stories that are open-ended, and indefinitely multiplex.

In the church today there are prominent efforts trying to counter this stream by reconstituting the single story, in which the Christian story is the only real story. These efforts are essentially *pre*-modern, and in the long run they will be destructive of faith because they isolate it from the wider reality. To enter into the post-modern world in the faith that the Christian story is only one of the expressions of the creative Spirit, and that it has no predetermined end, is no easy task, but it does open the way to relating this orienting narrative to others. For narrative is the traditional way of relating value, truth, and action, and it affords a network within which to test the adequacy of claims for truth and value.

What is to prevent the various narratives from simply running contrary to one another and destroying one another—say, the stories of the quest for truth, the quest for liberation of the poor, the quest for the expression of brotherly and sisterly love in the community of human beings, and the quest for the identity of a people? Often, indeed, these stories do conflict, but if we study them we find that there are directions of convergence as well as of conflict; and therefore there is the possibility of placing the various orienting narratives in relation to each other. They do not have to be "zero-sum games." For instance, the story of our nation may become fuller and more satisfying as it takes seriously its relation to very different stories of other groups. If we find that creativity is manifested in diverse and often fragmentary narratives, and find as well that there is a tendency that makes possible important convergences, this means that something more than *random* creativity is at work. There is a valuational and directional aspect of creativity which we can designate as the activity of the Spirit. While this is not Whitehead's language, it is the great merit of his philosophic vision that he recognized the multi-centered post-modern world, yet also saw this tendency toward convergence.[9] The effort of this paper is to articulate a view of Christ from this post-modern perspective, in dialogue with "severe" post-modernism.

Creativity and the Spirit

Before we turn to the question of Christ, it is important to note that it is one-sided to locate the work of the Spirit solely in the efforts to bring forth expressions of creativity that are new to the society. Such efforts—whether they be directed to transforming the society toward justice (as in the creativity of different forms of liberation activity and thought), or whether they be turned to the effort to transform our vision, imagination, and knowledge in new and creative ways—such efforts must be in the center of our understanding of the work of the Spirit. But a closely related, and often neglected, phase of the Spirit's presence is the process of growth of the individual person—what the Greeks called *paideia*, or the acquisition of culture, and what we, in a more restricted term, speak of as education. Education is a backward-looking as well as a forward-looking task, because it involves the person's interacting with a heritage. It may also be a long and usually painful process. One of Eudora Welty's characters says to herself that it took her till her middle years to know "how deep

9. For a brief interpretation of Whitehead's thought that makes this point explicit, see Michael Welker, "Whiteheads Vergottung der Welt," (with an English summary), pp. 249-272 in Harald Holz and Ernest Wolf-Gazo, eds., *Whitehead and the Idea of Process* (Freiburg: Karl Alber, 1984).

were the complexities of the everyday, of the family, what caves were in the mountains, what blocked chambers, and what crystal rivers that had not yet seen the light."[10] We shall look for the work of the Spirit in the growing awareness of and ability to respond to these complexities, as well as in the larger-scale processes which more obviously shape our common life. In such ways as these we need to expand the post-modern vision.

But the post-modern vision, even in its severe form, has much to teach us as well. Most importantly, we need to confront the way in which the system or network sets limits to our transformation, as Lyotard so clearly portrays the situation. We all know the end to which a self-regulating technological system will bring us—the premature end of life on earth. We rightly affirm a different vision, but our dialogue partner can help us to see the difficulty of the task.

We need not only effort and commitment—though these we need in far greater depth than they are readily visible; we need better clues about what we do. The general line is clear enough. In contrast to the monolithic self-regulating system presented by Lyotard, we need to recognize and activate smaller networks, which can undertake specific tasks, and can give expression to aspects of our humanness as well as a purchase for the transformation of the larger network.

Birch and Cobb see this clearly, and they offer some helpful suggestions. They strive to emphasize decentralization and decision-making by persons who participate in a particular aspect of the life of society. They point out as well the shortcomings of both capitalist and Marxist economics, which are usually taken to be the only alternatives. But decentralized, cooperative economic and social procedures are not doing particularly well in our society. I believe that it is as much because we do not have the theory, the understanding of what will work, as because of social rigidities. To my mind one of the exciting Christian intellectual tasks of today lies exactly at this point. Developing the needed theory is not a uniquely Christian task but one which is particularly appropriate from the point of view of the Christian vision and commitments.

This is the post-modern world, a world of networks of exchange, without an empirical center or a predetermined goal, but a world in which the Spirit is active, leading us toward a more human, less dominative, more liberated life, and a world in which the pressing issues seem to be

10. Ellen Fairchild in Eudora Welty, *Delta Wedding* (New York: Harcourt, Brace, 1945), 157.

largely immanent and practical. What roles does or can Christ play in this post-modern world? Is the specific profile of human meaning—or rather the particular bundle of related profiles of human meaning—that is associated with the image of Christ, valid or important as giving a concrete, historical direction to the activities of the Spirit? We affirm the activity of the Spirit, a Spirit distributed throughout this non-centered post-modern world, a Spirit which is expressed in creativity breaking the established forms so that new expressions may appear, and a Spirit which is also concerned for valuation (not all that is new is good), and which is seen also in the network which sustains and makes possible creative acts. Does this Spirit still need to be associated with Christ?

The Spirit and Christ

Let us address this question by looking backward to the period of Christian origins. Parts of the post-modern perspective will help us to relate what has actually been going on in biblical studies to the theological tradition, which is too often remote from biblical studies.

In the Christian interpretation of faith, Christ is the image around which all aspects of reality come into focus. Early Christianity moved quickly in this direction.[11] In doing so the early church masked the diversity of the ingredients that went into the image, though they were quite right in affirming that the new faith was a new "historical emergent"—in our terms, something that could not possibly have been predicted. Let us first look at the diversity of the ingredients. To do so I have only to refer to the recent re-activation of the history-of-religions studies of early Christianity. A number of important works take the general line of showing how the various liturgical, ethical, and theological aspects of the different forms of early Christianity functioned very similarly to analogous structures in the other faiths of this period, whether Jewish or Hellenistic (itself a distinction that these studies call into question).[12] Somehow these

11. See Reginald Fuller, *The Foundations of New Testament Christology* (New York: Scribner's, 1965).

12. We may cite as examples the work of Hans Dieter Betz on literary forms in the New Testament and that of Wayne A. Meeks on New Testament social organization. See Hans Dieter Betz, *Der Apostel Paulus und die sokratische Tradition: Eine exegetische Untersuchung zu seiner "Apologie" 2 Korinther 10-13*; "Beiträge zur historischen Theologie," 45 (Tübingen: Mohr, 1972); *Galatians: A Commentary on Paul's Letter to the Churches in Galatia*; "Hermeneia"; (Philadelphia: Fortress Press, 1979), and Wayne A. Meeks, *The First Urban Christians: The Social World of the Apostle Paul* (New Haven: Yale University Press, 1983).

micro-elements, when they were put together, effected a major historical emergence, at the center of which was the image of Christ. Thus, moving from our previous discussion, we assert that the Spirit was active in countless micro-events, which were symbolically elevated to major transforming power in the figure of Christ. I call this a "distributive Christology." Of course it is a modification of the old logos Christology.

To clarify, let me draw an analogy to the work of Norman K. Gottwald on the formative period of the Hebrew Scriptures.[13] Gottwald's proposal is that during the Joshua-Judges period the Hebrews established a radically egalitarian society [as far as socio-economic classes were concerned] that stood in sharp contrast to the hierarchical, authoritarian societies of the environing Canaanite culture. The stories of Moses, the Exodus, and the wanderings symbolically present God's establishment of this egalitarian society.[14] The "real" action was in the countless, nameless deeds of courage, resistance, and affirmation of common humanity that took place as the Hebrews forged the alliance of the tribes during the period of the tribal federation. That was where, in our language, the Spirit was at work in the micro-events, though Gottwald himself stays pretty strictly to a critical sociological analysis.[15] In their liturgy and symbolic memory, the activity of the Spirit was transferred from the micro-scale to the macro-scale in the great stories of deliverance.

The analogy to the distributive Christology which is demanded by current study of the New Testament is not exact. Gottwald can concentrate on only one kind of transformation, that toward an egalitarian society. The Hebrew Scriptures are by no means a single-issue collection; but other issues, such as those raised by the book of Job, can be deferred because they come at a later period. In contrast, in the New Testament

---

13. Norman K. Gottwald, *The Tribes of Yahweh: A Sociology of the Religion of Liberated Israel, 1250-1050 B.C.* (Maryknoll, N.Y.: Orbis Books, 1979).

14. Gottwald fully recognizes the formative role of the experiences of the "Moses group," but regards these experiences as preceding the history of Israel and as part of that history "only in the restricted sense that it was the experience of this Moses group, interpreted through its cult of Yahweh, which provided the basic, immediate historical catalyst, the communal forms, and probably a significant part of the repertory of cult symbols and practices for emerging Israel" (*The Tribes of Yahweh*, 38).

15. Walter Brueggemann, in his appreciative review of Gottwald's book, notes that the theologian will ask a range of questions that Gottwald does not address. See Brueggemann's "The Tribes of Yahweh: An Essay Review," *JAAR* 48 (1980), 441-51.

everything is happening at once, so to speak. This means that we have to look for the activity of the Spirit in a number of disparate areas and kinds of activity. The resulting historical process is not a single strand, but a complex interweaving of related trajectories. Mark and John may have had a source in common, but their creativity moves in different directions. Matthew and Luke share a concern for the Christian community, but in different ways. Yet many of the creative acts out of which Christianity emerged were taking place in the work of these writers and their communities. And no matter how far back we go, there are multiple strands. An older model traced them all back to a unity in Jesus. But even in Jesus we see the interweaving of varied strands of creativity. On the one hand, Jesus was a wandering charismatic who challenged the establishment religion and social structure. The cleansing of the Temple and the manner of his death are inescapable clues to this side of his story. Reading Jesus from these clues alone one finds Jesus the liberation preacher—persuasively argued, for instance, by George Pixley.[16] On the other hand, the healings are most naturally understood in the frame of making life more whole in the difficult present. Gerd Theissen notes how unusual it was for Jesus to combine these two worlds.[17] Some readers see the words about non-resistance as the central clue, and find a pacifist Jesus.[18] And the parables as read by Funk, Crossan, and James Breech erase the socio-political concern and deal with the fracturing of the individual person's world to lay her or him open to grace, to the unexpectedness of the gift of life.[19]

No doubt these different phases of Jesus' activity were symbolically united by him around the image of the Kingdom of God. But if we were to treat each one as a language game, they would be as difficult to unify as the modern activities which Lyotard has in mind.

Other aspects of the wider picture are equally well known. If we look in the dynamic of early Christianity for a Spirit of creativity and trans-

---

16. George V. Pixley, *God's Kingdom: A Guide for Biblical Study*, tr. Donald D. Walsh (Maryknoll, NY: Orbis Books, 1981).

17. Gerd Theissen, *The Miracle Stories of the Early Christian Tradition*, tr. John Riches (Philadelphia: Fortress, 1983), 178.

18. See John Howard Yoder, *The Politics of Jesus* (Grand Rapids: Eerdmans, 1972).

19. Robert W. Funk, *Parables and Presence: Forms of the New Testament Tradition* (Philadelphia: Fortress, 1982; John Dominic Crossan, *The Dark Interval: Towards a Theology of Story* (Niles, IL: Argus Communications, 1975); James Breech, *The Silence of Jesus: The Authentic Voice of the Historical Man* (Philadelphia: Fortress, 1983).

formation, which renews motifs from the Hebrew Scriptures and opens itself to aspects of its contemporary culture that can blend with these to open the way for an inclusive, open, humanly interactive society, we shall also recognize the Spirit in parallel forms in Judaism, with which Christianity was often in rather acerbic debate. Not only so, but if we see, for instance, one of the significant aspects of early Christianity to be that it was in good part more open to the full participation of women than were many of the other groups of the period, we shall also recognize the work of the Spirit in those aspects of Hellenistic-Roman society that made it possible for some women to have greater freedom—a locus of the Spirit's activity that has not been given attention in traditional theology.

Thus the early Christian world discloses itself as very like ours. The work of the Spirit is to be seen distributively, for the most part in micro-terms, and for Christians this activity was symbolically united and enlarged in the figure of Christ. To them, Jesus of Nazareth so fully represented the transforming power of God that he was identified with the expected deliverer-figure, the Messiah or Christ; the Christ figure also was elevated to be a focused representation of divine presence and eventually an aspect of divinity. In part because of this focusing and enlarging as a witness to the Spirit's activity, Christianity and the Christ became a major transforming force in the late ancient world—one which on the whole was liberating, though with very uneven results. This judgment can stand only if the creation of a new style of social organization, the Church, is regarded as liberating and humanizing. Despite its rigidity and the loss, for instance, of initial movements toward the liberation of women, and despite the controversies with Judaism and the intramural controversies in the Church, and despite the increasing accommodation to the environment, I would judge that Christ was a powerfully, if unevenly, liberating figure in ancient Christianity. The movement originating with Jesus, gathering a diverse bundle of concerns, giving dignity to the individual person's life both by giving him or her a place in a new social group and by proclaiming the weight of that person's significance before God, became a powerful if flawed renewing force in the ancient world.

Christ in the Post-Modern World

Now we return to the present, and to the meaning of Christ today, in the post-modern world. If it is appropriate to begin, as we did, by looking at the factors in this world that generate hope by thinking in general terms about the activity of the Spirit, what is to be added by focusing on the specific image of Christ or the memory of Jesus? If we find as well that the activity of the Spirit in early Christianity was distributed among many centers and many acts of creativity, which were drawn together into the image of Christ, does this image have sufficient unity to function today?

First, the Spirit is active in many ways which have nothing to do with human language or symbolism. But in those aspects of our life together on this planet which do depend on language and symbolism, the Spirit is mute if it cannot work through appropriate symbols. We are far from being as enclosed in language as some would tell us, yet the Spirit is not free to speak directly to us, at least to our conscious selves.[20] That is, the direct presence of the Spirit in our experiences must be given comprehensible form through language and symbolism before the Spirit's transforming power can be an inspiring part of our conscious, and to a large degree also of our unconscious, life. This is one great reason why the Spirit is not evident to so many today—because the Spirit is in fact mute insofar as no appropriate language is available through which she can speak to us. That does not mean that the Spirit will be without effect, but that we will only dimly apprehend the directions in which the Spirit is leading us. Thus, if the image of Christ can be a vital symbolic focus for the activity of the Spirit, it will be a major gift in dealing with the difficult world which we have sketched. The question is in large measure a pragmatic one: Does this biblically-rooted image still disclose the power of transformation that Christians have previously found in it?

A first answer would be: "Yes, it, along with several others, functions well." To answer this way would be to defuse the well-established Christian tradition of making this decision the sole determining one for the whole structure of one's existence. In a pluralistic world, we do not claim the exclusive presence of the Spirit in Christ that Christians have sometimes affirmed.[21] So one way to answer the question would be, essentially, to cool it: "No big deal; it is a good symbolism: use it when it

20. John Dominic Crossan, as in *The Dark Interval*, has been as eloquent representative of the total limitation of awareness to language. For a critique of this position, see John B. Cobb, Jr., "A Theology of Story: Crossan and Beardslee," in Richard L. Spencer, ed., *Orientation by Disorientation* (Pittsburgh: Pickwick Press, 1980), 151-64.

21. I have suggested earlier that "while most earlier encounters with this figure found an exclusiveness in Christ which insisted that Christ is the center of all meaning, Christ does not today impart the claim to be a universal logos that excludes all meaning which cannot be derived from it." See *A House for Hope: A Study in Process and Biblical Thought* (Philadelphia: Westminster, 1972), 167.

fits, when it is appropriate." There is much value in this approach, even though it runs directly counter to so much of the theology that we have been taught. For many purposes this answer works well. For example, consider the case of Margaret Mead, who gave a great deal of her time to church causes, especially to commissions of the National Council of Churches and the World Council of Churches. This aspect of her career was sketched by Roger Shinn in an article in *Christianity and Crisis* not long after her death.[22] If I were a pastor, I would be working hard to get people to take part in the work of the Church on these terms. Or think of the students who attend seminary to study the ministry, and end up teaching film or being social workers in a hospital. Most of them do not experience these changes as shifts in their fundamental commitment; rather, they have found more effective ways of doing what they are called to do, using symbols that are related to the Christ image but in which Christ is not explicit.

But I expect that the emphasis is usually somewhat different among those whose vocational journey runs the other way. I am thinking of the fact that seminaries everywhere in the United States are receiving a rising percentage of students who have tried some other vocation and then, later, are drawn to the ministry. Such students, I suspect, will be searching to find a more sharply profiled image of Christ, a function for Christ that is not quite so optional.

A way to this more sharply profiled image is to recognize more fully our limits as historical beings. To choose to enter the orbit of the explicit Christ image is to choose a place, not to stand—for we can never simply stand—but a place within which to move. To open oneself to the specific Christ symbolism is to move into the Christian Church. Sometimes this can be in the sense that "this is too valuable to leave to those who want to use it in the wrong way." Elisabeth Schüssler Fiorenza takes this view, in part, in her important books, *In Memory of Her* and *Bread, Not Stone*.[23] To express an open relationship to the Scripture, she calls the Bible a historical prototype, not an eternal archetype.[24] This means that historically

22. Roger L. Shinn, "I Miss You, Margaret Mead," *Christianity and Crisis*, 38 (December 11, 1978), 304-06. Professor Shinn has commented at greater length on Margaret Mead in the March 4, 1985 issue of *Christianity and Crisis*.

23. Elisabeth Schüssler Fiorenza, *In Memory of Her: A Feminist Theological Reconstruction of Christian Origins* (New York: Crossroad, 1983); and *Bread, Not Stone: The Challenge of Feminist Biblical Interpretation* (Boston: Beacon Press, 1984).

24. *Bread, Not Stone*, xvi-xvii.

we come from the story it records, and it tells of the breakthroughs of the work of the Spirit that are foundational for us, but nothing in it is forced upon us literally in its given form. Appropriating our heritage does not have to be the stance only of those for whom this already was a heritage waiting to be appropriated. It can also be adopted by those who find this the path to liberation.

Thus if the cluster of images that we call Christ is to be compelling in the post-modern age, it will be in the context of the particular historical community, the Church, that lives out of that heritage. To affirm the contemporaneity of Christ is to affirm the viability of the Church in at least some one of its lines of development. This does not mean that any form of the Church will be found adequate to express the meaning of Christ, but that unless there is some viable community, the image of Christ will become so diffuse that it will not have significant directing power.[25]

At the same time, we must recognize that Christ has become problematic in a way that I for one could never have anticipated. There are those who find Christ language unwelcome, perhaps even unacceptable, because the term "Christ," midway between "Jesus" and "God," tends to impart male gender to God (or at least to one person of the Trinity), through Jesus' having been male. We have to listen seriously to this kind of rejection of our traditional language and to the proposal that we not speak of Christ but only of the Spirit and Jesus. This practice would inevitably entail some loss, and this revision of our vocabulary would, in the foreseeable future, probably be only one form of Christian speech. But it might be an important linguistic venture. Thus I am suggesting that even those who are drawn by the Spirit to the cluster of meaning that we call Christ might cast about for another way of speaking about this meaning.

So far the discussion of the contemporary meaning of Christ has been cast in pragmatic terms: What would or does the image of Christ do for us? I see this as an appropriate way into the question. After all, if

---

25. This assertion does not overlook the presence of a Christ image in our culture that is effective outside the bounds of the recognizable Church; see the discussion in John B. Cobb, Jr., *Christ in a Pluralistic Age* (Philadelphia: Westminster, 1975), ch. 1. But the specific traits of this image that derive from the New Testament will easily assume quite different functions while retaining the form given by their history. Thus the "Christ Figure" in literature may be put to ends that are unrelated to its original function; see Theodore Ziolkowski, *Fictional Transfigurations of Jesus* (Princeton: Princeton University Press, 1972).

Christ were to be experienced as repressive, one would not want to remain bound to Christ, and that has been the experience of many modern people. I have tried to sketch the broad outlines of a way of opening oneself to the Spirit of God at work in the story that comes from Jesus, that is, a way of opening oneself to Christ that is freeing and hope-giving in that it brings together both those elements of challenge (and even, as we saw earlier, outrage) and those elements of sustenance and flexible structure which nurture community and human transformation. A Christian community focused upon and living from this mode of presence of the Spirit can and (I will venture to say) will be a strong factor in the seeking and finding of those patterns that will resist the technological cybernetization of life, encourage cooperative ventures and smaller networks within the overall society, and help to reconstitute the story of our common life in such a way that it gives up its imperialistic claims, whether of tribe or nation or religious group, as well as its imperialistic claims upon the fabric of the earth, and opens the way to seek common values or at least coordinated values within the human community.

But we cannot leave the question with a simply pragmatic evaluation. One of the perennial meanings of the figure of Christ has been the way in which it has led people to reach beyond a simply pragmatic assessment of their lives. To illustrate, let us think of the two central actions in the story of Jesus, for these give us an entry into aspects of God's dealing with the world which we can glimpse even if we cannot wholly comprehend them. I am speaking, of course, of the cross and resurrection. These actions, the climax of the story of Jesus, have repeatedly shown their power of opening to us dimensions that are beyond our daily common concerns, and these dimensions can make a tremendous difference in how we engage in those daily concerns, even though we do not come to these actions for pragmatic reasons.

First, Easter and the story of the resurrection of Jesus tell us that our commitment to hope has a dimension that reaches beyond whatever community could be built in our human society. Our deepest insight into the meaning of this hope is open to us in our care for another human being. As Gabriel Marcel put it, "To love a being is to say, 'Thou shalt not die.'"[26] This other matters! And matters to God! The resurrection story implies that the existence of the person is received—in some other

26. Gabriel Marcel, *The Mystery of Being* (Chicago: Henry Regnery, 1959), 153.

form—into God's presence. It may be that Whitehead's doctrine of the preservation of experience in the consequent nature of God is the adequate expression of this faith in our time. However, I believe that the traditional view, that God empowers our existences to continue in some form of new life after death, is one of those glimpses that faith affords us, and I do not see this faith as escapist, but as empowering action on behalf of immeasurably precious beings.[27] I am not impressed by the efforts to offer evidence of communication with those who have died, nor do I offer this faith as a remedy to the injustices of the world. I believe that the resurrection of Jesus was affirmed in faith by those whose lives were deeply sensitized to the guidance of God's Spirit by their association with Jesus and by the traumatic experience of his death; and just as then, this faith opens one to the worth and dignity of human life, which is capable of such a transformation into the presence of God.

If the resurrection helps us to affirm the profound worth of the person, who matters to God, the crucifixion story works the other way around, and gives us a glimpse of the opposite insight, that persons exist in a web of relationships which may call for going beyond the wholeness of the person. We could explore this from the point of view of self-transcendence, and say with Martin J. Buss that "self transcendence is an integral part of selfhood," or in simple language that giving and commitment to others is the way of life.[28] I believe this, though I also recognize the justified protests which are made when the emphasis on self-sacrificial self-transcendence is loaded upon a particular part of the community, say, on women.

But I want to make a different point, which is that the cross of Jesus Christ opens our eyes to the way in which something other than the pragmatic question is of final concern. To make the point, and to make it for those who believe strongly that faith leads to wholeness, let me (with perhaps a touch of the outrageous) quote from a great anti-modern, John Henry Newman: "There are wounds of the spirit which never close, and are intended in God's mercy to bring us ever nearer to him, and to prevent us from leaving him, by their very perpetuity."[29] If the resurrection shows us the infinite worth of the other, the crucifixion gives us a glimpse

27. I have presented this view in more detail in *A House for Hope*, ch. 7.

28. See Martin J. Buss, "Self-Theory and Theology," *JR*, 45 (1965), 46-53. The quotation in the text comes from a personal communication.

29. I have not been able to locate the reference for this quotation from Newman.

of something which transforms without removing our difficulties. Let me close with a commentary on this particular Christian imagery by quoting from a great Jewish interpreter of the Hebrew Scriptures, Martin Buber. He rendered the words of the Lord to Moses in Exodus 3:14 in this way: "I shall be there as I shall be there."[30] So, even in the cross, "I shall be there as I shall be there, even there."[31]

30. Will Herberg, ed., *The Writings of Martin Buber* (New York: Macmillan, 1958), 261.

31. In slightly different form this paper was presented as the Ernest Cadman Colwell Lecture at the School of Theology at Claremont, April 8, 1985.

- 16 -

Vital Ruins
Biblical Narrative
and the Story Frameworks of Our Lives

Conflicting Views of Stories

We are at an awkward impasse today in how we think about stories. On the one hand, in the construction of our personal lives, we use and need stories. We enter into them with imagination, and we find in them our most powerful route to moral values, as Robert Coles has reminded us in *The Call of Stories*.[1] Yet at the same time traditional story-patterns are being sharply challenged. Much of the literature on narrative shows us how contrived stories are, and how difficult it is to relate them to a larger world beyond the story. Equally challenging to the traditional function of stories is the distance which so many sense today between what I call the orienting stories of our culture and the experience of our time. The actual history of our century has been so chaotic and terrible that it is not possible to fit it into a traditional story pattern—at least, this is not easily possible. And apart from this, many of the ways in which we think today have no room for a story, in which the past lives in memory and in the expectation which memory creates, and in which the future beckons with the possibility of fulfillment yet at the same time with a deep sense of the precariousness of the outcome. Vast tracts of our understanding work with a pattern of a firm line of cause-and-effect, predictable but with no place for choice or for the drama of a story. Within the world of traditional scientific description, there is no place for narrative. The result is that if we are able to affirm our freedom, it is all too often a freedom

From *Southern Humanities Review* 24 (1990), 101-116.

1. Robert Coles, *The Call of Stories: Teaching and the Moral Imagination* (Boston: Houghton Mifflin Company, 1989).

which is cut off from the rest of the world so that it becomes a private venture.

So we face a situation in which there is an increasingly rich literature which helps us understand what narrative is and how the successive steps in a narrative are connected to one another; how our imagination expands the narrative which is actually related in words so that we can picture the whole story to ourselves, both the parts of the story that are actually told in the narrative and the "blanks" which we have to fill in; and how narratives are generated by tensions among the basic values which they express. We have never had so full an analysis of stories with which to work. Yet on the other hand, never have we so persuasively been told that stories are purely artifacts of the imagination, that they do not refer to anything beyond themselves, other than other language patterns, and that the coherence of life that stories create has nothing to do with "real life," which is aimless and without any pattern except that which we imagine for it. I believe that this separation between the imaginatively created story and our experience of daily life represents a severe impoverishment of our lives, and weakens our ability to become engaged in life. At the same time, the way in which scholars interpret narrative to us is thoroughly honest, and reflects not just the specific scholarly techniques, let us say of literary or structural analysis, but is also a clear statement about the lack of narrative pattern that we perceive in the world today.

Stories as Frameworks for Life

I hope that what I have to say will be in touch with the scholarly discussion of narrative. But I shall talk instead about how we use stories, what they mean to us. As Coles sees so clearly, one of the basic functions of stories is to place us in a larger world. I can put it that we see our own little story as part of a big story. This is one of the principal ways in which we find our identity, discover who we are. We are our stories. As a younger person finds a role model, usually in an older person, it is the story that you see in that other life that becomes a model for the story which you hope to see in your life. And the person who, consciously or unconsciously, becomes a role model is important because she or he represents a larger story. Through this other person you find that your little story can be part of an overarching story that gives it meaning beyond the moment.

We can understand our lives as coherent, so that what we have done and what has happened to us means something to our present life and points to a future, first, if our life feels like a story, in which memory and expectation give meaning to the present, and second, if our own life belongs to a larger story which has its own coherence, which makes sense of its past and its expectation. Stories are different from simple accounts of mere happenings, because stories embody *values*; even when a story does not come out in the way we hope it will, it puts things together by putting values on the things that happen in it. Stories are the great bearers of value in our culture, and, I dare say, in virtually any culture. Our finding ourselves in a story is a principal way of affirming the values that we believe in.

This ancient pattern of finding oneself by finding one's place in a story, in my own little story which, in turn, fits into a larger story, is still very much alive. Yet it is also extremely problematic. What *is* the larger story which gives meaning to my life, and to yours? On the one hand, it has to be the story of the society in which we live; on the other hand, in the past a still more overarching story has given meaning to the course of events in our society. In our tradition, it was above all the Bible which provided the larger story, even for those who had distanced themselves from the communities of faith which adhered to the Bible as authoritative. The interplay between a comprehensive, overarching orienting story and the little stories of individual people is very clear in the Bible. And the influence of its narrative patterns is still very strong even in our secularized culture, as well as in the Jewish and Christian communities of faith. We can well reflect about the biblical story and its influence on our own time, as a way of thinking about how viable "story" still is as an orienting framework for today. As we do so, I will not be unmindful of the extremely suggestive work on the forms of biblical narrative, such as that of Robert Alter and Meir Sternberg on the Hebrew Scriptures, or Robert W. Funk, Hendrikus Boers, and James Dawsey on the New Testament.[2] Yet our emphasis will be on how story functions to help us orient ourselves to life.

---

2. Robert Alter, *The Art of Biblical Narrative* (New York: Basic Books, 1981); Meir Sternberg, *The Poetics of Biblical Narrative: Ideological Literature and the Drama of Reading* (Bloomington: Indiana University Press, 1985); Robert W. Funk, *The Poetics of Biblical Narrative* (Sonoma: Polebridge Press, 1988); Hendrikus W. Boers, *Neither on This Mountain Nor in Jerusalem: A Study of John 4* (Atlanta: Scholars Press, 1988); James M. Dawsey, *The Lukan Voice: Confusion and Irony in the Gospel of Luke* (Macon: Mercer University Press, 1986).

Reading the Biblical Story

As we have learned to read it, for all its variety the Bible told a coherent story, the story of the human venture under the guidance of God. It was a rebellious story, a story of failure and loss, but one in which God never gave up, leading God's people through the wilderness, giving them a kingdom, sending them prophets, bringing them back from exile, and, finally, despite all the human fractiousness which in the crisis led to the crucifixion, sending God's Messiah to bring God and human beings together, an event which formed the hinge of history and provided a base point for interpreting all history after that time—a history which, on the one hand, was to be taken seriously in its own right, and, on the other hand, was to be lived through by you and me in expectation, in preparation for the final consummation and triumphant achievement of God's purpose as we already glimpsed it in Christ.

Augustine's formulation of this story, typical for the ancient church, strongly emphasized the need for those who stood within God's story to separate themselves from another, downward-moving story, and make the choice for the City of God. The Augustinian version with its strong emphasis on a single true story line, to belong to which one had to make an unequivocal decision against a competing story line, has been typical of most Christian telling of our story since that time.

A modern version of this classic way of reading the Bible, more inclusive and less judgmental than Augustine's, can be found in C. H. Dodd's *The Bible Today*, a book which I used many times in the early years of my teaching.[3] Dodd is particularly good at showing how the overall drama of the Bible as I sketched it above was built into the sensibility of our Western culture, for instance as the tale was illustrated in the stained glass windows of medieval cathedrals, with the prophets marching down one side and the apostles up the other, and also in showing how the overarching drama became, as he put it somewhat patriarchally, the drama of Everyman, as you and I recapitulate the big story in our little stories. Dodd's book is so good because it expresses so clearly what has been the prevailing story pattern which we read in the Bible, a pattern which has shaped how we think and feel about finding our place in reality through story.

---

3. C. H. Dodd, *The Bible Today* (Cambridge: Cambridge University Press, 1946).

Tensions in the Biblical Story

It was never easy to join oneself to the biblical story. For one thing, the story as the Bible tells it never corresponded very well to life. Life was often much more disorderly than the story. Probably the classic example of this tension is the so-called Deuteronomic history, which, in 1 and 2 Kings, resolves the tumultuous history of the two Hebrew monarchies into a relatively simple pattern according to which when they obeyed, things went well with them, and when they disobeyed, things went badly. Usually they disobeyed: "I will cast off the remnant of my heritage, and give them into the hand of their enemies, they shall become a prey and a spoil to all their enemies, because they have done what is evil in my sight and have provoked me to anger, since the day their ancestors came out of Egypt, even to this day" (2 Kings 21:14-15).

So on the one hand, the orienting story was a better story than daily experience—better in the sense that it was better-ordered morally. But biblical writers were strongly at odds on this point. In one of the Psalms we read, "I have been young, and now am old; yet I have not seen the righteous forsaken or their children begging bread" (Psalm 37:25). Other psalms and the whole book of Job express a bitter protest against this optimism about how well the big story of God's purpose and the little story of my life correspond. Of course, that stories are more orderly, more predictable than daily experience is one of the principal points of scholarly study of stories today.

But there was another, quite different problem as well. If the stories by which the biblical people oriented themselves were, so to speak, better, more moral, than life as experienced, on the other hand, from a moral point of view, biblical writers constantly remind us that the stories on which people relied were worse than they ought to be. The prophets especially repeatedly reminded their hearers that their story was too small, that the story to which they had joined themselves had to be revised to expand their vision beyond where they were. Amos astonished his hearers by reporting Yahweh as saying, "Did I not bring Israel up from the land of Egypt, and the Philistines from Caphtor, and the Arameans from Kir?" (Amos 9:7). Isaiah tells his hearers that the destructive power of the great empire, Assyria, is an agent of Yahweh's justice (Isa 10:5-11). The call for an enlarged vision of the story reaches a high point in the vision of the so-called II Isaiah, that the story of God would expand to the point that

God would bring salvation not only to God's people but to the "the end of the earth" (Isa 49:6).

Both of these points of stress on the orienting story are still very much alive, whether we are thinking of religious people who still live by the biblical story, or of the secularized echoes of the biblical story which are still so potent in the imagination of the people of the United States. How easily we imagine that the story of our country ought to go smoothly because we are such a good country; how baffled we are when we find that we may be coming to the end of the period when things go well for us as a nation! And we are even more deeply baffled to sense that this country is not uniquely gifted by divine purpose, but is only one of many countries, all of which have equal claims to "life, liberty, and the pursuit of happiness." Just as in biblical days, we need an orienting story against which we can discover ourselves, and we tend to think of the orienting story as established and adequate. We are disturbed when we find that the story does not work very well or when we sense that the values which it expresses are all too meager. We are reminded, just as biblical people were, that we cannot simply accept an orienting story, but also have to be critical of it.

Orienting and Disorienting Stories

But there is more. Among students of the Bible, a great deal of attention has been given to stories which disorient rather than orient the person who enters into them. Of course the classic stories of this kind are the parables of Jesus as they are commonly interpreted today. The parable of the Good Samaritan is a classic example. John Dominic Crossan sums up his interpretation of this parable as follows: "The point is not that one should help the neighbor in need. . . . But when good (clerics) and bad (Samaritan) become, respectively, bad and good, a world is being challenged and we are faced with polar reversal."[4] Now the position is reversed: instead of functioning as an overarching story which enables us to be integrated into a larger reality, the parable deals with us by breaking up the larger world to which we think we belong, for the sake of giving us a glimpse of a more profound reality than the overarching story has been able to embody. As I put it elsewhere, speaking of John Dominic Crossan's interpretation of the parables,

---

4. John Dominic Crossan, *In Parables: The Challenge of the Historical Jesus* (New York: Harper & Row, 1973), 64.

> The world in which the hearer lives must be broken for the hearer to have the possibility, the momentary opportunity, to glimpse the ultimate, the mystery of God. Crossan describes this basic process of coming to insight in the following way: the seeming naturalness of a parable compels a hearer's assent and leads into involvement in the story, only then to shock the hearer with the discovery that to give assent to the story necessitates abandoning the vision of the world the hearer originally brought to the event. Radical judgment and the possibility of redemption can suddenly but momentarily be glimpsed.[5]

Even Crossan would not force all of the parables into one pattern, but this is the model function of a parable, in his view and in that of many of our best interpreters. Many of Crossan's points were actually first formulated by Robert W. Funk.[6] Though through the centuries the parables of Jesus were usually interpreted more as illustrations of parts of the overall orienting Christian story, it is of great significance that the parables as a counterpoint to, or even a contradiction of, the orienting story is widely regarded today as the more appropriate way to view them. This tells us something about the time in which we live as well as about the parables.[7] What it tells us about orienting stories is that they are not self-sufficient. They are under strain because the are "too good to be true," and because on the other hand they are too exclusive to be true, as noted above. In addition, and most profoundly, the orienting story needs to be challenged and reoriented by the disorienting story, which reminds us that we miss the deepest insight when everything is too neatly organized into a story.

Doing Without Stories in Biblical Interpretation

Of course the problematic of stories in the Bible has been noticed by students of the Bible for a long time. All along there have been interpreters who spoke for the orienting story, like C. H. Dodd whom I mentioned, or Oscar Cullmann, whose work strongly emphasized Christ as

---

5. See above, pp. 52-53. See John Dominic Crossan, *In Parables*, and *The Dark Interval: Towards a Theology of Story* (Allen, TX: Argus Communications, 1975).

6. Robert W. Funk, *Language, Hermeneutic, and Word of God* (New York: Harper & Row, 1964); *Parables and Presence: Forms of the New Testament Tradition* (Philadelphia: Fortress Press, 1982).

7. Something like what I have sketched as the function of the parable in the message of Jesus is an important factor in the decisions of the "Jesus Seminar" about which parables of Jesus are authentic. See Robert W. Funk, Bernard Brandon Scott, and James R. Butts, eds., *The Parables of Jesus: Red Letter Edition: A Report of the Jesus Seminar* (Sonoma: Polebridge Press, 1988).

the central point in historical time.[8] But the most important New Testament scholar of the twentieth century saw the difficulties of biblical narrative clearly and cut the Gordian knot by eliminating narrative or story from the heart of the New Testament message. Rudolph Bultmann, in a series of works, offered a sharply different view of our experience of time. For him, the influence of the past was known precisely in the rigid determination of cause-and-effect. Past, including the past of the religious tradition, is imprisoning rather than liberating. And we would relate wrongly to the future if we tried to know it, for knowing would be a form of controlling, and we would not be truly open to the future. Since we cannot grasp God in the past or future, we cannot speak directly of God, but only of our response to God.[9]

Thus real life, authentic life, condenses into the present moment. There is no more story to faith, only the moment, for that is where we are free. For Bultmann the classic moment was the moment of encountering the proclamation of the Christian faith, but the same encounter could take place in meeting a fellow human being. Bultmann's reformulation of the biblical tradition was a powerful response to the loss of narrative meaning in the Europe of his time. His reading of the New Testament found so widespread and vigorous a response precisely because what he saw in the New Testament corresponded to the loss of story that people found in their own lives and in the wider social life of the time.

A Fresh Look at the Biblical Story

If the overarching biblical story framework which had traditionally given shape to the lives of countless "little stories" was already in ruins in the 1920's, as Rudolph Bultmann believed, how does it stand today? To speak to this question we should first go back to the traditional biblical story itself, and look at it a little more closely, and then return to our perception of the time in which we live and to the question whether our own time can and does have a story.

---

8. Oscar Cullmann, *Christ and Time: The Primitive Christian Conception of Time and History*, tr. Floyd V. Filson (Philadelphia: Westminster Press, 1950).

9. Among the many writings of Rudolph Bultmann, the following is particularly clear on the points made in this essay: "The Historicity of Man and Faith," pp. 92-110 in *Existence and Faith: Shorter Writings of Rudolph Bultmann*; tr. and ed. by Schubert M. Ogden (New York: Living Age Books, 1960). See also "The Meaning of God as Acting," pp. 60-85 in *Jesus Christ and Mythology* (New York: Scribner's, 1958).

The overarching biblical story is far from the unity which it has appeared to be. I have noted some of the ways in which it has always been questioned from within the biblical tradition. Critics of the traditional story like Bultmann were quick to point out that a prime difficulty in the "sacred history" approach to the Bible is that we cannot know how the end will turn out beforehand. If our common life has an element of true freedom in it, then even God cannot determine the outcome. The tension between human freedom and divine determination that this comment reflects is well known within the Bible itself, and this tension can be seen in the contrast between two basic components of the biblical story.

"Covenant" as a Foundational Story-Image

The contrast is between two images of "covenant." The covenant provides a foundation for the story and continuity between the moments of time in the people's experience. A covenant is an agreement. But the biblical covenant is not an agreement between equals. God is imaged as a great ruler who graciously extends favor to a lesser one. In response to the gift of the goodness of the unimaginably great God, the people respond in thankfulness and accept the pattern of life embodied in the claims of God. Thus the response to the covenant includes two moments: the moment of venture, moving into a new future opened by the covenant, and the moment of obedience, following the rules which attempt to specify what God's requirement are.

As time passed, Hebrew thinking about covenant developed in two parallel streams, which existed in uneasy alliance. The distinction between these two understandings of covenant has been most clearly drawn by J. Coert Rylaarsdam.[10] On the one hand, the covenant with Israel joined God's promises with the claim for obedience in a way that left the future open; it was clear that if they failed to respond, there was no assurance about how the future would turn out. This covenant, as I put it elsewhere, ". . . promised nothing beyond what could be given in the spatio-temporal world, and, equally important, its promises were joined to requirements; grace and demand were inextricably interwoven. . . ." But around the figure of David another covenant image developed, which included the unequivocal promise that God would provide a successor on David's throne perpetually—regardless of how the ruler or the people

10. J. Coert Rylaarsdam, "The Two Covenants and the Dilemmas of Christology," *Journal of Ecumenical Studies* 9 (1972), 249-270.

behaved. "The covenant with David, in contrast, was static rather than historical; it was absolute, and its absoluteness forced those who used its symbolism to project a future beyond this historical world, where its promises could be realized."[11] No doubt the covenant with David was very reassuring in chaotic times in Hebrew history, especially after the collapse of the monarchy. It embodied the affirmation that in spite of all, the promise of God will not be lost, and this affirmation is very important to faith. But the negative side was that the determinate form of the promise devalued the human response. The good end would, eventually, come whatever people did. Such thinking is all too evident still today. For instance, when we hear that God would not let us destroy ourselves with atomic bombs, we are hearing echoes of the covenant with David. It seems that the imagery of the covenant with David was central in the process which brought about the fixed and definite end to the biblical story—that is, this covenant imagery was an important ingredient in apocalyptic, the vision of a new world which would right the wrongs of this one. In turn, this apocalyptic imagery was central in the development of Christian symbolism for Christ. Most of what is problematic in the traditional Christian story is related to the focus on a single story line and on a predetermined end that we find in the covenant with David symbolism. The open-ended covenant with Israel symbolism can be adapted to suggest a story which is improvisatory, in which the outcome derives from the interplay of several forces, including the actual past and the surrounding events, the decisions of the people, and the influence of God.

Story Frameworks for Life Today

The discussion of biblical narrative, its different forms and its possibilities for theological interpretation, is not just a conversation among specialists. For, though I have said that the path of finding oneself by finding one's story is still very much alive, the same tensions between orienting story and disorienting story, and the same limitations of the orienting story that are suggested above for the biblical narrative are very much live options today not only among religious people, but equally among those whose orienting story, though derived from the biblical tradition at least in part, has been recast in contemporary political or social images. And there are many who are trying not to identify with any

11. See above, p. 142.

story—this is, after all, the stance of the whole existentialist way of interpreting life.

A character in Wim Wenders' film, *Wings of Desire*, says, "I don't belong in any story. And I like it that way. I'm free."[12] The barren, wasted scene in which she makes the statement strengthens the point. Another figure in the film is the wise old storyteller who reappears from time to time in the sequences; the point of his appearance is that no one listens to him or needs him. The film presents a world without stories, and even though the conclusion shows the young woman who denied that she belonged to a story joining with an angel-turned-human-being to create, so to speak, the story of their life together, none the less, this intimate story is wholly fragile and not in any way supported by the fragmented world which the film has presented. The suggestion that the only way to affirm one's freedom is to stay out of a story points to one of the central issues which we shall discuss below. Moments, at best fragments of stories, are where life is real, we are hearing. This vision of life is derived from the existentialism which Bultmann represented, but it is very different in that for Bultmann there was a centered self, and responsible decision was the only really human way to be, while what we are seeing and hearing today views the self as fractured, as a group of nodes of interaction; the different responses are not integrally related to one another. Not only is there no long-range purposiveness; instead of serious decision we are called to play, to wander without any purpose.[13] This philosophy of religion makes a valid critique of the rigid truth-claims and rigid ethical standards of much traditional faith, but its abandonment of purposiveness is not the creative direction in which to move.

The puzzle and disarray of story telling and narrative in biblical studies and in our own journeys through life are closely interwoven. We have to be honest to say that in the face of the disorders of our time, it is understandable that many think that we can no longer speak of an overarching story which gives meaning to our little stories. And it is also true that many have rejected the traditional stories because they find them repressive. At best, on this view, what lies behind our own personal stories and the narratives that we tell to cast light on them, is a set of values to which we have committed ourselves, but these are values which

12. I cite the script from memory.

13. As in Mark C. Taylor, *Erring: A Postmodern A/theology* (Chicago: University of Chicago Press, 1981).

we affirm without expecting them to have consequences in an actual story.

Finding a More Adequate Model of the World
Reality as Events

Without trying to evade the harsh events which have destroyed the shape of the traditional orienting stories, and recognizing that we have often told them in ways that made them repressive, it is important to try to see other reasons why narrative has not been valued. In pre-modern times it appeared that the world and human experience were of the same sort. We have feelings; it was appropriate to think not only of animals and trees as having feelings, but even of rocks and mountains. Modern thinking separated human beings from the rest of the creation, above all by supposing that human beings were the unique possessors of a mental life or spiritual life. Things or even, according to some thinkers, other living beings had no mental life. This is "substance thinking." What is most real in us, however elusive it may be, is mind or mental substance, while physical substances compose the rest of reality.

Thinking about the world as if it were made up of physical substances has worked so well for describing the mechanical aspects of our world, that many people have come to believe that this is the way to deal with "reality." It has not worked so well to think of ourselves as "minds," because then we have to deal with the stubborn fact that we are also more than minds. But at least the dualistic division between physical substances and mental substances did leave a place in the mechanical world for there to be also mental life. This view has not been so friendly to religious belief. The mechanical world seems to get along very well without God—although originally the mechanical way was developed by devoutly religious people who wrongly believed that they were glorifying God by denying that there is any other creative power at work in the world.[14] Substance thinking is so deeply ingrained in our imaginations that it is hard for us to escape it. And substance thinking is not friendly to story, for physical substances seem to react purely in a mechanical, cause-and-effect way, and mental substances, while they may have their private adventures, are hard to bring into the interactive, public world.

---

14. See David R. Griffin, "Introduction: The Reenchantment of Science," pp. 1-46 in David R. Griffin, ed., *The Reenchantment of Science: Postmodern Proposals* (Albany: State University of New York Press, 1988).

There is another way to think of reality, which opens the way to connecting the imaginative, dramatic world of story to the public world. That is to think of reality as events rather than as substances. What is real is the event of experience. There is no continuing "thing" that experiences—the experience is the event, the reality. It is, of course, a momentary reality, which gives way to a succeeding moment of experience. Events can be related to one another in ways that substances cannot. For a substance cannot act upon the inner constitution of another substance. It will simply act upon it externally, as in the classic physical laws of motion, in which motion is imparted from one object to another without changing the objects in any other way. If what is real, however, is a series of events, each of which receives the data of its past as constitutive but not as wholly determinative, and if the event organizes these data from the past into a new experience, which in its turn becomes a datum for further experiences, we have a model which makes room for the basic ingredients of story. Events do not have to display the continuity-in-change that is familiar to us in narrative, in which the constancy of some elements ties moment to moment, while new elements provide the change and drama—but they may be organized in this way. Indeed, it is our profound experience that there is such a dramatic continuity in our lives that provides a basic clue to the event-character of experience.

Increasingly the mechanical model is being found to be less and less adequate to a careful description of reality, even though it works well for many rough approximations. Though I am no expert here, and though when we move in this direction we may be challenged to deal with phenomena which we have been accustomed to dismiss as aberrations, there are many and strong reasons for moving beyond the mechanical substance model not only for the human story, but for all of our thinking. To do so would make possible a rapprochement among fields of imagination and thought which have fallen lamentably apart.

Internal Relations

Three dimensions of the event-model for reality are especially important for understanding life as a story. The first of these is that in the event model, the relations among events are not merely the external pressures of one event upon another, but are relations by which one event takes the elements of preceding events into itself as the data out of which it constitutes itself. In other words, the relations among events include internal relations, and not merely external ones. This is how relations feel in stories. They feel that way because that is how relations actually are—despite the narrow, external description of relations which has characterized so much of modern thought.[15]

Experience Includes Experience of Value

The second aspect of the event-model to which I wish to call attention is that on this model, experience is actually experience of value. From Kant on, most Western thinkers have supposed that values are attributed to the data of our experience by our own mental processes. Event-thinking recasts the model of experience to affirm that we experience values which are actually in the data which are available to make up a moment of experience. The components of the world have value to themselves, and not just to us. This insight of many writers on nature and of the whole ecological movement can be seen not to be a human imposition on the world, but a reflection of how things are. We are not the only center of value! We engage ourselves not only with other human beings, but with all that we encounter, with respect for the value of what we meet. This is not to say that the values of which we are conscious are read directly out of experience. Obviously it is not that simple. We do have direct experience of the world, prior to its being shaped by the forms of our consciousness. But the clear and conscious experience which has provided the model for experience in most modern thought is a derived, secondary form of experience. The values which we entertain uncritically are social constructions and have to be evaluated and criticized. But one ingredient in these values is indeed the values which are communicated to us by our direct experience, and it is possible to become more attentive to these values if we discipline ourselves to do so. We may add that from the point of view which I represent, we experience not only a group of often conflicting values, but also the central source of value, God, who offers to each experience an aim in which relevant values are coordinated.

Experience as Experience of a Network of Stories

The third point is that experience is always of a complex network of relationships. Narrative highlights one tract of experience, but others are

---

15. On internal relations, see Charles Birch and John B. Cobb, Jr., *The Liberation of Life: From the Cell to the Community* (Cambridge: Cambridge University Press, 1981), esp. 104-105. The whole book could be described as a sustained effort to reconceive reality on a model of internal relations.

always there, enriching or impoverishing the one that the story highlights. It may, indeed, be the case that in some of its aspects the biblical narrative overemphasizes the basic tendency of story to concentrate on one single line of experience. But at least some biblical writers are well aware of this danger, as I noted above in commenting on the problematic tendency of the overarching story to be narrow and exclusive.

Not Just the Human Story

For our thinking today it is important to draw a conclusion that has often been overlooked: the overarching story to which we can commit ourselves is not just the human story. Our reading of the Bible has almost always focused strictly on the story of God's purpose with human beings. That is rightly central, but the wider story is the story of God's purpose for all the creation. There is ample resource in the Bible for reading the story in this wider way. For instance, the Psalms and the wisdom literature often express a sense of the beauty and integrity of the natural world, a beauty which God enjoys, and which creates the responsibility for human beings to use this world with care and appreciation. In Proverbs 8, wisdom rejoices in the whole creation as God creates it, and not just in humankind (though she does rejoice in that); in Psalm 65 God's sustaining presence in the process of nature is celebrated.[16] These are only illustrations of a new style of recovering the overarching story that is required if such a vision is to speak to us today. It will also be of fundamental importance to learn from other traditions that have been more sensitive to the value of the earth than our city-oriented Christian tradition has usually been. Native American religion is has much to teach us here.[17] Such an ecological model is a natural outcome of an event-model of reality, for events are comprehensive unifications of experience that bring together the mental and physical poles of every event.

Life in a Network of Stories

Many students, both of the Bible and of narrative in general, have told us that we should abandon the traditional pattern of trying to struc-

16. For a study of biblical thinking about the earth, see Richard Cartwright Austin, *Hope for the Earth: Nature and the Bible*; "Environmental Theology," 3 (Atlanta: John Knox Press, 1988).

17. See, for instance, Jamake Highwater, *The Primal Mind: Vision and Reality in Indian America* (New York: New American Library, 1981).

ture our little story by relating it to an overarching story. Many of the reasons for this judgment are strong. The traditional overarching stories embody power claims that were uncritically accepted; that is to say, they were to some extent at least stories that undergirded ideologies. These stories, both the traditional biblical one and the social and national stories that were in good part derived from the biblical story, all too easily promised a happy ending to the chosen few. And the experience of our time has been unfriendly to the larger story patterns. It is not too much to say that the patterns given to us by the biblical narratives are in ruins.

Some of our best biblical scholars have reacted by focusing on the disorienting story, as I noted above. They tell us that it is only when the structure in which we feel at home is broken, that we may briefly glimpse at least that there is something "more," something beyond, even if we cannot say what that "more" or "beyond" is. I take the need for disruptive stories very seriously, and in my own work I have given some attention to how they work.[18] We do indeed need to have the familiar patterns broken, and we are indebted to scholars like Funk and Crossan who have recovered this dimension of the message of Jesus. But the sounder pattern is the alternation between orienting and disorienting story, which helps to keep the orienting story from becoming sterile, and this pattern has ample biblical basis.

The criticism of the traditional Christian story, that it is too exclusive, is well taken. All too often those of us who stand in this tradition have assumed that the deeper meaning of life was exhaustively presented in this story. The event-model of reality will remind us that, though we inevitably have a limited perspective, and though in faith we choose to explore the possibilities of a specific tradition such as the Christian one, we are actually continually in interaction with many lines of story, and we will be on a wiser and truer course if we are attentive to how these may enrich the tradition in which we stand. We should remember that this kind of self-criticism of the biblical and Christian tradition is actually an integral part of the tradition itself. Its ability to be self-critical is one of its great strengths.

While some very thoughtful interpreters of religion understand the interaction of different stories to be a matter of finding deep common elements in them, this route has a great possibility of losing the strongest distinctive contributions of the different traditions. It may be precisely what

18. See above, chapter 4.

is not in my tradition that is most valuable to me in another one; and it may also be that some elements of my tradition that are very familiar to me, and possibly in part overlooked, are of greatest value for the interaction of traditions. There are, indeed, common elements in very different religious traditions, and we may discover and celebrate these. But the deepest learning will take place as we affirm our basic insights in contrast to what the other tradition has to teach us, and learn to transform our vision so that it may include that new without losing what we already affirm.

But it is a different matter to say that we are to live without an orienting story. If one reads those who make this claim attentively, one often sees remnants of an orienting story despite their disclaimers. It is usually a story of the cry or the movement toward social justice, but the abuses of the available forms of the story of human liberation have rightly made these critics draw back from either the Marxist story or the Christian story in their traditional forms.

The response which will enable us fully to become engaged in life is not to abandon the quest for an overarching story, but to work to recast the story imaginatively so that it may be both more inclusive and more honest to life as we experience it. But honest does not have to mean reductive or cynical. We can no longer honestly affirm that either we or God knows how the story will end. And we recognize that the total story includes terrible loss and waste. But an adequate story will show how creative possibilities may be expressed. Its openness will not be the randomness of some forms of post-modern "wandering," but openness to the transformative possibilities that we can both find and make. This kind of openness is as deeply built into the biblical tradition as is the grasping at a definite promised end that was so marked a characteristic of the traditional way of telling the story. To put it differently, there will always be times when an adequate orienting story challenges us to believe in possibilities that seem too good to be true. While one of the functions of such a story is to enable us to feel at home in the world, this function must stay in balance with the other one, of promising us that things can be better than we have found out how to make them. This may turn into escapist thinking, but it does not have to do so. It is important to be free to question the accepted limits, whether of traditional economic thinking or of our widely-accepted individualism. On both counts, event thinking can uncover possibilities that, indeed, do not have to come to pass, but which are genuine possibilities, beyond the "zero-sum game" thinking that often seems the only possibility when you are thinking about exchanging momentum among substances.

Thus though we cannot go back to finding our place in the biblical story just as it used to be told, this story is still a vital source for shaping our vision of life. If we are able to let its vital insights speak, we shall be able to find an open, improvisatory overarching story, which does not have a predetermined end, and which does not allow us to regard ourselves as specially privileged, but which does set us free to commit ourselves to action and also to thought, in both cases as explorations of the possibilities that are as yet unrealized. Such an open vision may be widely influential both in religious communities committed to the Bible, and among those who resonate to the values of this story though they set it to work outside of the churches, as we work and live together to find a more human world[19].

19. In slightly different form, this essay was presented as a Franklin lecture at Auburn University in February, 1989.

Afterword

These essays, written over a period of more than twenty years, still represent very well what I would want to say about their subjects. Of course there are topics which I would carry farther today, especially the relation of texts and thinking to their social setting; and I hope that I would be able to write more penetratingly if I were to recast some of what I have written. But I have let them stand as they appeared, not even adding references to more recent works that are relevant to their topics.

I have made a very few changes. Biblical quotations now appear in the translation of the New Revised Standard Version Bible. I have silently altered some expressions which were androcentric in their language, and here and there clarified an awkward expression. Otherwise I have not attempted any revisions. Inevitably, in such a collection as this there are repetitions. I trust that the reader will forgive these, and move quickly through them.

Looking back over what I have written, I realize anew how much I owe to the various dialogue partners whose names appear, sometimes often, in the various essays. I have chosen a few well-defined positions to set against my own, to clarify my own search, and to learn from deeply as I interacted with them. To mention only one person, as I re-read these essays, I was freshly aware of how much I am indebted to the work of Rudolf Bultmann, even as I distance myself from some of his positions. In the language of the day, I could say that his brilliant and profound modern formulation is the indispensable background of my move to the post-modern.

Some years before the date of the first of these articles, I began to explore the fruitfulness of process theology for biblical interpretation, spurred precisely by my sense that the dissection of time into discrete moments in the existentialist interpretation missed something important in the biblical message, while at the same time the sacred history perspective was not fully accessible to us today. Various avenues of exploration of this interaction are shown above; I still find this an exciting frontier for thought and for personal and spiritual life. In the course of this exploration I have been particularly in touch with the work of John B. Cobb, Jr., and David R. Griffin. But no one perspective is a panacea; while working with process thought I have tried to be alert to other possibilities, especially the developing literary interpretations, here originally stimulated, like so many others, by my teacher, Amos N. Wilder.

"Margins of Belonging" suggests in the first place the inadequacy of our traditional academic boundaries. One cannot really "belong" in a traditional academic discipline; understanding comes alive as one moves back and forth among what have come to be regarded as separate intellectual activities. A creative future for theology will come from such interdisciplinary work—but "interdisciplinary" as well in a sense that reaches beyond academia to the springs of theology in the life of the church.

But the "margin" has wider implications as well. The varied uses of this image most obviously fall into two types: those which suggest that real or decisive meaning is to be found at or beyond the margin, and those which propose that it is by staying within the margin that things fall into place.

The margin, limit, boundary, or frontier, as something that it is good to respect, to stay within, has not been so widely used an image in the discussion of religion, culture, and philosophy in the liberal tradition. Yet this image—the margin as a sign of our finitude—is one that we shall be finding more and more frequently. The precious distinctiveness of the many religious and cultural groups, and the corresponding deep pluralism that expects and respects profound variety, were not squarely faced by much of the liberal tradition that has shaped our discourse. A world separated by boundaries which make communication difficult and sometimes impossible is a dismaying prospect. But "guarding our boundaries" will be an increasingly prominent motif in cultural and religious writing. Minority and excluded groups need to define themselves as separate, as bounded. This is a lively motif among women and among Afro-American thinkers, to mention only two. And in Christian theology, one can point to such a work as Stanley Hauerwas and William H. Willimon's *Resident Aliens*, which puts a strong emphasis on baptism as a separating mark, and which calls for the church to understand itself as a group of aliens, a colony in a world from which they are essentially distant.[1] Hauerwas and Willimon find separateness necessary both for the church's own integrity and for the sake of a truthful critique of society. And much of the writing about the post-modern world emphasizes the social, linguistic, and religious boundaries that break the world into separate groups which often find it difficult or impossible to communicate with each other. I respect and learn from this re-emerging stress on difference and limit, though it is not my central point as I use the image of the margin.

On the other hand, the margin as bounding the exhausted, static established area, beyond which the only vital possibilities lie, is an image which we also encounter a lot. D. J. Leahy's "edge" is the point at which we venture from the finite into the infinite, and at the same time lose the separateness which pits us against the other; here the image of the "edge" runs in the opposite direction from the separating boundary just noted above.[2] Such imagery is close to the image of total apocalyptic reversal, familiar in the many works of Thomas J. J. Altizer. Altizer notes the importance of the "boundary" in ritual, and laments the weakening of this imagery in contemporary Christian liturgy; but his use of the image entails what we may call a total passing; the "collapse of our past as the way to an apocalyptic and eschatological future."[3] Here the temporal image communicates the same message as the spatial image of the boundary: it is by passing from the exhausted, dead, already-formed area that we come into the new, fluid, and living one. Though both Leahy and Altizer hold that the sterile, already-formed culture and faith are taken up into the new, it is only by recognition of their death that the new may be welcomed, by a total reversal.

Others use the image of the margin with a more open attitude toward established cultural and religious structures. Stephen J. Moore insists on the "necessity of an iconoclastic moment in biblical studies (for [himself], at any rate)—a revision, though not a rejection, of such foundational concepts as Bible and exegesis," and finds in this iconoclastic moment a "spring-like quickening of [his] intellectual *and* spiritual sap" like that which he once experienced which he discovered historical criticism; to cover both moments of discovery he cites Kierkegaard, "For

1. Stanley Hauerwas and William H. Willimon, *Resident Aliens* (Nashville: Abingdon Press, 1989).

2. D. J. Leahy, "To Create an Absolute Edge," *JAAR* 57 (1989), 773-789.

3. Thomas J. J. Altizer, *Total Presence: The Language of Jesus and the Language of Today* (New York: Seabury Press, 1980), 92.

to begin thinking such thoughts is to approach the boundaries of faith."[4] Moore's boundary, with its combination of dread and adventure, will indeed be passed, and the new world will not hesitate to reshape any item from the old, but in contrast to the more radical edge of Leahy, there will be many recognizable patches in the new, interestingly illustrated by Moore's acute observation that there are many parallels between the dissection of organic meaning by source criticism, and the dissection of meaning by deconstruction of narrative coherence.[5] It will be by its more limited claims about transcendence that this new hermeneutic will be defined. Thus here the image of the margin, though it is structurally very different from the rediscovery of boundaries noted first, is conveying a related message.

My own affinity with the image of the margin comes from recognizing that we need always to press to the edge of our understanding and insight, and be willing to give up any item that we assume to be established, but not because the exciting and valid is beyond; rather it is in the interplay between what is at the margin and what is established and tested (but may need to be tested again from a new point of view) that we deepen our insight.

Another way of putting it is to ask how sharp a break with the existing pattern of life or thought does it take to awaken us? The mood of much theology today is very much in the direction of pressing for the need of a very sharp break and a rude awakening, and this is the case in a wide spectrum of theological positions. The widespread use of the term "post-modern" is an indicator. I also use this language, though I have strong reservations about it. Often the term "post-modern" is used to imply that we can easily escape the past. But the interplay between past and present is more complicated than that. We both live in and from our traditions, and creatively reshape them at the same time. This is what happens even when we think of a total new beginning. It is wiser to develop a post-modernism that is directed toward a drastically new "paradigm" and also lives out of the vitality of the past.

I also believe that it is possible to write and live from a Christian commitment and at the same time live and think in the public world. Some elements deeply embedded in the Christian perspective lead in this

4. Stephen J. Moore, *Literary Criticism and the Gospels: The Theoretical Challenge* (New Haven: Yale University Press, 1989), 177.

5. Ibid., 164-166.

direction. Other elements which cut differently and claim an exclusive possession of truth and life need to be relativized and freshly understood, recast so as to find their place in the open and improvisatory story of a community which both claims reality for its own insights and life, and also welcomes the reality of the insights and life of other communities. This was very much the goal of the liberal tradition. The move to a post-liberal world is sometimes greeted as if we could return to separate realms of discourse for separate communities. What is correct in this proposal is its criticism of the usually unconscious domination in the claim for universal validity of the liberal tradition. But that does not mean retreating to a private realm of discourse. It is too simple to think that all are ultimately saying the same thing. But it is not wrong to affirm what at the end of the final essay above I call an "open vision" in which no one speaks from a privileged position, but in which we speak from deep conviction and also learn from our differences, while at the same time we know that our imperfect and fragmentary vision none the less springs in part from the very shape of reality, and is not merely our own creation.

Index of Ancient Texts

Biblical Texts

Genesis (Joseph narrative)—82ff.

Exodus, Book of—209 n. 14
Exodus 3:14—217

Deut 5:15—58
Deut 20:5-9—34

Joshua, Book of—209

Judges, Book of—209

2 Samuel (David narrative)—82ff.

2 Kings 21:14-15—223

Job, Book of—7, 223

Psalms, Book of—7, 233
Psalm 37:25—7, 223
Psalm 65—233

Prov 3:28—17
Prov 8—233
Prov 10:1—18
Prov 10:25—17
Prov 12:—17
Prov 25:6-7—17

Isaiah 10:5-11—223
Isaiah 49:6—224

Amos 9:7—7, 223

2 Macc 7:11—34
4 Macc 9:1—34

Matthew, Gospel of—210
Matt 5:44—20
Matt 7:7—21
Matt 7:24-27—17
Matt 8:20—19
Matt 8:22—19, 76
Matt 10:38-39—25, 29, 32, n. 21
Matt 16:25—25
Matt 17:20—19
Matt 20:16—18
Matt 21:21—19
Matt 23:12—18
Matt 23:24—20
Matt 26:26—76

Mark, Gospel of—83, 89-100, 149, 210
Mark 8:34-35—19, 25, 29, 76
Mark 8:36—18
Mark 8:37—33
Mark 10:25—20
Mark 10:31—18
Mark 10:43-44—18
Mark 11:23—19

Luke, Gospel of—85, 210
Luke 6:27—20
Luke 6:47-49—17
Luke 9:24—25
Luke 9:58—19
Luke 9:60—19
Luke 10:30-37—7, 44-60, 224
Luke 11:5-8—17
Luke 13:30—18
Luke 14:7-11—17
Luke 14:11—18
Luke 17:6—19
Luke 17:33—19, 25, 28
Luke 18:14—18

John, Gospel of—86, 90, 210
John 4—86
John 8:58—76
John 12:25—19, 25
John 15:5—76
John 15:13—34

Acts of the Apostles—85

Paul—3
Rom 2:14ff.—43
2 Cor 6:7-10—32-33

Other Ancient Texts

Apophthegmata patrum—67-73
Asher ben Yehiel, Rabbi—34 n. 31
Augustine—45, 86, 222
Babai—72
Didache 1:3—20
Epictetus—32
Euripides—33
Evagrius Ponticus—70-73
Gershom, Rabbenu—34 n. 31
Gregory of Nazianzen—72
Gregory of Nyssa—72
Herodotus—30 n. 15
Iliad—176-177
Menander, Sayings of (Syriac)—30-31
Menander, Sentences of (Greek)—33
Odyssey—175-176
Origen—71, 73
Philo—32-33
Pindar—33
Pirke Aboth—63
Plato—31, 32
Plotinus—71
Rashi—34 n. 31
Qumran *War Scroll*—34
Sextus, Sentences of—16
Sittenkanon in Omenform (Moral Rules in Omen Form)—18
Talmud Babli—34
Thomas, Gospel of—15, 21, 22 n. 10, 164
Valentinus—72
Xenophon—30
Zen Koan—73-76

Index of Modern Texts

Abe, M., 41, 75
Allo, E.-B., 38
Alter, R., 10, 81-88
Altieri, C., 165, 166-168, 170
Altizer, T., 107-110, 165-166, 170
Aragon, L., 105
Arnold, M., 168
Arvedson, T., 14
Austin, R., 233

Balthasar, H., 71
Bamberger, J., 70-71
Barley, N., 25, 40
Barth, K., 1, 169, 202
Beardslee, W., 1-11, 16, 22, 66, 78, 161, 166, 212
Beckett, S., 106, 132
Bennett, C., 33
Betz, H.-D., 208
Birch, C., 171, 203, 207, 232
Blake, W., 103, 166
Boers, H., 1-11, 194
Boozer, J., viii
Borges, J., 67
Bouyer, L., 70-71
Breech, J., 210
Breton, A., 106
Brown, N., 108
Brueggemann, W., 209
Buber, M., 217
Bultmann, R., 2, 7-8, 15, 16, 49-51, 52-53, 57-59, 63-64, 66, 94, 150-151, 183-186, 188, 226, 229, 237
Buss, M., 216
Butts, J., 225

Cadbury, H., 63, 64, 65
Carlston, C., 57
Chadwick, H., 16
Chang, C., 74
Christian, W., 111
Cobb, J., 38, 41, 60, 79, 111, 138-140, 143, 145, 146-147, 153-154, 170, 171, 203, 207, 212, 214, 232, 238
Coles, R., 219, 220
Crossan, J., 4, 7, 9, 26, 28, 29, 39, 48, 51, 52, 55, 57, 58-59, 65, 67-68, 77, 96, 98, 210, 212, 224-225, 234
Cullmann, O., 225
Culpepper, A., 86

Daly, M., 189
Dawsey, J., 221
Derrida, J., 168, 200
Descartes, R., 197
Dihle, A., 29
Dinkler, E., 29
Dodd, C. H., 6, 8, 15, 45, 48, 51, 61, 222, 225

Economic Justice for All, 195
Edwards, J., 102
Eliade, M., 127, 128
Eliot, T. S., 168, 198
Emerson, R., 105

Farmer, W., 90
Fenn, W., 62
Fenton, J., 75
Fiorenza, *see* Schüssler Fiorenza
Ford, L., 113
Frankenberg, W., 71
Franklin, B., 103
Frederick the Great, 31
Frei, H., 1, 10, 97, 98, 127, 152, 169, 203
Fuchs, E., 14
Fuller, R., 208
Funk, R., 4, 7, 9, 14, 21, 27, 51, 52, 53-54, 55, 57-60, 66, 210, 221, 225, 234

Gadamer, H.-G., 185-188, 195
Galileo, G., 197
Gilligan, C., 174
Goethe, J., 5
Gottwald, N., 209
Gray, F., 39
Griffin, D., 230, 238
Guillaumont, A., 72

Habermas, J., 192
Harrington, M., 158
Hartshorne, C., 113-114, 198
Hauerwas, S., 238
Hazelton, R., 65
Hegel, G., 115, 165, 167, 168
Heidegger, M., 2, 126
Highwater, J., 233
Holtzmann, H., 90
Holtzmann, O., 90
Howell, N., 173-174, 179
How, W., 30
Hume, D., 115
Huxley, A., 104
Hyers, C., 74

Janzen, J. G., 118
Jeremias, J., 14, 48, 51
Johnson, R., 68
Johnston, C., 196
Johnston, W., 73, 74, 76
Joyce, J., 166
Jülicher, A., 2, 4, 7, 14, 15, 46, 50, 52, 53, 58, 62, 182
Jüngel, E., 14

Kafka, F., 106, 132
Kähler, M., 92, 93
Kant, I., 115, 118, 151, 165, 169, 182, 200, 232
Kelber, W., 83-84, 96
Keller, C., 11, 175, 177, 193
Kermode, F., 10, 97, 98, 149-150, 152
Kierkegaard, S., 123, 239
Koester, H., 15
Kümmel, W., 89

La Rochefoucauld, F., 39
Leahy, D., 239
Leclerc, I., 71
Leisegang, H., 33
Lester, C., 99
Lewis, C. S., 31
Linnemann, E., 14
Lull, D., 60
Luria, I., 105
Lyotard, J., 1, 192, 199-202, 204-205, 207

Mallarmé, S., 105
Marcel, G., 215
Marx, K., 173
Marxsen, W., 95
May, J., 187
McFague, S., 65, 177
Mead, M., 213
Meeks, W., 208
Meinong, F., 158
Melville, H., 103
Merton, T., 70, 73
Metz, J. B., 161
Metzler, D., 193-194
Michie, D., 97
Miller, P., 102
Milton, J., 103, 168
Miranda, J., 58
Mould, E., 64
Mühlenberg, E., 72

Newman, J., 167, 216
Newton, I., 197
Niebuhr, H. R., 193-194
Nietzsche, F., 116
Northrop, F., 104

Ogden, S., 138, 140-142, 144-145
Ong, W., 84

Palmer, R., 186
Pannenberg, W., 107, 134
Parsons, T., 200
Patte, D., 51
Percy, W., 132
Perrin, N. 26, 37, 48, 65
Petersen, N., 96
Pixley, G., 210
Pound, E., 198
Pregeant, R., 60

Rauschenbusch, W., 188
Reitzenstein, R., 71
Reverdy, P., 105
Reynolds, C., 153, 195
Rhoads, D., 97
Ricoeur, P., 27, 65-66, 84, 155
Robbe-Grillet, A., 106, 132
Robinson, J., 14

Rorty, R., 200
Rubenstein, R., 104, 108
Russell, B., 158
Rylaarsdam, J., 138, 142-144, 146, 227-228

Schopenhauer, A., 116
Schmid, H., 17
Schneidau, H., 84
Schüssler Fiorenza, E., 181, 188-192, 195, 213
Schwartz, H., 59
Schweitzer, A., 91
Scott, B., 225
Scott, N., 87, 105-106
Sebba, G., 31, 99
Shah, I., 76
Sherburne, D., 121
Shinn, R., 213
Sloterdijk, P., 191
Stählin, G., 33
Sternberg, M., 221
Strauss, D., 91
Streeter, B., 63
Suzuki, D., 73-74

Tannehill, R., 85, 96
Taylor, M. C., 1, 202, 229
Teilhard de Chardin, P., 76, 134
Te Selle, S., see McFague
Thébaud, J., 192
Theissen, G., 210
Tillich, P. 77, 126, 156
Toynbee, A. J., 104

Valéry, P., 105
Via, D., 14, 48, 51, 58, 96

Waddell, H., 69-70
Walker, W., 90
Watts, A., 104, 108
Weeden, T., 60, 96
Weiss, J., 91
Weisse, C., 89
Welker, M., 206
Wells, J., 30
Welty, E., 207
Wenders, W., 229
West, C., 173
Westminster Confession of Faith, 101
Wettstein, J., 33
Whitehead, A. N., 2, 112, 115, 117-123, 155-160, 169, 178, 198, 203, 206
Wilckens, U., 14
Wilcox, J., 113
Wilder, A., 14, 21, 63, 64, 65, 68, 69, 78, 94-95, 99, 153, 162
Willimon, W., 238
Windisch, H., 33
Wittgenstein, L., 167
Woodbridge., B., 60
Woolman, J., 109
Wordsworth, W., 168
Wrede, W., 81, 92

Yeats, W. B., 198
Yoder, J., 210

Ziolkowski, T., 214